3/98

My Son, My Sorrow

The Tragic Tale of Dr. Kevorkian's Youngest Patient

Carol Loving

New Horizon Press   Far Hills, NJ

Requests for permission should be addressed to:
New Horizon Press
P.O. Box 669
Far Hills, NJ 07931

Loving, Carol

        My Son, My Sorrow: The Tragic Tale of Dr. Kevorkian's Youngest Patient

Library of Congress Catalog Number: 97-66563

ISBN: 0-88282-161-X

New Horizon Press

Manufactured in the U.S.A.

2000 1999 1998

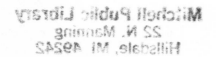

Contents

Dedication...v

Author's Note..vii

1.   Young and Invincible....................................3

2.   Search for Tomorrow 31

3.   Down, Down, Down 55

4.   Family Sorrow..75

5.   The Rapid Decline 89

6.   Enough is Enough.................................... 111

7.   A Strand of Pearls 125

8.   Losing Ground 137

9.   Cumulative Suffering 153

10. Desperate Measures..................................165

11. Our Helpless Family.................................175

12. They Call It Respite.................................187

13. The Good Doctor 205

14. Time to Say Goodbye 211

15. Flight to Freedom 233

16. The Long and Winding Road............... 247

17. The Final Phase 257

18. Life After Death...279

This book is dedicated to my surviving children

Hannah, Drew and Luke

and

my grandchildren

and

to the memory of

Nicholas John Loving

Author's Note

This story is based on my actual experiences and reflects my perception of the past, present and future. The personalities, events, actions, and conversations portrayed within the story have been reconstructed from my memory and the memories of participants. In an effort to safeguard the privacy of some individuals, including some members of my family, I have changed their names and, in some cases, altered identifying characteristics.

Part I

The Descent

1

Young and Invincible

One warm and light-filled summer afternoon, as I lay stretched out on the bed in my seventh month of pregnancy, I found it impossible to sleep due to the tumbling going on inside me. My belly was a ball of activity. Finally things settled down and then the baby decided to roll over. I watched with fascination as it turned from the left side to the right. I held my hands on the flesh of my bulging, shifting abdomen as the baby moved his arms and legs from the right side of my abdomen to the left side. His back and rump crested my belly as I watched and ran my hands gently along his back. The baby stretched his legs before settling into a snug position, and a pair of little feet came to the surface of my flesh below my left rib cage.

For a few seconds all was quiet, then I felt more kicking. But how could the baby be kicking me in my right set of ribs when he'd just rolled his body over and had his legs nestled on my left side? Suddenly the answer struck me. The reason for so much activity was because I was carrying twins.

Carol Loving

But, why? Why on earth had God given me not one, but two babies to cherish and love? Who was I to deserve such a blessing? I didn't know the answer, I only knew twins meant something special.

I reported the discovery of twins to my doctor on the next visit. But my doctor said, "Carol, I think there's only one baby, not two." My doctor was firm in his statement that I was mistaken, sticking to his notion that I was going to have a big baby. He offered the fact that he could only hear one heartbeat as evidence that I was incorrect. He even gave me the opportunity to listen to the single heartbeat through the stethoscope.

I knew there were two babies in my womb, but the doctor had dismissed the idea. He said one big baby. What did he know? Was he a woman? Did he have a womb? Was he me? He heard only one heartbeat beneath the wall of my abdomen. To him, that was proof that there was only one child. But I knew better. This was not my first pregnancy. I had two adorable little girls. One from a teenaged marriage which was over before the baby was born, and another, Hannah, with my present husband. Never before had my belly been so big. Beyond my physical appearance was what I felt inside. It was the abundant activity in the womb that told me I was blessed with two, not just one.

I had been scheduled to give birth on Labor Day, which was September fourth of that year. But it was three and a half weeks prior to that date when I actually went into labor, with my doctor still insisting there was only one child. I experienced three hours of heavy, intense labor, which afforded me not one moment of relief between the rounds of contractions. Instead, each contraction started before the previous one was completed. It was the most strenuous delivery I ever experienced. I anxiously watched, by way of the large mirror, as the doctor assisted my first born son, Drew, into the world at 11:25 that morning. He was red, tiny and nowhere near the size the doctor had anticipated delivering.

Soon it was obvious that there was another child waiting to be born, the child only I believed was there. The baby was in breach position. The doctor reached his latex-gloved hand inside me to facilitate the birth of my second child, but he was unable to turn the baby around to allow him to move head first through the birth canal. Despite the difficulty, my second son, Nicholas John entered the world at 11:40 that Friday morning. I watched nervously in shaded silence as he was born with an umbilical cord tangled about his body and wrapped twice around his neck. It was obvious from his blue color that he was in distress. My heart beat furiously as the doctor worked to get him to cry. Finally, he wailed out loud and I thanked God for my twin baby boys. I felt truly blessed.

My husband Marc and I wanted to raise a family of beautiful, well educated children to grow, prosper and do well in life. By the time our twins were born, we had been married a little over two years. I was committed to motherhood. My husband appeared committed to a career in the Air Force to support his wife and to raise his children. Shortly after the twins arrived, my husband signed up for his second four-year hitch. Marc was an immigrant from the Ukraine, who came to America as a child. We hoped that when the children grew up and left the nest, we would have a pension waiting for us. We would still be young enough to invest in our personal lives. The mixture of his old world blood and my Virginia breeding created a beautiful blend of colors and features for each of our children. However though we agreed on our children's future, my husband was strangely cold and unsupportive. He refused, for instance, to even take me to the hospital when our daughter was born and was unavailable much of the time to help me during my pregnancy. But I wanted above all to keep our family together. So, I kept the peace and suffered in silence.

The second baby, Nicholas John, came into the world weighing only four pounds, seven ounces—five ounces less than his brother Drew. They both measured out as eighteen inches long from head to toe. Drew and Nicholas were put directly into incubators and the doctor said I could not take them home until they reached the weight of five pounds. Nicholas lost four ounces of birth weight in the first twenty-four hours and his twin lost five. At that time, home was a two bedroom apartment in Amarillo, Texas, where my husband was stationed in the Air Force for one year. We had driven to his new post from Edwards Air Force Base in California, after our beautiful daughter had been born.

The hospital actually let our twins go home when my first born son reached five pounds, since Nicholas trailed by only a few ounces. I was ready to nurture and care for their every need from that first day. Because they were twins, I expected them to be very much alike, but, in fact, they were very different from each other right from the start.

Drew was a quiet and content baby. Nick's chemistry was different, very different from his sibling. He was an over-active baby inside the womb, and that characteristic carried over into his existence outside it. His excessive activity produced a demanding appetite and caused him to go after my breast with aggressive sucking. By the time he was four months old, his demand for nourishment forced me to give him several ounces of milk from a mug. He took his milk in large gulps with great glee and excitement. Once the major part of his appetite was satisfied, he would relax in my arms like any placid baby, happy to satisfy his natural urge to suckle.

It is not uncommon for an infant to turn from his stomach to his back early in his development, but it is a more difficult task for the infant to go from his back onto his stomach. Nick took the challenge as soon as he was brought home and placed in his crib. As if showing his progress, he would flip over on his back and then twist his little body back on his stomach. Physically, he proved to be far more accelerated than his twin. All babies rock back and forth on their hands and knees, but not to the extent that energetic Nicholas John did. The more he rocked, the more he was inspired to continue. Five, ten minutes of rocking was not long enough. Twenty or thirty minutes, sometimes longer, was what it took to satisfy his vigorous nature. And as he rocked back and forth the look on his face was one of absolute joy.

Nick was literally a bouncing baby boy. In fact, the more freedom of movement he had, the more glee projected from his heart and expressed on his face. He loved to hold on to my thumbs with his tiny hands and bounce up and down on his little legs, taking great thrill and pleasure in his ability to assert his drive for life. The more he bounced, the stronger he became. At four months, he began pulling himself up in his crib by using the bars. I will always remember the day in December when he made it up on his feet. I helped him secure a firm grip by wrapping his little fingers around the crib rail so he could stand as long as his strength would allow. Joy of achievement beamed from his face and I grabbed my husband's camera and snapped Nick's picture to capture his happiness.

Nick was motivated by challenge from the very beginning. His desire to move forward made a major impact during his fifth month of infancy. That was when I learned he not only exhibited excessive stamina and unparalleled physical endurance for one so young, but also had a very strong competitive drive. One day, I had placed my twins on the living room floor. I stood several feet away and encouraged them to crawl to me. Both were delighted to crawl to Mommy. Nicholas, in merry spirits, stopped halfway to look up at me with a big, beaming smile. As he did, his brother Drew continued on his diligent way. Before Nick got back into the pace of his crawl, the race was over. His twin had reached me first.

I picked up my number one son to kiss and congratulate him for his win. What happened next was shocking. Little Nick started to cry like he had never cried before, thrashing about on the floor. Sometimes babies can cry so hard they can't catch their breath. It makes your heart clutch, but the baby eventually does catch his breath and returns to a normal cry. So at first, I wasn't alarmed, but Nick's wailing grew. He cried with every ounce of energy he could muster. He cried so hard he was gasping for breath. His arms buckled beneath him and he rolled onto his side, his face turning red. He still couldn't breathe.

My heart raced inside me. Putting Drew down, I grabbed up Nick. I put him on my shoulder and patted his back. He still couldn't breathe. I laid his body along the cradle

of my legs and blew into his mouth and nose. Still no movement. I was scared to death. He had turned purple. I flipped
him over and pounded his back. Finally, finally the muscles of
his diaphragm began to relax and enabled him to take short
breaths. The panic that had built up in me regressed with every
breath he took as I rocked him gently in my arms and spoke
loving words to him.

From that day forward, although Nick loved his twin,
he never allowed Drew to take away from him the position of
number one. Nick was walking at seven months as long as he
held onto something for balance. By nine months, he was running across the lush green world of grass. There was
absolutely no stopping his progress. What a great pleasure it
was to watch his early developmental skills.

My husband's tour of duty in Texas came to an end in
the summer of 1968. We moved the family to the southern
coast of Mississippi, where we found a comfortable house in
Ocean Springs to rent for the next two years of my husband's
new tour.

That August, the twins celebrated their first birthday.
The spry little fellows weighed less than twenty pounds each,
but they were healthy, happy and bright. Nick and Drew were
very affectionate children and learned to play well under my
supervision. With their sister so close in age, it was like having
triplets. I devoted my days and nights to my children and my
husband, whose silence increased with the passing of time. I
had to quietly take Marc's aversion to all of us. However, I tried
not to think about it and instead kept my mind on my children.
I came to the conclusion that the joy of motherhood was worth
the pain of my marriage.

Carol Loving

I was determined that the upcoming holidays would be happy ones, and they were. For each child I prepared a special gift. My gift to Nicholas was to be a hobby horse. It took hours of patience to put it together. But it was well worth the effort as it turned out to be the favorite object in Nick's young life, his source of joy and pleasure. He bounced back and forth on that horse for hours at a time, sometimes with such great force I feared he would fly right off. Of course, he never did, but he derived great enjoyment from riding the horse. Nick loved the physical freedom and activity he found in the continued motion that called for great stamina on his part. It was a thrilling achievement and his first sports activity.

I knew my children were above average in intelligence. They all questioned the world around them, and it was my job to teach them well and prepare them for school. I devoted much time to their development, spiritual, as well as educational. I read to my children every day from the Bible and from children's stories. They learned to read at a very early age. I gave them constant praise for all their efforts and loved the gift of motherhood. Loving my children was just as enriching for me as it was for them.

Nick continued to excel in physical stamina as he grew into a toddler. Every developmental stage he went through, he set records with each level of accomplishment. Nick was energetic, always happy and determined to stand on his own two feet.

In the summer of 1969, Marc wanted to move from Ocean Springs to Biloxi. I wanted to stay where we were. We lived in a good location, and I wanted my husband to buy the home we were renting. It was an equal distance from both of our in-laws, and I felt it was a wonderful place in which our family could grow up. By that time, I had also given birth to another child, a third son. We named him Luke. Five years of marriage had given me four children.

My husband got his way, and we moved to Biloxi. His tour of duty came to an end in Mississippi during the summer of 1970. After seven stateside years, Marc's next tour was supposed to be overseas. We hoped for Germany. This would take us past the halfway mark in my husband's twenty year career. Instead, he was assigned to a one year tour in Vietnam.

The question was, where should the children and I go while he was there? Should it be New Jersey and the Ukrainian community, which was my husband's heritage or should I go to Phoenix where my family lived? I wanted to be with my family for the year my husband was overseas, but Marc felt it would be better for the children to be exposed to their Ukrainian culture. His mother, Baba said that we could rent the downstairs quarters of her large home.

There were many reasons I didn't feel it was a better choice. A primary one was that his mother was a staunch Catholic and had disapproved of me. Fortunately, she decided she didn't want to put her renter out in order to have her grand-children around. We moved the family to Phoenix the year the twins turned three. Their father left for Vietnam soon after in September. I felt proud that I was keeping my children nour-ished and happy that year in Phoenix without the head of the household present.

At first, Nick's reaction to the separation resulted in a series of nightmares about war. He'd wake up in the middle of the night, sometimes in a cold sweat, and crawl into bed with me. Nick wasn't looking for a place to run and hide—he wanted to talk about his dreams. I never once failed to listen as he articulated his thoughts and feelings on violence. By listening to my young son, I discovered he knew more about the conflict in Vietnam than I did. Eventually, the bad dreams stopped, but the special bond I shared with Nicholas continued to grow.

The twins turned four in the summer of 1971. And, shortly thereafter, their father returned home from Vietnam. He didn't let me know he was on his way. Just showed up at the door.

During his time overseas, Marc's moods had grown darker. I often wondered if my husband had become the violent man he now was, because of his recent combat experience. However, since he had become so explosive, I dared not ask and didn't know. I quietly took the abuse.

Soon he turned our entire lives upside down. "I've decided not to re-enlist," he announced. This meant there would be no check coming in every two weeks. Marc said he wanted to play music to earn a living. But my husband wasn't a professional musician. I couldn't believe he was throwing away our future so he could play the drums all night and sleep all day.

I begged him to re-enlist. "You have to for the sake of the children. We have four beautiful children and my daughter, as well. How are we going to eat and pay the bills and secure them a future? The Air Force is our financial security." But Marc wouldn't listen. He wouldn't re-enlist. He wouldn't get a regular job. He just hung out in bars jamming each night with friends.

The little money that we had saved soon flew away. The bills kept coming. My husband refused to correct the irresponsible direction he was taking with his life, and with ours. I decided I had to do something and quickly. Without an education, I soon learned jobs were sparse and menial. I enrolled in a short night school nursing program. At least I could keep food on the table and a roof over our heads. After several months, I was qualified to take a job in a nursing home on the graveyard shift. I had a house and children to care for during the day, and I worked all night. Sleep was a luxury I seldom had time for.

Weeks turned into months and my husband still was unemployed. When it was light he slept. When it was dark he left the house. Marc didn't do any kind of work at all, and he brought in no money. As our financial situation turned from bad to disastrous, I became more and more worried. "I beg you to be responsible for the sake of our children," I said. "Please get back into the Air Force before it's too late." That day Marc walked out the door without any intention of doing what was morally right. He never returned. Alone and destitute, I was forced to file for welfare.

A few months later my husband was picked up by authorities for not supporting his children. The last time I saw him was in a court of law. He was dressed in prison stripes and shackled at his hands and feet. After he got out, he disappeared, and the course of our lives changed forever. Abandoned. We were all alone. A mother and five small children, with no means of support. I called his mother in New Jersey and told her we needed help. She taunted me and said it was my fault. "There is nothing I can do," she decreed.

"But there is," I pleaded. "You can have us move to New Jersey and live in the downstairs quarters of your home.

Carol Loving

It's empty. If you won't help that way at least take your name-sake granddaughter, Hannah, so she can have the benefits of church, school and heritage. Please," I begged. "At least save my daughter from poverty. We're going to lose everything." But she just repeated that there was nothing she could do. My family said they couldn't help either because they were immersed in their own problems both financial and health-wise. At that time, welfare was well under two hundred dollars a month, and the household bills totaled well over four hundred a month. I picked up a food box offered by the state once a month. Food stamps did not exist in Arizona. We were given corn syrup, rice, flour, powdered eggs, a few cans of vegetables and two large cans of a meat product that smelled and looked like dog food.

Although poverty and everything that went with it hit us like a sledge hammer, the strength of Nick's young character never faltered. Nick felt a strong sense of loyalty to me and his siblings. At six years old, he came to me and said "Mom, I'm ready to take over as head of the family." I held him to me, too overcome with emotion for words. His strength of character was vibrant. I promised myself to treasure it and him forever.

However, many of our neighbors looked upon our fatherless and penniless home with disdain. We were a family of white trash to be run out of town. A cluster of malicious neighbors banned together with hypocrisy in their self-righteous hearts, and they used their collective force to chastise my children and me. They knew I worked all night, and that my first daughter now twelve, was old enough to babysit, but the neighbors made phone calls to both the police and the Child

My Son, My Sorrow

Protective Services with outlandish accusations about me. The neighbors told authorities that I neglected my children, who, according to them, commonly went from door to door dressed in only dirty underwear asking for handouts. They told the authorities I didn't feed my children, I didn't clean them. I neglected them and left them alone all night. The powers that be warned me if the complaints continued, I could lose my children. The State would take them away.

And the State did just that. It happened in the summer in 1972. I still did our grocery shopping and laundry after the children were asleep. Even though I had to quit my job to be home with them. Each time I left my house, one of the malicious people who lived near us called the authorities. Within weeks after I gave up my job, so I could be with the children, who according to the authorities needed more of their mother, the police walked into my home and took my children away from me. How was it possible for police to have the power to walk into my home and take my babies away, I asked myself? How could those who were supposed to protect us compound the tragedy I was already facing by tearing my heart out?

The experience of separation from my children drove me almost to insanity. It was hard for me to believe I would ever have my children with me again. The only thread of hope I had as I bore the pain and suffering of persecution came through my personal faith in God.

If I wanted my children back, the authorities said, I had to prove I was worthy. I had to go back to work. I had to pay my husband's bills. Round and round the wheel went. If I worked I was blamed. If I stayed home, I was chastised. I became angry and frustrated, so they labeled me mentally ill. That meant I had to see a mental health doctor. In the eyes of the State, I was an unfit mother.

Hannah was put in a foster home in Mesa. Luke, my youngest boy, was put in a foster home in Apache Junction. My precious twins were put in a foster home in Phoenix along with their adorable half-sister. The State paid total strangers three times the amount of money to have my children live in their homes than they gave my children to live at home with me. I asked myself continually, where was justice? Where was the father of my children? Why was he riding free? Why didn't the State go after him? Why were the children and I the ones being punished? The children were all I lived for. They were my world. How, in the country that boasts of freedom, could I have my babies taken from me? How could the government take innocent children away from an innocent mother? Next the authorities wanted me to give my children up for adoption. The authorities said that under the circumstances, it was the right thing for me to do. Except for my brother, Rick, my family was wrapped up in their own problems, ignoring the torment I was experiencing at twenty-six. Maybe it was best to give my children up for adoption, my parents suggested. How could they believe such heartless propaganda? "I'll never do that," I vowed.

I went to work at the county hospital. Paid debts which the divorce papers said I was not responsible for paying. Went to the required appointments to have my brain washed. And all but killed myself. God got me through what turned out to be the most desperate year of my life. He proved to be what I needed most.

My Son, My Sorrow

The separation had been horrible. It was the most difficult for Hannah, an intelligent, sensitive child who at the age of six had suddenly been torn away from her companions, as well as from her mother. Hannah was forced to live all alone with strangers who were cold and unfeeling people. They sent word they did not want me to enter their expensive home with a swimming pool in the backyard. They didn't want me to see my daughter, though I insisted and they looked at me as if I was trash. Hannah only got to see me and her family about six times during that year.

Luke's situation was not any better. He was given to a minister's family who, like Hannah's foster parents, didn't want me to have any contact with my boy. They clothed him in long white dresses for the year he was under their roof.

According to Arizona statutes, the government could not take children away from the parents for more than one year, unless abuse occurred in the home. So one year after the children and I had been torn apart, the government let me have my children back. It was the summer of 1973.

I was thrilled to be able to celebrate—as a family— Nick and Drew's sixth birthday that August. All the children except my youngest were enrolled in school once the semester began. Despite my working hard, to my horror, we were forced to go back on welfare again. In addition to the monthly check, the state now supplemented the income with food stamps. Food stamps made a considerable difference. I vowed we would become independent. I enrolled in a junior college and after class I tutored students. I received a thousand dollar loan for the school year and a matching one thousand dollar grant from the Federal government based on need. I filed my papers after the welfare went back into effect so I wouldn't lose the benefits. I hated being deceptive, but the fact that I was getting an additional two thousand dollars for the next twelve months helped us survive. I didn't feel good about it, but we had to live and I had to equip myself so we could get off handouts. The extra money made life a little better. I bought some new clothes for my children and even was able to take them out for pizza every couple of weeks. I tried not to think about what would happen if the welfare department found out about the extra income.

I was doing the best I could to keep our lives afloat. The neighbors who had reported us simmered to see me back with my children. Between the summer of 1973 and the summer of 1974, they went on the war path again. I was on welfare probation, and each call they made to the authorities threatened the future of my family. There I was, working wherever and whenever I could in order to be independent and to support my small family. On the one hand, they complained I was a welfare cow, and on the other, when I worked, that I neglected my children.

Then, just when things appeared to have hit rock bottom, my brother introduced me to Paul, a gentleman, who loved the children and me. Not only was he good with and to my children, he was also sympathetic to the difficult circumstances surrounding our lives. Unfortunately, the neighbors used his presence to step up their exile campaign to the authorities. As a result, Paul wanted to take me and the children to Colorado to live. For three years, I had been forced to live through an unbelievable world of hell from which I saw no end other than the total collapse of everything I held dear. My children were my life. I was determined not to lose them again. So, when the twins turned seven, Paul and I and my family headed for the cold country in order to try to make a new life.

It was in Colorado that Nick got his first taste of basketball. The instant he picked up the ball he could feel the magic. On the first try, whoosh! A basket. What a feeling. He was already good at boxing, track events, and many other activities, but basketball was his key to happiness. Nick was short, but that worked to his advantage to fire up his speed while advancing to the basket where he sprang from the floor to score.

Nick was exceptional in all areas of his studies, too, and the schools in Colorado were quite good. In addition, Nick took band classes and played the drums, at which he was a natural. Nick also enjoyed sledding and ice skating and the all around fun that snow brings to children. But, despite the friendly atmosphere, our stay in Colorado only lasted a year. The lack of available jobs prompted another move.

Sadly, my oldest daughter stayed behind in Colorado with relatives from her father's family. We just didn't have enough money for all of us to live on. However, I knew her father's relatives would give her a good home and would care for her spirits.

We left for Tennessee in the summer of 1975. Since Paul was an artist and had many friends in the art community, the children had the opportunity to work with a couple of artists that summer. Nick explored his artistic talents, and at eight years old, he created a clay figure of himself. It was a beautiful work of art: a taut, lean figure showing a commanding young man in motion, captured in the thrill of winning a race.

Carol Loving

We lived in a cabin at the time without running water or electricity, but treated it as an adventure. Nick vigorously hauled water from a spring and chopped wood. Once, he cut a deep gash on his finger while chopping, and with courage and calmness he told me about it. We cleaned it, and I put golden seal powder in the open wound to begin the mending process. It healed without incident.

For five months we stayed in the cabin and saved every penny we could. At the end of 1975 we moved onto a one hundred acre farm in Allons, Tennessee. We were the caretakers. The children were happy and healthy, pink cheeked from the fresh air. There was a horse for them to ride, cattle to graze, cows to milk, a good number of goats, dozens of chickens, a tobacco field that stretched beyond the boundaries of the human eye and a quarter-acre garden plot next to the farm house. We were all very happy. It was there that I married my friend and companion.

It was a wonderful environment for the children, providing a good balance of work and play. Never had we had such an abundance of food to eat. The children were exposed to outdoor picnics and down home country people who were the salt of the earth. But Paul and the owner didn't get along, so another move came.

This time we moved our family to Cookeville, Tennessee. A college town. We rented a nice home in the summer of 1976. Between silversmithing, for which Paul had a natural talent and welfare for the children, we were able to get by until winter came. Paul looked for a weekly paycheck to supplement his silversmithing, but found nothing and he moved us again. We moved into a house in Murfreesboro, Tennessee over Christmas week.

My Son, My Sorrow

Another home. Another town. Another school. The economy was hurting us. Everything was rising in cost. After six months of struggling in Murfreesboro, we decided to return to Phoenix to look for work. Because of all our financial troubles, we sent Hannah across country ahead of us to stay with my sister in Tucson. I had called her out of concern for my daughter and was surprised to hear her say Hannah was welcome for the summer.

Job hunting was difficult. When I applied for welfare for my children, the case worker offered to help. "I can put the boys together in one foster home for ninety days so you can get on our feet." he told me. He also said he would provide each of my sons with a one hundred dollar clothing allowance. At this time the twins were nine and Luke was only six. We were all in dire need, we had been through a lot as a family. I foolishly agreed to accept this unusual offer made by the State.

I stayed in a bare cottage by the freeway, while Paul toured the summer circuit of arts and craft sales in the South trying to sell his art. I called the boys from a pay phone everyday. It was all I could do to hold on to my sanity until I could see them.

At last, the day came when my brother drove me from where I was staying to where my children were being held in a temporary shelter. Bam! The door was shut in my face. I watched as the foster parents pulled my children back from the window where their faces were pressed. They were not going to let me see my sons, and they were not going to let my boys see me. Raging inside, I walked away quietly and immediately reported the actions of the foster parents to the authorities. I ranted and raved and demanded my children be returned to me immediately. It took forty-eight hours, but in that time Nick and his brothers were back by my side. We only had one bed and each night one of my sons slept on the bed with me and spent the next night sleeping with his brother on the floor. But, at least, we were together.

Paul returned and so did Hannah. I joined an agency which entered me in a nurse's pool, and we began to reconstruct our lives once again. With everyone in school, I worked the morning shift in different hospitals and cleaned the house and did chores from afternoon until evening. Despite his tender age, Nick looked out for his brothers and sister. In addition to all the housework, I cooked for my children, helped them with their homework, organized constructive activities to enhance their perception of life around them, and supervised their play. Nick was ten years old by this time and very much his mother's protector. He was also very fond of his stepfather who seemed to return the affection. Paul was there for them, listening to their problems and helping them when he could.

For the next three years, Paul moved us all around the valley. The children changed schools twice a year. Nick realized he would never be able to join a school basketball team or a school band. Nevertheless, it did not stop him from enthusiastically participating in athletic activities and music on his own. He won numerous ribbons and honors for his athletic abilities. He even won the President's Physical Fitness Award in the sixth grade. Nick was always placed in the gifted classes. He was intelligent enough to be put ahead a grade. Just like when he was a baby, Nick thrived on challenge. Grew from challenge. Developed through challenge. But as competitive as he was with Drew and the other siblings, he shared all he earned or was given.

My Son, My Sorrow

I finally located my children's father in the Spring of 1980. I had an address for him in Michigan. I turned the information over to the authorities in the hope of getting back child support. He had walked out of our lives in the fall of 1971. Now he owed over eight years of unpaid child support. But the action the State took was a joke. All the courts ordered him to do was to pay eight dollars a week for each child. This gave them spending money, but it only lasted a few months because Marc just stopped paying it.

That summer, discouraged with his own inability to move ahead and the responsibility of another man's children, Paul threw in the towel. I was desperate and abandoned again. Suddenly their biological father offered to take the boys. With nowhere else to turn I was forced to put Nick and his brothers on a bus to live in Michigan with Marc.

Then another blow was dealt. Hannah was under the spell of a man who exhibited domineering behavior. She and I had moved into a small house together. But that didn't last long. My daughter could not give up her relationship with her boyfriend and I felt I had no way to force her to, though I begged her to end it. She disappeared with him and I was left alone. I searched as best I could, but she was nowhere to be found. I didn't know where my daughter was, and my boys were in Michigan. Everything I lived for was gone. I looked back at the path that led to the present point in time, and I agonized. Was I wrong to keep my children once they were snatched away from my bosom just months after their father abandoned us? Maybe their lives would have been better if I had listened to others and turned my children over to the state permanently. Maybe it would have been better if they had never seen me again. One thing I learned from my bitter experience was that our government does little to aid helpless women and children.

In November, out of the blue, I got a wire from Michigan. My boys had been put on a bus and were due to arrive in a matter of hours. To my infinite joy, Nick and his brothers, my three musketeers, were back under my wing. I had returned to school and was only renting a bedroom, and though we still had nothing, we were happy to be back together.

Unfortunately, the landlord doubled the rent on our cramped living quarters as soon as the boys arrived to share it.

Then another blow. My mother went into the hospital for tests and was dead a few hours later, just like that. It was extremely difficult for my father, and I longed to comfort and care for him. I thought it would be a good opportunity for us to rent a home together where he could, at long last, come to know and enjoy his grandchildren.

But even that was not possible. After my mother's funeral, my sister snatched my father away and took him to Tucson to live with her and her husband.

At Christmas, my sister Lee invited me and the children and my brother Rick down to Tucson. Although we felt estranged from my sister, we did love our father, and did the best we possibly could in the plastic atmosphere that existed when we were all together under Lee's roof.

Our bad fortune continued. When we got back to Phoenix, we found a note on our bedroom door. Evicted. We had to be out at the end of the month. I wanted to rent my sister's house because with our mother gone and our father in Tucson, it was empty. It was an older two-bedroom with a monthly mortgage of under a hundred dollars. It would have meant a place for my boys to live. One place, one school, and an opportunity for a little stability from the relentless poverty of the past nine years. But my sister refused. She wouldn't let us use it even for the one evening I tried to slip the children in so we would not have to face a night out on the street in the drizzling rain. Instead, we ended up at my brother's tiny cottage New Year's Eve. The next morning, I set out on foot and covered a five mile radius until I found a place to live. The landlord let me put half the required amount down so I could get caught up.

During the months that followed, Dad, who was grieving over the loss of my mother, began to drink heavily. My sister tightened the reins, trying to keep everything under control.

The next four years were very difficult, but I was determined to finish school and get my bachelor's degree. To pick up some extra money, I tutored students in English after classes. Most of them were of Asian descent and I quickly fell in love with the people and their culture. My college offered some courses in Mandarin Chinese, so I enrolled and soon became fluent in the Chinese language.

Rice was our main staple and the only means of stretching the food dollar. Early in the morning we went to get it. After walking nearly a half hour, Nick and I would take the bus to the Chinese market. We would haul the twenty-five pound bags the great distance from the bus stop to our apartment. Was there another teenager in Phoenix who would tote heavy sacks of rice through the streets of Phoenix for his mother? Drew, smaller and slighter than his twin, could never have helped me carry the load. So the burden was forced onto

Carol Loving

Nick. He never complained. Nick would hoist the sack, sometimes two, on his shoulder as we transferred from one bus to
another and walked the remaining distance home. When it was
too hot for me to walk home from my job at the college, Nick
rode down to the school on his bike to pick me up. I sat on the
seat while he stood and managed the pedals. He was always
there for me and for his brothers. Though our lot was hard the
love we all shared was rich and fulfilling. Even at their ages
the boys were never idle and always found part-time work.

I worked. I studied. We all prayed for a better future.
Meanwhile, I struggled to keep a roof over our heads. In 1983,
the welfare department demanded I enroll in a technical training
program, or my allotment, one quarter of what we received, was
going to be stopped. I refused to let the State deny me the right
to an education which could eventually help my children and me
to rise in the world above the poverty level. I stayed at the
University. My share of welfare money stopped. This only
meant I had to work harder. However, I soon learned that the
State had another rule. No more money or food stamps for children once they reached the age of sixteen. Two more quarters of
my income were cut. The State never forced their run-away
father to pay back child support, let alone current payments to
his children. I felt completely besieged.

Then one day, one of the students I tutored, knowing
of my mastery of Chinese, began to tell me of good jobs
teaching English in Taiwan. Because the Chinese people's
need to compete in the western world was so great, the pay
was extraordinary. I was given names, addresses, and phone
numbers of contacts in Taiwan. Desperate, I wrote in Chinese

to prospective employers. Immediately I was offered a good position. Praying this was our chance, I told my children we were going to Taiwan to live.

At the end of 1984, I took my sons to the Republic of China.

Spending time in Taiwan enriched my life, and my children's lives not only because we were exposed to another culture, but because we were able to see that family and loyalty to one's family is a strong foundation that does exist in some parts of the world.

During the next six months on the island of Taiwan, Nick's outgoing spirit made him well loved by the Chinese. They were absolutely captivated by my children, but especially by Nicholas's red hair, green eyes, and the splash of freckles on his face.

The school boys in Taiwan all had their hair cut down to a GI buzz, and out of respect for his Chinese friends and the culture, Nick decided to follow suit. He had his beautiful, red curly hair buzzed down to the scalp. Luke did the same, always wanting to be like Nick. I can't think of a more beautiful way for a mature seventeen year old to show his respect for his Chinese counterparts. (To this day, Nick is fondly remembered by his close friends in Taiwan as I periodically speak to one of the wonderful boys, now a young man, he made friends with.)

Of all of the children, Nick learned the most living among the Chinese, and he developed a genuine respect for them as a people and for their rich culture. He loved the food and the beautiful faces of the Chinese girls. And Nick was quite impressed with the strength of the family and the emphasis the people placed on education. The excitement of living in a different culture enriched us all.

One day in February, 1985, Nick came home insisting excitedly, "Mom, you have to see this." He clasped my hand, called his brothers and led us out of the house.

We became a part of the massive throng that swept through the streets for the Chinese New Year. Out of nowhere, noise drew closer. Drums pounded. Firecrackers exploded. Lions danced on stilts. All of this amazed us. Then, through the throng appeared the fierce looking dragon. We were swept away by the dragon which seemed to go on forever. It was a moment of magic in which we were awed and inspired. After six months in China, Nick had amassed friends and admirers, just as he did wherever he went. He was even beginning to communicate well in the language. Despite all this, Nick loved his native land and believed his future lay in America.

"I want to return to Phoenix and move on with my life," he told me. Nick wanted to join the American Armed Services, so he could pursue an education. In June, when he was seventeen, Nick flew away from the nest. Several of his Chinese friends came with us to take Nick to the airport. We all wished him well on his trip back to America. I hated to lose him again, and his brothers were especially sad. Yet I realized it was time for him to grow. He was young and strong and healthy. He was intelligent and a natural-born leader. He was filled with enthusiasm, good humor, and a sparkling wit. I loved my son and his spirit to succeed and hoped we all would be reunited soon.

My Son, My Sorrow

Since I was now working for a publishing company and earning a very nice living, I paid for Nick's ticket back to the States and gave him a good sum of money to get started once in Phoenix. My son was a confident young man ready to take on the world. I was very proud of him.

2

Search for Tomorrow

When Nick returned from Taiwan, he called his sister, who had chosen to live with the young man who had for several years caused her great heartache. Hannah and her boyfriend drove him to his Uncle Rick's place in central Phoenix, and Nick stayed with my brother for a while to get his feet established firmly on the ground. It was a generous sacrifice for Rick to make, because his living quarters were quite cramped, but Nick was his favorite nephew.

As soon as he was settled, Nick spoke with Army recruiters to learn what was required to join and what the benefits would be. Since I had taken him to Taiwan, Nick missed the last half of the twelfth grade. Before he could enter the Army, he had to have a high school diploma or a General Education Diploma. Since Nick didn't have time to go back to school because he had to earn money for living expenses, he settled for the GED.

Then Nick learned that because he was still seventeen, he had to have a letter from his high school and a letter from me to permit him to take the GED test. He decided to take the test right after his eighteenth birthday. In the meantime, in addition to studying for the GED, Nick badly needed immediate employment and began to ferociously job hunt.

Family and friends were happy to have Nick back in Phoenix. As always, Nick was most concerned about those loved ones he feared were experiencing problems, and so he was very worried about his sister. He wished she could see that she had great potential to move forward with her life. Nick wanted Hannah to go back to school, so that she could support herself and the child she was expecting if necessary. Nick was just as concerned with his twin still living in Taiwan. Nick wanted Drew to come back to the States and do something with his life. Now that he was putting his own plans into motion, Nick wanted to see the rest of the family reunited. "I'm happy, young and alive, and I have the world by the tail, but I want you all to share my future." he wrote.

Nick found a job at a pizzeria and studied whenever he got the opportunity. In the dead heat of August in Phoenix, he celebrated his eighteenth birthday. As planned, he took the GED examinations. Of course, he passed. Time to celebrate! Nick and his best friend, Charlie, got together in the evening after Nick had closed the pizza shop. They drove to Papago Park on the eastern border of the city. They climbed the large rocks, looked out over the city, and talked about their futures. It was to be a joyous occasion. The night to celebrate Nick's passage from the youthful constraints of childhood into the adventures of manhood.

Nick eventually left his uncle's place and moved into a spare room in Charlie's parents' home where Charlie was still living. His friend's parents were school teachers, and they were especially fond of Nick. Nick gave up his work at the pizzeria and increased his earning power by working with Charlie in the small painting business he had started. It was work he had done with Charlie and his father in the summers while the two boys were in high school. By September, prodded by Nick, Drew felt that it was time to return to Phoenix to focus on building a life for himself. He needed to take responsibility for his independence. I gave Drew, as I had Nick, money for his pocket and he too stayed with Hannah who had married her long time boyfriend, despite our misgivings. Nick was very glad to have his twin brother back. But he still wanted Luke and me to return to the States. I missed my twins and my daughter. But, for the first time, I had a good job and was saving money.

After financing trips back to Phoenix and start-up money for my twins within a three month period, my savings were sorely depleted. I, once again, began a saving plan. "When I have enough to finance the shipment of our belongings back to the States and establish a household once we arrive, Luke and I will return," I wrote.

During this period, although lonely for my children, I stayed busy and enjoyed living and working among the Chinese. I tried not to agonize about my three children living halfway around the world. I told myself I had to accept the fact that they were young adults and that they needed to establish their independence and build their own nests. The separation was hard. Nevertheless, as long as my children moved forward, I was content.

Nick celebrated Christmas 1985, proud that he was self-supporting and considering both college and the army. He was earning a goodly amount and saving money too. He had been back in Phoenix for only six months and was already focused on the upcoming year. He made plans to use it to his best advantage. The new year of 1986 arrived and with it came the unexpected. Luke was fifteen and a rebel who needed to have a male role model. He refused to settle down and was headed straight into trouble if I didn't accept his demand to be sent back to the States.

I had no intention of placing the burden of Luke on Hannah or on the twins. But, I realized he badly needed his brother. Despite the fact that it would be a disruption in his life, Nick understood his brother's urgent need and offered to take on the responsibility for Luke. With the concern of a parent, once Luke was returned to the States, Nick found a place where he and his twin brother could comfortably live. There he could provide a stable environment and assume the responsibility for getting his younger brother enrolled school, looking after his welfare, and keeping him off the streets. After several months passed, Nick wrote that he was glad his plan to enter the army had been put on hold by Luke's return. He believed, due to the timing, there was a chance he would have been shipped off to Libya.

Maybe, I thought, fortune was finally smiling on us.

By June, I had not seen the children for a full year. I hated the extended separation from Nick and the others. We wrote letters and sent cards across the ocean. I sent money to the children whenever possible to help with necessities or offer fun. We spoke long-distance whenever we could afford it. But it was not the same as seeing each other. My children were unanimous in their belief that I should return. However, I was paying off my own school loans and could afford to help them only because of my job. I had to earn more money where it was possible, and that was what I was doing. "I still don't have sufficient funds to transport myself back to America," I explained. "When I do I will return," I promised my children.

In the meantime, summer moved into full gear. My twins turned nineteen. They worked, helped their brother, and started to save for education expenses.

Once again, turbulence intervened. Drew lost his job. It was weeks before he found another, and a couple of more weeks before he had any cash to stem the cost of living that inched up like a tide coming in. This misfortune took a bite out of the boys' savings. It also shed light on the reality of poverty that hovered over us since the day their father walked out. Nick said during a long distance call, "I can see with great clarity now how hard it was for you as a mother to keep a roof over our heads, put food on the table, and supply us as we grew with the shoes and clothes we needed for school and play." Nick's new role of maintaining a home for his brothers had helped him gain insight into my world and a deeper respect for me. He added, "I can't understand how you managed." I didn't know either.

Filling me with pride, Nick and Drew enrolled in junior college for the fall semester. Full time work. Full time school. They had to walk or rely on the worst bus system of any large city in America. I sent what money I could to help them. I commended the twins on their diligent effort to move forward.

As the holidays approached, I was so lonely for my children I could no longer bear the separation, and so I flew back to Phoenix for a visit. When I arrived home, I was disappointed to learn Nick had dropped his classes due to financial burdens. Soon after, Drew dropped his classes too. In the meantime, they worked and saved what they could. Nick, seeing the anguished look creep into my eyes told me, "Mom don't worry, we'll get there." But I did worry. That's what mothers do.

My daughter gave birth to a baby boy. He was a little angel who endeared himself to us right away. The most important thing was that Hannah, Drew, Nick and Luke, were all under one roof for Christmas, at my brother's place. This had not happened in a long time.

Nick surprised me late Christmas eve by walking in the door with a fresh evergreen tree. Though we were going to forego it as a luxury, he and his brother scouted tree lots that night. It was close to midnight when someone gave them a well-shaped tree around six feet in height. They carried it a great distance on their shoulders to get it home. The very act itself was Christmas fulfilled. Though humble and modest in material wealth, it was a Christmas of immense joy and love, one we shared with my brother Rick and Del, a friend we considered family.

My children were old enough to look back and reflect on Christmas past. They were able to remember that despite the fact that there was never much money for material things, there was always good food, good people, love and lots of fun. They talked about the years we spent with Paul and all the places he took them. They still loved him, especially Nick, and they were sorry he wasn't with us to celebrate our reunion. Life had gone on. The love we had as a family was the glue that held us together. I was amazed at how fast the years were passing. "I guess we made it after all," I said happily.

In January, 1987, I had to return to Taiwan. My possessions were still there, and I had to make enough money to get back home permanently, with a cushion to sustain me until I found a decent job. It was hard to tear myself away from the children, but finally with embraces and tears, I left Phoenix. Nick went back to college for the spring semester. Unfortunately, halfway through he had to withdraw a second time because of the demands of working six days a week. When he told me, I worried about his plans to move forward to a better future. But with each phone call and letter, Nick impressed upon me, "I'm working hard and I haven't given up."

I wanted to give him money to go back to school, but Nick wouldn't accept it. "Mom," he said, "its the first time you've been able to save. I'll take out a loan. I don't want you to worry. I'm still considering the Army to secure an education." Nick remained active in sports, shared good times with family and friends, and had high hopes for his future.

However during October, 1987, a disturbing letter backed up by a very persuasive phone call from Nicholas forced me to pack up and get back to the States without delay. Grandpa wasn't in Tucson with my sister. He was in Phoenix in a nursing home. I was shocked. I had seen my father when I'd been back for the Christmas holidays, and he didn't appear ill or debilitated. How could it be he was in a nursing home? Not my father. A nursing home was an institution where unwanted people suffered until death took them away. How long had he been there? Why was he there? I made immediate arrangements to leave Taiwan after Nick's call. I spent the trip across the ocean dismayed and confused. As soon as I got off the plane, I demanded to be taken to him. Rick drove me to the nursing home.

The figure I saw on the bed was a far cry from the person I had seen when I was back in Phoenix last December. I didn't recognize my father. He was a mass of bones curled up into the fetal position, lying helpless in a strange bed in the corner of a room where no on could see him. He was completed neglected. The staff had even lost his dentures. I learned later that was quite a common occurrence in nursing homes. His skin was dehydrated. He had a huge decubitus at the base of his spine. His mouth was crusty. His tongue was dry and split. His breath was putrid. He could not muster the strength to speak. But his eyes begged for mercy. I set my nursing skills to work, and for the next several hours I attended to my father. I massaged and lotioned every inch of his dying body while I spoke comforting words to enrich his mind and soul. Words of love and of what good times still lay ahead.

How could this have happened? Why had my sister placed him here? I wanted to take care of my dad. He certainly didn't deserve to die in a nursing home. It was wrong. It was cruel. I wanted to take him to Nick's and attend to his every need until his very last day. I wanted my father to share in our love, wanted to give him life before his death. However, after my second visit, my sister had him transferred to another nursing home, even further from central Phoenix where we lived. She let me know that she was making the decisions.

But I told my children that Grandpa was soon going to heaven, and we all needed to see him. We needed to pay our loving respects to him before he passed away. We went to the new nursing home and gathered around his bed. One branch of the family he would have cherished had he been allowed. We let Grandpa know we loved him, and that we were okay. We were able to make it. He didn't have to worry. Hannah set her son down at her grandfather's side so he could set eyes on his great-grandson before he left this world.

It was his last day on earth, and I knew it. While my children stood around his bed, a nurse had me sign a form for my father. It was a form that had been overlooked, a form my sister had not signed. A form that said 'hands off' me while I die. I spent the entire day with my father and remained until early evening. It was only the third occasion I had to spend with him. Once again, I cared lovingly for his body, his mind and his soul. I thanked God for bringing me back in time to attend to my father in his hour of greatest need. My father passed over to the golden shores of the heavenly kingdom just ten days after I returned from Taiwan. My sister, just as she did when our mother died, made funeral arrangements without consulting me or my brother.

My three sons, with the assistance of their Uncle Rick and Del, carried Grandpa's coffin out of the church where my sister arranged the open casket ceremony. The funeral party was made up of people who were her family and friends. My sons slid the coffin of their grandfather into the back of the hearse with honor, pride and respect. After the service at the cemetery was over, my sister invited everyone but me, Hannah and her family, Nick and Drew, Luke, Uncle Rick and Del to gather at her house on the outskirts of Phoenix to honor our father. What made her carry so much hatred in her heart for me was beyond my comprehension. But I decided, however, with my father dead, I had to pour my energy into reconstructing my life. Despite their love, I felt myself an intruder in my sons' lives. I took up space living with my twins, who were now twenty years old and didn't need their mother underfoot. I wanted to get back to work and return to college to begin a master's program, so I would have the education which would change our lives. But I had no car, and the cost of school was prohibitive at the time. Going would mean more loans. I didn't want to live in Tempe, to share an apartment with students half my age after being separated from my children so long.

I began working two jobs. Nick insisted on relinquishing his quarters to Drew and to me. Nick told me point-blank, "You just can't make it on your own Mom." Humbly, I accepted. I split the cost of living with Drew, while Nick took a place with a long-time friend with whom he had worked in the restaurant business. By the summer of 1988, things looked better. The twins and I rented a three bedroom apartment together. I bought an old Honda Civic that proved a benefit to all of us. I shared the car with Nick, who was now twenty-one.

After six months went by, the economy started getting worse. A sizzling summer began early. One of my jobs didn't work out, and the other came to an end shortly after I had started banking some money. I felt dejected. No matter how hard we worked we couldn't seem to get on a firm footing. Our money was going to landlords, utility mongers, and auto insurance companies.

To economize we moved to a smaller two bedroom apartment. After scouring the want ads, I found a job, while Nick went through the process of deciding what was best for him. I convinced Nick he had to reach a decision now about his own future and to build on it.

The Air Force looked good to Nick and Nick looked good to the Air Force. He went through the battery of tests. There was one flaw, however, and I felt it was all my fault. If Nick had a high school diploma, which he did not because I took him to Taiwan during the last half of his senior year, he could have signed up on the spot. Nick did have a GED, but Air Force rules mandated that anyone with a GED had to have a certain number of college credits to join.

Nick gave the Air Force very serious consideration, but he then got swept up in the incentives the Army waved under his nose. The Army didn't care about the GED. And the Army hitch was half the time. Three years instead of six. At this time, Nick was twenty-two. He could join now and be out of the Army at twenty-five. If he went into the Air Force, he would be twenty-eight when he got out. As an added inducement, to show him the Army really wanted him, the officer told him he would be inducted into the military band.

Nick was at the crossroads and had to make a choice. He decided he could not pass up the opportunity to play in the military band, so he signed his name to the Army contract. But, wait! Nick had a surprise in store. As the stream of paperwork started the ball rolling, his plans came to a sudden and abrupt halt. Juvenile records indicated that Nick had been charged with arson when he was twelve years old. The records also stated that he had been exonerated of the charges, and cleared of all accusation or blame. No felony ever took place. But someone in the Army wanted to play games. What was the story?

Carol Loving

The Army wanted to know all about the incident. But why should something Nick did at age twelve give the Army any trouble? Why was there a juvenile record in existence when Nick was an adult? And when there was no real wrong-doing attached to the past, why did the Army want to make a big deal over nothing? The incident was blown out of proportion and had taken place in 1979. That year Paul moved us to a trailer neighborhood where trailers had been converted into houses. It was on the far northwest edge of Phoenix, in Peoria. Nick was twelve years old at the time. He and Luke were playing with the boy next door in his backyard. The kid had a plastic squeeze bottle with a few ounces of gasoline in it.

And being curious and somewhat mischievous, as young boys often are, they wanted to see if they could make a lighted trail. The boys decided to find an open expanse and hiked for a couple of miles in the nearby desert that spread across the vastness where the housing development came to an end. They looked for a place where there was no dry scrub of any sort, and they soon found the perfect spot, a deep dry wash with a mud run along the bottom. There wasn't anything flammable anywhere around so the fire would be contained. The neighbor boy squeezed out a trail of gasoline along the bottom of the wash and put the plastic container with the remaining solution at the end of the line. Then went back to the starting point and put a match to the gasoline. A small flame ran across the bottom of the wash and began to die out when it got to the plastic container. That would have been the end of it, but the desert and the Law intervened. A cop stumbled onto the scene. The neighbor boy ran. My boys panicked and trying to hide, they ran into a nearby tunnel in the ground. The cop threatened to use tear gas on the children if they did not come out. When they did, my sons, only nine and twelve, were hauled away. Nick was charged with arson.

However, when the judge learned what happened, Nick was exonerated of the charge. The cop had taken an ordinary juvenile act of mischievous curiosity on the part of the three boys and turned it into a felony. There was no malice. No fraud. I felt they deserved a strong talking to, and perhaps community service.

Now, ten years later, that incident became a issue. The Army wanted Nick to expunge his juvenile file, so Nick went down to the courthouse and complied with the request. But the Army wasn't going to let it go at that. The officials wanted Nick to supply two letters from professionals to vouch for his character. Nick complied. He got a letter from Charlie's father, who was a teacher and another letter from a college professor and long-time friend of the family. Then an army official said they wanted him to spend six months in the Reserves to prove he was of worthy character. Nick felt this was one step over the line. He had defended his honor and character. He was not going to spend six month in the Reserves. Did the Army want him or not?

The Army broke down. The recruiter in charge of his file defended him to the ones above. After weeks of making Nick jump through hoops because of one innocent boyhood experience, the Army finally said "Welcome aboard." However, somebody up the chain of command had to play hard ball and attach a stipulation. The Army welcomed Nick with open arms, but he would have to choose something other than the military band. The excuse was that Nick had never taken a class in music theory. He didn't read music. He played by ear. Nick couldn't believe this when he heard it. He knew he could learn music theory at the drop of a hat. Nick agonized over whether to join up under the new stipulation. It was painful, but without the music he decided not to do it.

I stood by and watched once again, as the system worked against my son, just as it had against me. There was a bitter taste in my mouth. The system had been working against us since his father closed the door on his Air Force career, and left us like a dirty bundle of sticks on the side of the road. Nevertheless, I tried to be hopeful, to look at the good side. Nicholas was an astute young man who possessed high moral character and true leadership qualities. He was gifted in many ways. He was intelligent, perceptive, and a very good communicator. But I agonized, where was his future? Where was he supposed to look? Was it in music? Was it in sports? Was it in the field of communications? What about his education? Should he go to trade school? And, if so, which trade? With all his plans, I never would have thought he would be struggling with his future four years after he left Taiwan. He had been filled with determination when he flew back, ready to grab hold of the world, pick it up in one hand and spin it around on the tip of his finger as he did a basketball.

The 1990's started off with an incident which seemed to be just bad luck at the time, not a portent of events to come. The twins were at a rock concert filled with a mass of people. Nick and Drew were standing down front, close to the bandstand, which was encompassed by security. Nick wanted to get away from the crush of bodies inching forward. He asked two security officers to help him over the wall so he could leave. As they were lifting him over the top of the wall, the two officers dropped him. Nick slammed to the ground. His neck was injured and he was in severe pain. Drew was able to help him to the entrance, and they left. As soon as I saw Nick, I knew he had to be seen by a doctor. I rushed him over to the hospital emergency room. The doctor examined him and told us he had a soft tissue injury. He prescribed pain medication, and I drove to an all-night pharmacy to get it filled before getting Nick back to his apartment.

In the past, Nick had his fair share of bumps and bruises and knocks and punches, as an energetic, athletic individual. But he had never been injured like this before. The pain was ferocious, and when it finally wore off, Nick was left with constant pain of a lesser degree in the left side of his neck where the injury took place. The pain lingered for months. Later, Nick would trace the path of his future back to the night when going to a concert with his brother irrevocably altered the course of his life.

In August 1990, Nick and Drew turned twenty-three. They were sharing an apartment together. Nick was still in a quandary over his future. He thought of becoming a physical education teacher and athletic coach. I thought it was a good path to follow. I offered the funding to help him obtain his goal, but Nick refused to take my money. He also thought a trade school might be an alternative. It was far less expensive than paying for a four-year degree. What was Nick going to do? He still wasn't sure. During the next few months, Nick began to put on weight. For no reason understandable to any of us, his metabolism seemed to have changed. He was at least fifteen pounds heavier than usual. One hot afternoon as the summer sun shone down on us, it seemed, to me, as I scrutinized him that Nick's skin had taken on the aged look of someone who had reached mid-life. It struck me in an odd way, and I worried over the change in his body. But I never said a word. Nick was more concerned about his future than a few pounds that he couldn't account for.

Once again, a bad blow fell. My boss let me go, but at least I had a nest egg to get me through until I found new employment. I now lived in a studio apartment. Nick was working two jobs. His original job hours had been cut back to the point where he had to find a second one. He labored day and night.

In May, 1991, I finally found work which would allow me to save money and provide me with the time to write. The owner of my apartment complex hired me as the complex's manager. Nick was happy for me. I turned forty-five and my children gave me a wonderful party at our favorite Chinese restaurant. It was truly one of the happiest birthdays my children ever gave me. All four were in their twenties now. They were each very handsome and happy, all except Hannah, my beautiful daughter who still suffered silently under the rule of a very abusive man. Nick, with his striking good looks, was the life of the party and kept a smile on everyone's face that night.

It was early winter of 1992 when Nick and several of his fire fighting friends drove up to Tonto Rim outside of Flagstaff to get away for the day. The land was smothered with iced evergreen trees. Fresh snow from the night before was piled on top of previous snow making a white velvet landscape. Nick, along with a close friend, ventured away from the roadside where they had parked and trod the snow-bound hill surrounding them. When they decided to return to the roadside, they argued over which way to go to get back to the truck. Suddenly, they could not agree, and each went his separate way. Nick's friend made it back to the truck where their other friends were waiting. Nick did not return. His friends drove to the closest telephone and reported Nick missing.

Dressed in jeans, a sweater, and a jacket he had with him, Nick knew his clothing would be sufficient for daylight temperatures. However, when the sun went down and the temperature fell to below freezing, Nick began shivering. He had to keep walking. He had to keep moving. Glittering snow was everywhere and everything was soaking wet. Nick had a lighter with him, but every branch and limb and sprig was too wet with new-fallen snow to catch on fire. He tromped through the snow all night to keep the blood in his body circulating, and he ate frozen snow to keep from dehydrating. By the hours that preceded dawn, he was so cold and exhausted that he had sprawled out exhaustedly at the base of a tree. He drew his knees up to his chin to retain as much body heat as possible, and looked out over the universe trying to figure out what it was God had in mind for him.

Nick didn't know if he was going to freeze to death or if he was going to survive to see the dawn. He was cradled and protected by the snow that surrounded his exhausted body in the chilling temperature, which had now fallen to twenty below. All he could do was look up to the heavens. Communicate with his Creator. He told me later that as he lay in the snow, he suddenly felt a warm, glowing sensation radiate from within his body. It actually kept him warm. And there was more. This radiant energy moved up out of his body and hovered above him, and he was sure it caused him to survive the night. The next morning, Nick got up from the ground and made it over the hill where he found rescue workers getting ready to set off in search of him.

I learned more about the night later. By then, I would attach a new and more ominous significance to the experience.

At their next birthday the twins turned twenty-five. A few days later, Hannah gave birth to a beautiful baby girl, who sadly was born with severely clubbed feet. My poor daughter, it seemed her life was plagued with one heartache after another. Nick had always been concerned about his sister. The relationship we saw between Hannah and her husband was now like an active volcano. And a newborn child with special needs was one more reason for the irrational man she married to push a few more abusive buttons. We were distraught, but so long as Hannah loved him and wanted to remain in the relationship, we could do nothing but love and support her.

We were invited to a wedding in October. Charlie, Nick's best friend, was getting married. Where had the years gone? Where were they taking us? Though Nick was only twenty-five, he was discouraged, because he had begun to notice he was losing the edge that made him exceptionally agile at most of his athletic endeavors. Even when he played a friendly game of basketball in the evenings with his friends, Nick felt awkward and almost clumsy. He told me worriedly, "I'm just not running down the length of the court at my normal pace and I stumble a lot. I don't know what to think about this slow-down except that it must be attributed to my age."

My Son, My Sorrow

I chuckled as I replied, "Guess how that makes me feel!" He threw back his head and laughed his infectious laugh. "Seriously Nick," I told him, "you're not a teenager anymore. You just have to accept that and move on."

"Yeah Mom, but twenty five is a little early for a slow-down," he shook his head, then went on, "Maybe you're right, I guess."

In January, 1993, Luke, who had been living with his brothers, was working during the day and going to trade school in the evening. He wanted to save money for a place of his own and asked me to put him up for a while. As long as my children made the effort to move forward, whatever their egos or my slim savings, I felt compelled to help. I took Luke back in and spent much time talking to him about his future. I helped him all I could.

About this time, Nick had gotten a better job. He was making more money and was more interested in the work, but still very concerned about the direction of his future. He was also worried about something else. Another disturbing symptom. Periodically, when he spoke, certain sounds of his speech slurred. It was perplexing to all of us. It didn't happen all the time. But, when it did, it sounded like Nick had a little too much to drink. I knew this couldn't be, so I didn't question him. After all, I had told him he was a grown-up and I didn't want to be a meddling mother.

That March, Luke announced that he wanted to use Nick's car to get back and forth to school at night. Nick let him. While on Luke's way home from class someone sideswiped the right side of the car. A hit-and-run driver.

Carol Loving

Although Luke was fine, the damage rendered the car completely useless. Nick no longer had transportation. Without a car, he lost the one job he had that he really wanted. Back to square one.

At that time, Nick was staying at Drew's apartment. Under stress, the twins had a big fight and Drew wanted him out. I was shocked when Nick called me and asked, "Mom, can you pick me up and let me stay with you?" I couldn't believe my sons were fighting so badly that Drew wanted to put Nick out when his brother was already down on his luck. But Nick gathered up a few things and we went to my place. He was so upset that his twin had thrown him out, he cried. A sight I rarely saw.

Three people in my small cramped apartment was too much for me to bear. I explained the situation to Luke, who agreed to find another place now that his school and job situation were more stable. I let Nick have the bedroom to himself, and I slept in the living room. I offered my son all that I had. A place to stay. Time to map out his life. Financial help to get another car. The use of my car to keep his self respect. I assigned odd jobs to Nick around the complex so he made a little money while he went to trade school. I told him, "Stay as long as you need to get your thoughts in order and to get your life's direction on the map. I'm here to back you up in every way." As I knew he would be for me one day.

With the extra support from me and his success at the trade school, Nick soon regained his good spirits. Although there was still some tension between them, he and Drew were friends once again. Nick was the picture of life. He'd lost the extra pounds he'd put on a couple of years before. His

50

favorite team, the Suns, were having a banner year under Charles Barkley, so the city fathers organized a parade. He and Uncle Rick went to it. More than a quarter of a million people showed up.

Several days later, my brother came over when Nick was at work and told me some disturbing news about my son. Something that had taken place the afternoon of the parade unnerved Rick. "Carol, I'm worried about Nick," he said pensively. "Nick and I were racing down the side of the road on our way back from the parade, and Nick couldn't keep up with me. He seemed to be having trouble with his legs, especially the right one. You know how fast he used to be. I felt uneasy watching him."

Then Rick told me something he had kept quiet for months. "Before Luke had his misfortune with the car in March," Rick explained, "Nick and I went biking early one morning. We both loved the challenge of pumping up Squaw Peak. The bikes were equally good, but Nick had trouble keeping up with me once I overtook him on our way up the steep hill. I looked back to find that he had come to a complete stop. He couldn't peddle his bike. His right leg was spasmodically jerking, and Nick couldn't stop it. He had to wait for it to stop on its own. Nick told me it was just a muscle fatigue or something."

Unable to win a race. Slowing down. *Something is not as it should be.* Alerted now, I began to watch Nick more closely. What was wrong with him? Suddenly, I noticed that he was quick to lose his temper over little things. That wasn't like him. Another problem was the leg spasms that my brother described. It didn't make sense that Nick would have less endurance than his uncle who was fifteen years his senior. I had to ask myself, what was the odd physical manifestation hanging like a cloud over Nick's life? Nick pushed me off whenever I tried to investigate. But, I was concerned about Nick. And Nick was very worried about himself. Much more than we knew. Every one of us.

Not even a month later, Nick began to complain of tightness in his jaw. We discussed his wisdom teeth as the possible cause, and thinking it might help, Nick had the teeth extracted. Nothing changed. The tightness remained. Though no one suspected it, his body was, indeed, a barometer of what was to come. Something none of us could foresee. But in other ways, things were going better. Over the summer, Nick explored many career paths and decided to focus on a four-year degree in business communications. At last, I thought, he would have the successful future for which I prayed. Nick and Drew turned twenty-six that August. Classes began a few weeks later. However, what should have been joy at knowing what his next stop would be turned into a knot inside his stomach. He had begun to have more difficulty pronouncing his words. It occurred more frequently. Then almost constantly. Nick now had to struggle to say certain words at all. It was forcing him to move from a life as a vibrant, outgoing, extrovert to that of quiet introvert. Nick dropped his communication class.

A few weeks later, inexplicably exhausted by work and school and needing the money that his job brought in, he dropped the rest of his classes. Nick seemed to have given up with his life, his dreams and his hope for the future. "I'm a failure," he told me. "I have to do some mundane job like I have now forever, so I don't have to talk to anyone." I felt unhinged by the things Nick was experiencing. I had no idea it was the struggle he was undergoing, forcing his body to perform, that made him leave school, experiencing more and more limitations. Nick looked absolutely vital, vibrant and handsome. But he was becoming weaker and weaker. My anxiety over something I couldn't understand grew. Then over the next several weeks there was another change in our life pattern which created more worry for me. I hardly saw Nick at all. He seemed to be leading an active life, but I couldn't shake the feeling that, though we lived together, he didn't want to see me or he didn't want me to see him. Either way I became increasingly uneasy.

3

Down, Down, Down

The weeks passed. There was no doubt now that Nick was avoiding me. He went out to run track early each morning trying desperately to regain the strength and control over his body that he was losing. He'd come back to the apartment late at night when I was asleep. One morning, I saw Nick enter the bathroom. Clearly, he was limping. I couldn't tell if it was his foot or his ankle that hurt. I called out, "Did you wrench your ankle?"

"Damn it no!" he snapped. I was startled when Nick yelled at me. Whatever the problem was with his leg, he sure didn't want to talk about it. I kept silent.

That fall, as always, Nick, his brothers, and his friends liked to get together to tumble their young bodies together in endless games of football. I went out to watch them. Another shock. Nick, who had won so many athletic awards for his sports ability, was awkward and uncoordinated. The tips of his fingers couldn't seem to grasp the ball, and without a solid grip he couldn't make a good pass. Also, his right leg kept giving out on him, causing him to stumble and fall. No one could figure out what was happening to Nick to make him perform so poorly on the field. Like his family, every one of his friends were in denial of the fact that something was wrong, very wrong, with Nick. That afternoon, when Nick, their former star athlete, could not perform with the ball, they convinced themselves he must have had too much to drink. What else could it be? Nick was only twenty-six. Young and strong like the rest. It couldn't be something physical, they and I reassured ourselves. Illness and infirmity was something far out in the future. A distant time when their hair would turn gray and their bodies would grow infirm.

Late that night, when Nick returned to our apartment, I was sitting on the bed in the living room when he entered through the front doorway. I gazed intently at him as he limped over and sat down beside me. I said nothing, allowing my eyes and ears and all powers of perception to work for me as Nick told me about the game and how weak he felt. "I think I need to see a doctor," he said slowly. Something had to be very wrong if Nick, who had always been so healthy and shied away from "the medicine men," as he called them, now wanted to see one. I went numb. I couldn't move. My heart suddenly felt heavy.

As Nick got up to leave, I watched my usually agile and spirited son limp away dejected and down-trodden. I would have done anything in the world to change the image in front of me. After a few minutes of communication with my Father in Heaven, I slowly walked to my son's room. He was in the dark, seated on the floor with his legs out before him.

My Son, My Sorrow

When I was inside the room, I flipped on the light. I was shocked to see his right leg shaking in a persistent spasmodic motion. As I looked closer, I saw his knees were swollen and purple from the trauma of activity in the football game. With trepidation, I asked my son, "Do you feel like you're becoming paralyzed? Is that it?" That proved to be the question that broke the dam.

Anguish took hold of my son, and he wailed out from the very depths of his soul. He sobbed with a heart-rending sound that wrenched every fiber of his being. "I don't know what's happening to me. I feel like I'm becoming a cripple," Nick cried.

I broke down in tears along with him. I put my arms around him. We sobbed like children. We had to know what was happening to him. This was not a time to wait and see. We had to find out now. Even though it was the middle of the night, we had to find out what was wrong. I telephoned Luke. "I need you to come to my place and help me take Nick to the hospital." He got there soon afterward. Together we helped Nick get up off the floor. With Luke providing physical support, Nick limped his way to my car. Taking his own car, Luke went to pick up Drew to meet us at the hospital.

The night was moonless; the streets were quiet as I drove Nick to Saint Joseph's Hospital, not far from our home. While waiting in the emergency room, Nick joked and reminisced about past emergency encounters. Then he was silent for awhile and when he broke the quiet, he said, "Remember the time you brought me here—the night of the concert—when I received that blow to my neck?" Suddenly, I realized that was the beginning of Nick's physical problems. It took me a few moments to remember that night, to try to recall what the doctors said.

"I remember sitting in this very spot waiting to see a doctor," Nick continued. "They took an x-ray and gave me a prescription for pain." Confused, I shook my head.

"Maybe the hospital overlooked something when you were seen by the doctor," I suggested. "Maybe this is related to whatever happened then." Our minds scrambled for answers as we waited. Our thoughts and conversations were interrupted when Luke and Drew showed up.

We all sat there silently until the hospital staff called Nick's name. I accompanied him to the examination room. A doctor eventually showed up and began to ask Nick a lot of questions finally saying, "You seem to be a well-developed, well-nourished young man." I smiled. The doctor referred to the slurring that Nick told him had been occurring over the past year as dysarthria. He noted, too, that Nick had a progressive weakness affecting the right extremities, both upper and lower, and that Nick's gait showed a pronounced limp in the right leg. These problems were evident to us all. What we wanted was an answer. Instead he continued to put long names on the symptoms. "Nick has chronic bi-temporal headaches along with occasional paroxysmal blurred vision. Optic atrophy is also noted."

"What does all this mean?" Nick asked. The doctor shook his head. The symptoms were ominous. He said, "Nick is subject to a slowly evolving constellation of neurological deficits." Finally, he admitted he did not know why. "Possibly the cervical spine, possibly the brain stem."

The evidence of optic atrophy made the doctor think of multiple sclerosis, but Nick did not have the list of customary complaints attributed to the disease. The doctor ordered a blood count on Nick and he wanted a CAT scan. Nick and I were taken to another floor to have the scan done. I sat in the waiting area and watched TV as I waited for my son. After a long while, when no one came to get me, I realized I had been abandoned. I learned Nick had been taken back to the examination room.

"The doctor wants to admit me into the hospital for a twenty-three hour observation period to rule out a spinal cord tumor and multiple sclerosis." It was past midnight by the time Nick and I found ourselves in a room on the neurological floor. Luke took Drew home and then Luke returned to see if there was anything he could do before going home himself.

Nick was hungry. I asked Luke to come with me to the cafeteria, so I could pick up a sandwich and milk for his brother. On the way to the cafeteria Luke began to cry uncontrollably. In a mothering way, I told him, "I know how you feel, I'm crying on the inside, but I have to be calm and you have to get control of yourself so we can help Nick." We returned, and Luke, more composed now, said good night to his brother, since he had to work in the morning. I stayed with Nick and we talked for a while.

Nick was calm, as he usually was in times of crisis. "Mom, I'm relieved to be here so I can discover what's wrong," he told me. As I stood by the side of Nick's bed, held his hand and spoke softly to him, I scrutinized my son; I saw a handsome young man with a radiant, healthy glow. It didn't look like anything serious could be wrong to me. The hour was late. Nick was tired. Ready to sleep. All we could do was be trustful, knowing all things are ultimately in God's hands. We said good night and I bent over to kiss him.

Early the next morning I returned to see Nick. We were both morning people, and I wanted to share a brief visit first thing so Nick would feel my support. An MRI was on schedule soon, but no specific time was given for the procedure. Nick was upbeat and except for the limp I noticed when he walked to the bathroom, he looked great.

"I have to leave to open my office, but I'll be back at lunchtime." As I walked to the door, "Keep your spirits up. this will soon be over."

"Spirits up." Nick gave me the thumbs up sign. "Don't worry, Mom, piece of cake."

At one o'clock, I returned, but the MRI still had not been done. Instead, there was a team of interns making their rounds. The group of budding young doctors who went into Nick's room were standing around Nick's bed when I entered. The tall, dark-haired leader of the fledglings began scraping a tongue depressor along the sole of Nick's foot. He leaned toward the others conspiratorially and stated, "The procedure I just demonstrated is an indication that this patient has had a stroke." Stroke! Was he out of his mind?

When the doctors left the room, Nick and I discussed the top banana and what he had said about a stroke. "That's the craziest thing I've ever heard," I declared. Even the man in the other bed had to laugh. "A stroke doesn't come creeping along like a caterpillar; it comes swooping down like a bat." It was growing late, I was forced to leave Nick again and return to work. Nick's roommate was being discharged that day, so Nick was left with a room to himself, with the exception of strangers, all dressed in different uniforms, coming and going as the afternoon moved on. People came in to clean. People came in with food. People came in to draw blood from his arm. Nurses buzzed in and out, busy, busy, busy. But no one came to get Nick for the MRI.

When I went back to the hospital around 6 P.M. and I found Nick still waiting for the MRI to be done, I couldn't believe it. Although I should have known better because that was the way hospitals were when I worked in them. When Nick was admitted, we thought he would be home by Monday night. We certainly thought we would know something about his condition by now. The reality was, we were at the mercy of an impersonal system that directed the lives of people and then pronounced sentence. We were finally told the MRI would take place that night, sometime before midnight. As the evening wore on, Nick and I laughed at "the white ghosts," as we labeled them, who seemed to disappear and rarely spoke as they came in and went out of his room in the deepening darkness. We visited in his room for a couple of hours. For the second night in a row, I left my son in good spirit and mind.

Later he called and told me that not long after I went home, someone finally took him to a distant location in the hospital, where he sat in a wheelchair and waited and waited before the test was actually conducted.

"They slid me into a long, cold tube to do the MRI scan. It lasted about two hours," he said wearily. During that time, Nick had to lie perfectly still. He was not returned to his room until several hours later. "It was silly to think I was going to be out in twenty-three hours. It took twenty-three hours before I got the MRI scan. I may grow gray hair here, but I've told the nurses not to worry, I've become a permanent guest."

Everyone who came in contact with Nick had been pleasantly charmed by his good looks and amicable personality. He was a joy for any nurse to have as a patient because he was kind, courteous, witty and positive. For a second night, my son rested his head on a hospital bed, unsuspecting of the insidious execution of his electrochemical system, already underway and unstoppable.

I paid Nick another visit the next morning before I went to work. He gave me a rundown on what the doctors planned for him that day. "All they want is more blood. I think they're undercover vampires and ghouls," he joked. Then he said more seriously, "They plan to do a lumbar puncture on me."

I cringed upon hearing that. From my nursing experiences, I knew it was an extremely unpleasant procedure, and unfortunately, as routine in a hospital as drawing blood. It was my gut feeling that the lumbar puncture would reveal nothing. I told Nick as much as I knew about the procedure, and that it could be painful. I also told him he could expect an intern to do the dirty work and he would have to remain very still while a large, intrusive needle was inserted into his spine. Doctors seldom succeeded in locating the right spot the first time, so he should expect the painful invasion into his spine more than once. "When it's over, it's important to lie still, flat on your back for hours." I explained. "Or you'll have the worst headache of your life."

When the doctor had made rounds earlier they told Nick that they dismissed Monday's idea of a stroke. "Gee. A stroke of light for the modern medicine man." he kidded the doctor.

My Son, My Sorrow

Nick and I talked about the limp in his right leg and tried to figure out what it was we were dealing with. His right foot seemed to be the problem. It didn't fall to the ground in a heel-to-toe motion. The ball of his foot came down first. It dropped before the heel. "It drops like there is no control over the tip of the foot," I exclaimed. Describing what I saw brought tears to my eyes.

But, my son, so adaptive and logical, looked at his leg and said, "I can handle it. I can live with it. After all, its not like I'll be helpless." I said nothing.

I returned to the hospital after one o'clock. Nick was flat on his back. He looked pale and tired. The lumbar puncture had taken place at noon. As I had told him, he had to remain still for hours. I took his hand and bent over the bed to kiss him. His face was contorted. I could see the pain was intense. At that moment, I hated the medical profession for inflicting this pain on my son.

Although Nick was exhausted and needed to rest, a phlebotomist came in to take more blood from Nick's arm. So much blood had already been taken from his left arm that it had become bruised and tender. I demanded the phlebotomist take a few extra steps around the bed to draw the blood from Nick's right arm—an area that had not been punctured so much.

Since Nick was completely fatigued from the pain induced by the lumbar puncture, I left him closing his eyes, drifting off into much needed sleep. I would see him again in the evening.

That night at the hospital, a group of doctors were in the room once again discussing Nick's medical condition. "We now believe we are looking at multiple sclerosis," a tall, thin, balding one stated.

I protested, "We really have no history of MS in the family."

But Nick interrupted. "We have no idea what my father's gene pool has contributed to my blood when it comes to possible medical problems." The M.D.s all nodded ceremoniously. After they left, we began to talk about their theories. Nick was sitting up and looking better, but still dealing with pain in his back. "If it doesn't mean a wheelchair, I can live with it. One thing I don't want to become is one of Jerry's kids. I'm too tall," Nick joked. We laughed when he said it, and couldn't remember if Jerry Lewis was associated with Multiple Sclerosis or Muscular Dystrophy. Either way, my laughter only thinly masked my worry.

Nick and I then took a slow walk up and down the corridor outside his room. He had been in the hospital for two full days. We didn't really know anything more than we did Sunday night when he entered. "Maybe it is MS." I said.

"The doctors said they would have to continue searching and schedule more tests," he replied. They wanted medical information on Nick's father's side of the family. Nick wanted me to contact his grandmother Baba, to see if she could provide us with any background on both her and her late husband's family.

"I will call her tonight," I promised. Nick was drained after two days in the hospital.

"I'm really looking forward to a full night's sleep." It was about nine in the evening when I left my son in a peaceful spirit. We were both tired and unaware of what the next day would bring, if anything.

My Son, My Sorrow

On Wednesday, I was back at the hospital at nine in the morning. Nick was well rested and was recovering from the procedure the day before. The pain in his back had reduced greatly. He was, as usual, filled with wit and a keen sense of perception that challenged everyone in an unexpected manner. Nodding in unison, the team of doctors, dressed in white jackets, huddled around his bedside again. They buzzed with great wonder and curiosity. "We've ruled out Multiple Sclerosis overnight," the same tall, balding physician said, "and we haven't as yet found other clues." They wanted to do a PET scan that day along with other tests.

Within a few minutes the doctors moved on, and Nick and I were left alone. I told him, "I spoke to Baba and there isn't any information she can give us. She said families in Europe were torn apart during the war years, and she doesn't know a thing."

Leaving Nick, I felt even more worried. A lot of activity had taken place since Sunday night. But the doctors were as mystified as when it all began. Exhausted, I planned to rest on my lunch hour and return to the hospital after five o'clock. Around two in the afternoon, Nick was taken to have a PET scan done. No conclusions had been reached when I returned to see him. Shortly thereafter, an attendant came along and wheeled Nick away to another area of the hospital where a technician conducted several neurophysiological tests on him. I went along with my son and sat through the procedures which took place in a small area with lights dimmed very, very low. The testing lasted a couple of hours. When we got back to Nick's room, I said goodbye and returned home to eat. Then I went right back to the hospital to be with my son.

Carol Loving

On Wednesday evening, we still didn't know what was wrong with Nick. The doctors wanted to keep him one more day. If by then they didn't know anything, they would send Nick home. I kept telling myself he was alright. Nothing serious could be wrong with him. A friend called the hospital that night while Nick and I were together. In fact, many friends had been phoning or visiting. Their chit-chat relieved the anxiety of waiting and kept Nick's spirits high.

After the call, Nick explained to me what the doctors had in mind for the next day. "They want to run a series of neuromuscular tests tomorrow morning and afternoon, in a last ditch effort to get to the root of whatever this is. They said they'll test me again to rule out the possibility of a terminal condition." He winked and smiled. "Guess if they can't kill me off quick, they'll go on to look for less serious stuff."

I tried to return the smile, but the word 'terminal' struck my heart. Catching my look, he said, "Mom, please relax. It can't be anything much since I still have a good appetite and that's your usual tip-off, and they're going to send me home after tomorrow's test."

I was glad he was going home the next day even if we didn't know what the problem was. I was his mother. Somehow I'd protect him. We watched a little television together. Then, since tests were to begin in the morning and no one indicated what time the tests would end, we decided it would be best to wait for Nick to call before I came to the hospital. Once again, I studied my son. He looked good, very healthy, regardless of the unknown malady that had a mysterious hold on him. Nick was very positive, and we were both

My Son, My Sorrow

happy the hospital stay was drawing to an end. I left my son to the comfort and security of his inner spirit.

The phone rang in my apartment Thursday morning about eleven o'clock. It was Nick. His voice was empty, hollow and distant. "Ma, it isn't good." That was all he said.

With a faltering voice of my own, I stumbled over words, telling him, "I will be right there." I hung up the phone; I didn't know what to think.

I crumpled and cried out in defiance at what was going on inside me. "No, no, no, no!" That was all I could utter. A flood of tears poured out of my eyes, nearly blinding me. I choked on them. Shaking I tried to orient myself, but I questioned my own ability to drive as I locked up my apartment. I battled the army of tears that still had control over me as I left the property. Slowly, I made the first turn heading toward the hospital. I drove through the streets of Phoenix, tears still cascading down my cheeks. They would not stop. I made it to my destination and parked in the lot across the street.

The distance I now had to travel by foot to reach my son was measured in pathways and corridors and elevators and hallways. All spotted with people. Their presence made no difference to me, as I ran through them determined to reach my son. Finally, I was forced to stop at the elevator to take me to his floor. There, a world of strangers also stood waiting. I could hardly catch my breath. One of the doctors involved in Nick's case was among the crowd of people waiting for the elevator. The look on his face as he recognized me told me he knew, and he tried to get me to sit down. "No, I don't want to sit. I have to get to my son." I sobbed.

Carol Loving

The elevator opened and everyone crowded inside. The doors closed. We inched up. At last, I reached the neurological floor and my trail of tears continued to spill out on the long journey to get to the wing where Nick was. I told myself that I had to stop crying before I got to Nick. I was down to a whimper by the time I passed more doctors and nurses in the hall. They stood silently, watching as my feet carried me quickly on my path. I was determined to get full control of myself before I saw Nick. And somehow, I did, when I rounded the nurse's station and made it down the final corridor to my son's room.

Opening his door, I saw Nick seated on the side of the bed. His face looked like a condemned man in a cell that seemed to swallow him up. He stared at me as I drew closer.

"Have the doctors told you the news?" he asked. I shook my head and sat down on the bed beside him. Nick held my eyes, "I have Lou Gehrig's disease." The life swept out of me. I knew little about the disease, except that it was deadly.

"Around nine o'clock," Nick explained, "the doctors conducted an electromylogram on me. They call it an EMG." The procedure required piercing the length of Nick's arms and legs with needles wired to a machine designed to measure the electric waves associated with his skeletal muscular activity. "It took about two hours, and I had some pain," Nick continued. When it was finally over, he was returned to his room.

"Then the senior doctor involved in my case came in," and asked "Have you ever heard of Amyotrophic Lateral Sclerosis?"

"I wondered what he was trying to say. He went on to tell me that Amyotrophic Lateral Sclerosis was also known as

My Son, My Sorrow

Lou Gehrig's disease. As soon as he said the baseball player's name, I knew I was going to die. He told me there was no cure for the disease." With that the doctor added that Nick could leave the hospital. "I asked him, 'How long am I going to live?' But the doctor could not find it in himself to be honest. He said it was impossible to say. He turned and left the room. Then I picked up the phone to call you."

No one had seen Nick since the doctor who announced his impending death sentence left. None of the interns. None of the nurses. We sat side by side for a while, both of us in a state of shock. My mind felt like sand. We tried to comfort each other. Finally, there seemed nothing to say, and so we waited in Nick's room to be discharged. Still, no one came in. When the doctor said Nick could leave the hospital, he apparently meant right then and there. That was it. Case closed.

Walking out in the hall, I flagged down a doctor and made him come inside. He looked very surprised and said, "I didn't know you were still here." It was the same doctor who had been waiting at the elevator who had asked me to sit down.

He said, "You can leave. There's no paper work to fill out." He, too, refused to give a definite answer as to how long Nick would live. "It could be a few years, it could be fifteen." the doctor said frowning.

He went on without giving us a chance to comment. "Barrow Neurological Institute, a sister institute, offers an experimental drug study for people with Lou Gehrig's disease. Nick can participate in the program if he's interested. Involvement in the study will eliminate the bill for his hospital stay, but the program doesn't offer any promises. It's an experiment." Then he turned away, not looking at either of us.

Carol Loving

I filtered something into my understanding as I listened and looked at the doctor. It was something I sensed: Hopelessness was in the air. The doctor. His words. His body language. All conveyed hopelessness.

Now that Nick had been diagnosed with the fatal disease, everyone was avoiding us. There wasn't even the normal hum of hospital activity outside his door. Nick, once the popular patient, had suddenly become the leper of the community. He was no longer of interest to doctors and nurses who could do nothing for him.

My son and I left the hospital knowing the name of his disease. Knowing he was going to die of a rare and dreaded condition no one seemed to want to talk about. But we refused to give up.

"The present is no time to weep. It's the time to eat, drink and be merry. Laughter before tears," Nick told me. "It doesn't bother me that I'm going to die. I'm not afraid of death. It's part of life and that goes on. I've been given a very good life."

One thing was firm in his mind about the death sentence he had been given. "I don't want to become helpless. I'll never accept that. I'll have to die before it ever gets to that. Promise me you'll help me." I agreed with my son and said I would be there to help him in the end.

"In the meantime, you have a lot of living to do," I told Nick. He could still drive, so hugging me first, he took off. He had a lot of thinking he needed to do on his own.

It was a month before Nick saw the doctor at Barrow Neurological Institute. We went to the appointment together, and I noticed that Nick was put through the same neurological examination as the doctors had given him at the hospital. We were given a brief overview of the drug study program. Some information about the experimental drug designed to slow the degenerative process of Lou Gehrig's syndrome.

Nick has never liked needles, and his immediate reaction to the drug study was no. But then he began to think out loud. It was certain he was going to die. Maybe he could tolerate the injections if it was going to do some good. What harm could there be in giving the program a try? It wasn't going to kill him. Or was it?

Nick eventually told the doctor that he would join. The doctor was pleased. He told Nick, "Under the program you are eligible for Social Security benefits." He then wrote a prescription. A pill to reduce excessive salivation that was building up at night in Nick's sleep, due to muscle loss in the throat. Nick didn't like the pills any more than he liked shots, and it didn't make sense to me to try to swallow a pill when the act of swallowing was already being hindered by the disease.

While Nick shared his time with family and friends, I spent my time at the library doing research on Lou Gehrig's syndrome. I read everything from complex neurological studies compiled in the New England Journal of Medicine to personalized stories of individuals afflicted with the dreadful disorder.

I found out that Lou Gehrig's disease, or amyotrophic lateral sclerosis, is an electrochemical disorder that causes progressive muscular atrophy, twitching and muscle spasms. It does not affect everyone in the same manner or at the same rate of degeneration, however, it is irreversible. The cause of the disease is unknown yet it is believed that a severe blow to the body or exposure to toxic chemicals may contribute.

Carol Loving

As I read further, I discovered what would happen to Nick's body through each stage of the sickness. In the beginning stage, as ALS attacks the motor neurons in the brain, the muscles controlling speech, swallowing and chewing are affected. ALS sufferers often notice changes in their voices. Also, many develop an unexplained weakness and stiffness in their hands. I thought back to the day when Nick played football with his friends and had so much trouble grasping the ball. Now I realized that this was one of the warning signs of the disease.

As the syndrome continues to destroy the body's muscles, speech becomes impossible. Movement of the arms and legs becomes even more difficult as the muscles stiffen, and eventually the arms and legs cannot move at all. However, unlike those who suffer from paralysis, the sense of touch remains intact. Sufferers can feel an itch, but they just can't lift their arms to scratch it. They can feel a gentle touch, but they can't return it. And it is the same for the other senses. Patients can still see and hear and taste and smell. Though Lou Gehrig's disease destroys the body, it never affects the mind or the senses. My heart ached when I learned this. I knew people died from the disease, but I never fully realized how awful the death could be. I thought of what was in store for Nick and winced. Though I could barely stand to go on, I had to learn as much as I could about what the future held for my son.

I discovered that people who contracted ALS could live seven to ten years, or could die within months. No one has found a way to extend the lifespan of those who suffer from the disease. Almost a century after discovering this syndrome, medical researchers still have no cure for it.

My Son, My Sorrow

I could remember the grim, dying faces of those who suffered in the nursing homes and hospitals I'd worked in. I could remember the old and the sick, abandoned and left to die alone. I could remember eyes that begged for mercy from those who had enough courage to look at them. "I will never let Nick die like that," I swore. We had a rough road before us, but one thing was for sure, Nick could rely on his family.

4

Family Sorrow

Just as there are in the heavens, stars that shine brighter than others, so it is within the cluster of children I brought into the world. One radiated more light than the others. Nick was that brightest and most shining star. He was born a leader, ready to take the reins of our struggle as a family. He was a much better decision maker than I was. Nick loved his family and he was always concerned with helping his siblings and me to maximize our individual abilities and achieve our highest potential.

Now, he was going to leave us. Called to move on, Nick accepted the end of his life, but it saddened him to know that his death meant we were going to have to make it on our own. We would have to make do without him. Could we do it? He had to wonder. He was concerned. The idea that I would be lost without him saddened him. And, in the short time he had left he was determined to give all he could of himself to me.

As a child, Nick was full of love, and as he grew so did his capacity for giving of himself. The bond that developed between us over the years had been well nurtured. The children and I were a close unit as they were growing up, but I shared something special with Nick. Together we had a rare gift of communication. The ability to listen and learn from each other and transcend to a deeper level of understanding. A spirit of sympathy flowed in our embraces and Nick knew I needed them. And now that death stood nearby, he embraced me with every encounter. He held me with fondness and affection and the special love shared between a mother and her son. He gave me something to hold on to for the moment. He may have felt weak in body, but the hugs he gave me were strong.

The reality that Nick was going to die sent shock waves into the heart of each family member. Everyone was overcome when they learned Nick was going to die of ALS, Lou Gehrig's disease. Everyone had to cry in order to accept the truth, but Nick didn't want us crying around him. "It is time to eat, drink and be merry, not sad," he told us. Nick was right. We should cry our tears in private. I had the greatest struggle controlling my emotions, at first. There wasn't a moment when tears were not right on the edge of my eyes, waiting to fall. Everyone's pain was so deep that no one could believe another's grief was greater than his own. Everyone loved Nicholas John.

The nature of Lou Gehrig's disease renders the victim powerless. Powerless to himself and powerless to the world around him. Powerless to the people around him. Powerless to the modern impersonal world of medicine which doesn't minister to the pain and suffering of the helpless and dying. Nick would have to end his own life in order to escape the suffering this earth had in mind for him. Life had presented the forecast of an early death to my son and he accepted it like a noble young man. Yet, before it was all over, we were destined to find ourselves faced with a disease worse than death. We were going to learn first hand the untold horrors of Lou Gehrig's syndrome, the physical and mental torment this neurological process is for the victim and the lack of power the medical community has to either treat the disease or help the victim and end the person's suffering.

Luckily, we didn't know at that point, our opponent had more power over the human body than we could ever imagine.

During these first days after learning of Nick's terminal illness, helpless was the only word to describe us as a family faced with the uncommon and devastating neuromuscular disorder some called creeping paralysis. We were helpless to aid Nick. Helpless to prevent the tragic effects due to unfold with time. And that made us feel even more impotent. We watched awe-struck, incapable of stopping the electrochemical strangulation of muscular life that had begun its take-over of Nick's body, robbing him of mobility. Together or individually, there was nothing we could do to bring this destruction to a halt. As a family, we wanted to do everything for Nick. Yet, all we could really do was live each day with him and give all the love possible. Nick had always helped his family, and now it was time for his family to help him. Could we do it when our own lives appeared to be crumbling as well?

For Drew, Nick's death sentence was almost unbearable. He and Nick were fraternal twins. They came into the world together. They complemented each other. They were like a hoop and a basketball. The reality of Nick's condition unleashed a torrent of tears and thoughts, emotions and pain for Drew to deal with. This only intensified when he learned more about the disease and began to understand the prognosis. His love for his twin was so deep, Drew was sure that no one knew the agony he felt when the waves of sorrow kept coming from within continued. I did what I could to comfort my first born son. In my heart arose a special sorrow for Drew; no other sibling could match the relationship he had with his brother. Each twin was losing the other. It was agonizingly painful for both. I knew well the intimate bond that sprung from my womb and the love they shared.

For Luke, grappling with the loss of his brother meant the loss of his hero. It also meant the loss of the only father who never abandoned him. Nick had always been there for Luke. Nick was there to help him make it through the procession of schools they attended. The different states and museums and parks they visited. The roads traveled and homes where we never remained long enough to establish any roots. In one way or another, Nick was always there to keep Luke on an even keel. Now Luke was going to lose the rock he had come to depend on. He was now forced to face life without his protector. Luke looked up to Nick and the idea of losing him was impossible to deal with. He too believed, without a doubt, that no one in the family suffered the agony of our tragic loss more than he did.

For Hannah, the loss of her brother Nick would be not only hers, but a loss for her children as well. Hannah now had two beautiful children who loved their Uncle Nick. Hannah herself was exactly thirteen months old when her twin brothers were born and the three grew up in close harmony. Nick and Hannah shared many adventures together while growing up. They were separated a few times during their lives, but separation never unraveled their love. Everyone must leave the nest and enter the adult world eventually. It was evident Hannah's life was a mountain of stress. She had been dealt one blow after another. Now, her brother was going to die.

I was lost in sorrow. I had watched all my children suffer in their early years from their abandonment by their father and from poverty. Why on earth was God taking my son Nick from his family? Why? And, why on earth by Lou Gehrig's disease? I cried at each thought of the despair to come. But when in the presence of my son, I set aside my private pain and laughed with Nick, who accepted his fate with a noble heart. If he could accept it, why couldn't the rest of us? We just couldn't, not yet.

In my solitude, I asked myself *should it not be me instead of my son who should die?* The only comfort I could find in my heart was in knowing God was going to release my son to a better world and to a better life. And if anyone in the family deserved better, it was truly Nick.

After we all recovered from the shock of the news that Nick was going to leave us, we attempted to cope. But we had no real concept of the extent of what was in store for Nick or how bad this thing called Lou Gehrig's syndrome really was. There was no way we could grasp the horror that was going to unfold or the physical deterioration that was going to occur in accelerated motion. How could we think about tomorrow when we couldn't see through the tears of today? We heard and read about ALS but there was no way we could fathom Nick, the athlete of the family, becoming as weak and helpless as an infant child. Confined to a lifeless body that clung to his bones like an albatross around his neck. There was no way to imagine the awful suffering that was destined to unfold like a specter of abject horror.

My brother Rick was the closest living relative we had. My brother didn't play the games that break down the love and communication between members of a family. Throughout our lives, my brother and I had strengthened the bond that began in childhood. Rick had always loved my children, especially Nick. Since my brother never married, he always looked upon Nick as the son he never had. He had first worried about Nick when he noted the bewildering signs of muscular loss the spring morning when they went biking, but had ignored them telling himself they didn't mean anything. Uncle Rick didn't want to believe the diagnosis of ALS. He didn't want to believe Nick was going to die. He loved his nephew too much to accept it. My brother cried as we all did. In the beginning, Rick wanted to believe that if Nick went to see another doctor, he would be cured. Then, when he accepted Nick's prognosis, Rick's anguish was far too much for him to deal with. Unfortunately, he tried to erase his pain with the spirit of alcohol, rather than the resident spirit within his being. My brother's inability to deal with Nick's illness brought his own life to the brink of destruction and, at times, almost destroyed the close relationship we shared.

Nick's half-sister, who had distanced herself from us over the years, was shocked and saddened when she heard the news. She tried to re-enter the family, but our lives had changed so much over a generation of time that she had no idea who we were, and we were similarly estranged. Now there was no time to bridge the gap.

Baba, the children's paternal grandmother had seen little of them once her son walked out on his family. Although she did not want to help me or my children after my husband abandoned us, she had to be told of Nick's disease. A few years earlier when the twins turned twenty, they had invited Baba out to Phoenix for a visit. Baba got to see her grandchildren and her great-grandchild. When the twins were twenty-one, Baba had them visit her in New Jersey, but the visit was not one which drew grandmother and grandchildren together. Still, we let her know that Nick was going to die. It was up to her to decide how she wanted to be remembered by her grandson. I let her know that she could stay with us a few days to visit with Nick, for the sake of closure in their relationship.

Nick's father had walked away from the beautiful children he created for reasons unknown to me. I think that something must have disturbed him deep inside long before we ever married. Before Marc left, he spent years abusing me, both mentally and physically. He gave me four children in four years, and then left us with barely enough on which to survive. I was too young to know what I was getting into when I got married in 1965. But I did get four beautiful children. I knew the news of Nick's illness would get to him through his mother. Nick didn't want to see him.

Friends are family in the heart. Nick had friends everywhere. It didn't matter what part of the country or what part of the world we lived in. People were drawn to Nick, to his captivating personality, his intelligence, his kindness, and his ability to relate to others. His oldest and dearest friends were in Phoenix. For them, it was inconceivable that Nick could be dying. The thought left them numb and wondering how fate could remove such a companion from their lives. With the diagnosis now known, these young men and women were forced against their will to swallow a bitter pill and accept the fact that someone good was going to die prematurely. It was not easy for any of them. They were too young to fathom death coming like a marauder into their midst.

Nick's stepfather, Paul, was a man full of love and ideals. He gave a lot of himself to my children. He was patient and fun and good at directing their minds into educational activities. But, Paul was also a weak man who left us when the going got tough. Nevertheless, the children, especially Nick, held a special place for him in their hearts. It tore Nick up inside when he learned Paul was going to divorce the family and walk away after six years. Nick looked up to him. Enjoyed being with him. Wanted to be just like him. Paul backed out because he was not the man he thought he was. He valued his material well-being above the welfare of the children. Regardless of his mistakes, I thought I should let him know that Nick had been stricken with Lou Gehrig's disease. In case he might want to see him; he should be able to say good-bye.

I debated for a few weeks whether or not I should contact Paul and let him know that Nick was desperately ill. I knew he was somewhere in Flagstaff. I finally decided to see if I could locate him by telephone. I didn't want to tell Nick what I planned because I didn't know if I would find Paul or if Paul would want to see him. I felt Nick would welcome the opportunity to see Paul, especially before his physical condition got any worse. I called information and made the connection. I told Paul the sad news. I couldn't see the expression on his face, but I sensed the awful finality of my words took his breath away and left him with a hollowness inside. He said he would visit Nick the next time he made it into Phoenix. Later I told Nick that I had spoken with Paul and tears welled up in his eyes to know that he was going to see the man who had been so much like a father to him.

When Nick's symptoms had first presented themselves, we had all reacted pretty much the same. No one wanted to think or believe that something was wrong with someone they loved. Denial. It was no longer possible to look the other way. Now was time for friends and family to let go of denial and accept the reality that the one they love was going to die. Everyone had to understand that the paragon of strength and manhood, Nicholas John, was going to be pulled down into his grave like a ravaged old person drained of all his strength.

We could no more hold back the progression of time or change the course of Nick's destiny than we could change the course of the universe. Bravely, my son faced the prospect of his own death and physical conditions worse than death. He knew each day that he lived, for as long as he lived, meant a downward acceleration, with the worst always yet to come. Days would eventually arrive with stark cruelty and make the passage toward death all the more difficult to endure.

Noble acceptance of his fate and gratitude for the life he had been given would be forced through a grating sieve of pain. He would end up in searing rage against the disease that forced him to suffer, yet refused to let him die. Through all this, my son had to prepare for the departure of his immortal soul and the separation from his family. He had to put his full trust in the mercy of God.

All this he accepted. Pity was the enemy that Nick didn't want, and wouldn't accept. Lou Gehrig's syndrome was irrevocably destroying the healthy body that had once made him so dynamic and energetic. As sad as the imminent physical limitations were that he was presented with, it was impossible to envision the extent of deterioration his body would endure. Or the crippling effects it would have not only on Nick, but on every member of the family. Nick had seen the lame and broken hobble their way through the streets of Taipei when he was seventeen. It had touched a resounding chord of pity inside him to see unfortunate souls trapped inside helpless bodies. Nick did not want to be one of these invalids.

Nick was on a roller coaster ride as he fought the battle to retain what limited control he had over his body. The ride continued. It would carry him to the end of life's road. It was a ride his siblings and I would share. We thought we were enduring the worst. However, we were, as yet, ignorant that the force of what was to come would whip us around and thrash us into a blistering constellation of grief. In fact, it would be so earth shattering that by the time the roller coaster came to a halt, I would be the only remaining member to hold on until death. During this tempest passage, Nick's cluster of emotions would become a maelstrom inside his heart. Increased speed in the degeneration of his body would untether an emotional whip to snap and pop like hot wires out of control.

My Son, My Sorrow

We would be called upon to address every thought and emotion that arose with the final chapter of his life. It would force us into opposite roles. In the midst of my own torment, I would become the pillar of strength Nick needed. The pillar he had always been for me. We were going to become suffering soul mates. But the bond of love so strong in our lives would carry us through. Though the struggle would exasperate the temperament of our spirits, and our hearts would clamor wildly with enraged suffering, the spirit of God would protect us and carry us to a noble end.

Nevertheless, as Nick passed through the stages of dying, each one of us, including myself, would let him down in one way or another. Simply because we were human. As everyone failed him in different ways, at different times, he would become discouraged with the people he loved. He would be angry with us, and he would turn away from us. As each stage of the syndrome led to greater devastation and physical decline, Nick would be forced to watch his family crumble under the emotional burden. He too would crumble. Lou Gehrig's disease was destined to cripple the family. The stark, bleak reality of watching Nick's stature change from that of a strong, young man of noble character to a weak and tottering old man imprisoned in his death bed was so grave a burden for all to bear, that we too were emotionally withered.

From the beginning we agreed, however, that no matter what was to come, we would never surrender our loyalty to Nick and shove him away in a nursing home. My son was not going to die isolated in an institution the way my father was forced to do.

Carol Loving

What was next? How much suffering could we bear in one lifetime? Abandoned in a snowfield, survival had been a blizzard which for a short while retreated, but now the storm was bearing down harder than ever before. Round and round, faster and faster, my desperate thoughts came, went, and came back again. At times, I felt strong. At others I became weak and asked myself would I be able to bear the loss of my son and the anguish to come? Again I asked myself why was Nick being taken away from us? Why Lou Gehrig's disease? Why not me instead of my son? In light of my strengths and weaknesses, was I really going to be able to assist my son to the end? Would I be able to survive the duration of his creeping paralysis and then manage to go on without my son? What did our Father in Heaven have in mind? Would I even know the answer? I had no idea what the next moment would bring. I simply had to accept and adjust and do my best.

Nick accepted death without a problem. He said simply, "Everyone dies." He believed in the next world. What he didn't yet understand was the method of death inflicted upon him would be particularly gruesome. Nick's body was sentenced to die while his heart pulsed on. Without a doctor to help him pass on to his reward in heaven, Nick would become an object of inactivity. A mind imprisoned, restrained and bound by a straight jacket made of dead flesh. Without ending the battle with the terminal condition, Nick would become a helpless, inanimate mass. Would he consider taking his life before the condition did? What else was there to do? Yet, he realized that if he had the strength to squeeze the trigger, it would destroy those he loved. That reality was an effective buffer to postpone the idea and share what he could of his present life with others.

My Son, My Sorrow

At this point, all we wanted was a reprieve, an extension against Nick's sentence. However, I knew there would come a time when all of us would want death and final peace for Nick. Death for the sake of compassion. Death to end a suffering existence. Death for the sake of mercy. Death in exchange for life in the receiving world of heaven. I would cry out loud for the death of my son, and the freedom it would give to him. Nick would scream for mercy from the dictates of the medical profession. We would damn the doctors for their inflexible approach to the process of dying. We would curse the government that enforced the laws that kept doctors and medical professionals from offering mercy to those suffering. Deciding Nick's fate, his life, his death. Nick would be forced to die as the government and medical community dictated, and the family would be shackled together to witness the torment and torture. We would be forced to search for an effective means of helping Nick regardless of consequences that would follow. Nick would beg for death. I would pray for strength.

When the time came, I would be faced with the task of finding a way to end his god-awful suffering. I would have to end my son's life to stop the heartless and cruel torture inflicted upon him by those who claimed ethics were their guide, but were really blinded by materialism. It would become a battle between my son and a system that ignored suffering and treated us in a cold, condescending manner. Everyone knows you can't fight the system, but, if I had to smother my son to death with a plastic bag to free him from the rules and beliefs of a few officials, I vowed I would.

5

The Rapid Decline

As long as Nick could walk, he planned to remain on his feet and do as much as possible. He wanted to take a part-time job, but the idea was a short-lived inspiration that gave way when he began to lose control over his body. Yet he held his head high and made room for everyone in his heart.

In turn, those who loved him wanted to show their feelings for Nick by giving him something special. Charlie, knowing Nick's love of sports, came up with a couple of tickets to a Cavaliers game. That game he shared with Charlie was a heartwarming experience for Nick. When he and Charlie left the apartment, Nick turned to me in the doorway and teasingly said, "See you in the next world, Mother." His face was radiant. His humor made me laugh at myself for mustering even the slightest quiver that I might not see him again once he passed through the door for the evening. My maternal instincts had me hovering about him like a hummingbird. His hesitant and worsening limp made my heart cry, but his laughter was good medicine for my soul.

Carol Loving

Thanksgiving had always been Nick's favorite holiday. He had always liked to take charge of the bird, make sure there was plenty of food and drink for family and welcome friends to enjoy. There was no reason for the tradition to change as long as Nick was mobile, and able to manage the preparation of the special foods for which he was known. There was no reason why the music couldn't play, and the televised football game couldn't be cheered on between talk and laughter that wove its way between the generations gathered together. There was no reason not to celebrate the spirit of brotherhood on a day set aside once a year for that purpose. The sounds and scents of the holiday would fill the apartment. Like so many turkey days before, we would eat to the utter satisfaction of all.

Certainly there was always sorrow in my heart. But, as long as Nick's face was raised, smiling and shining above others, I could set aside my sadness and enjoy the best of what the day provided. And, as holidays go, it was a good one. Filled with delicious food, fun and laughter, Nick was generous and fun-loving with everyone. Holidays were for hugs and I still thrived on those from my children regardless of the fact that they were no longer little fledglings. Nick and I always united in spirit when we embraced, and the embraces Nick gave to me during this period of Thanksgiving kept my spirits high. Hugs amid laughter. Hugs among tears. Hugs for all to see and hugs held in private. Hugs that tugged at the soul. And hugs that had to be given before Nick could no longer stand on his own two feet and put his loving arms around me.

Soon after the holidays were finished, Nick's papers to start the experimental program came through. Nick was keeping his physical activity to the minimum so he could remain upright and walk, albeit with a heavy limp. According to the research I'd read, it was important for him not to exert the use of his muscles, for that only created more electrochemical damage to the body. What did the study require of him? Far more than they dared to tell, but we couldn't know that from the hopeful explanation.

The program would start off with a three month plan of regular physical activity to determine the rate of muscle loss that he was undergoing. After that, the second stage would begin. The double-blind experiment required Nick give himself intramuscular injections twice every day for a period of three months. Injections were of an unknown substance. A placebo or the experimental drug. After six months, the third stage would begin. Nick would knowingly give himself two injections a day of the experimental drug. A drug designed to slow down the process of Lou Gehrig's Syndrome.

A week or so after Thanksgiving came Nick's first scheduled appointment at BNI. Nick drove himself to the facility, and when he returned several hours later, he looked beat. "I'm exhausted. Completely exhausted," Nick said. His face drawn, he sat down on the couch next to me. His eyes were red and weary. Before long, he shifted his position and put his head in my lap as he stretched his body out on the couch. In minutes, he was asleep. The appointment had obviously been too much for him. I sat quietly with his head resting on my legs, completely unable to imagine what he had been through. I had no idea that he had endured hours of strenuous physical activity working out with weights. Working out with weights! Doing exactly what the books tell you not to do having his sickness, because it creates further electrochemical damage to the body.

Carol Loving

Nick slept through to the morning as a result of his initial visit at BNI. Although he didn't want me to know what they had put him through, he told his brothers the appointment was exhausting, and he was wrestling with the idea of not going back. But he did. His next visit was a week later. Between the two appointments, he lost ten pounds. In the next session of strenuous physical workout, blood was drawn as a matter of routine. A painful EMG was repeated on him. To Nick, who was feeling worse and worse, it all seemed for naught. He saw himself as a human guinea pig in the laboratory of a mad doctor experimenting with human life. When he returned home this time, he was even more exhausted than the first. In fact, the treatment appeared to accelerate his decline. Nick struggled with his decision of whether or not to continue.

It was both a rational and emotional judgment for Nick to work through. He was concerned about how we, his family, would feel if he quit. Nick knew if he didn't participate in the study, we might be devastated thinking the only hope for his recovery had collapsed. But Nick was beginning to feel very strongly that involvement in the program only instilled a sense of false hope in both the patient and the family. My studies on the disease and evaluation of the program led me to think, despite my fervent hopes, that Nick was right. Nick agonized over the matter. He cancelled appointments, rescheduled appointments, and then cancelled again. We all felt despondent and grief stricken, as Nick became more convinced of the treatment's uselessness.

Time passed. Suddenly the holidays were upon us. Christmas, 1993. Nick's half-sister wanted us to go to her place to celebrate. In truth, I knew Nick would be more comfortable at home where everything was on one level. It would be easier for him to navigate, and get around and enjoy the holiday. His sister's house had multiple levels.

By this time, it was extremely difficult for Nick to go up and down stairs. However, Nick decided to go to his half-sister's. "It will make her feel better," he said.

I didn't like the idea because I felt it was Nick's comfort which had to come first, but I loved my son and his willingness to give of himself to others. Even at his own expense. "As long as everyone, including Uncle Rick, and his dog are invited," he said, "let's go." I worried and agonized about a possible fall, but we altered our plans. It was more important that Nick made the decisions which concerned his body and his ability to live to the fullest.

We went to his sister's house on Christmas Eve to have dinner. Though she tried her best to make it festive and to communicate, so much time had gone by with her not being part of our lives that we had little to say to each other. There were too many silences. It was a difficult night, but we all got through it. My heart shuddered with Nick's every upward motion, and with the difficult task it was for him to maneuver himself up and down stairs. Yet, he did. Nick was not going to let the obstacles of the environment get in the way of his enjoying himself. We all ended up having a good time and even stayed up late playing a trivia game. By noon the next day, I drove back to my place and watched basketball with my brother while Nick and Drew went back to Drew's place.

As the year drew to an end, Nick was still walking, but his gait had changed dramatically since he had been diagnosed. Though I hated to admit it, he was thinner and he was weaker. Nick felt more weighed down by the progress of his condition than when he was first diagnosed, but he still looked handsome, as he stubbornly resolved to stay active until it was no longer possible. I could do nothing but admire my son's resolve as he stood proud and tall while the disease within him slowly robbed him of mobility. My heart crumbled a million times watching the daily battle my son waged with Lou Gehrig's syndrome. Luckily, I didn't know the worst was yet to come.

Nick came to a firm decision with the new year. "I'm not going to continue to participate in the experimental drug program," he declared. In between actual visits and cancellations, Nick had gone to three of the sessions. Witnessing Nick's condition afterward, I had come to believe the doctor played Frankenstein with total disregard for the consequences his abusive behavior would have on my son's body. Just as we'd feared, the physical requirements diminished any energy Nick had and accelerated the process of electrochemical toxicity current in his body. Injuring and killing even more neurons. Nick felt that by further eliminating the vital impulse of life designed to animate the muscle of the body, the doctor was accelerating his death. The doctor made demands of him. The doctor took from him. He gave Nick nothing in return. "If I put myself through what the doctor requires from me each week for the next three consecutive months, I won't be able to pick up a syringe to give myself a shot."

The experiment was accelerating the pace of the degenerative disease. Nick felt it and I felt it, too. I felt it was malicious for the medical community to exploit my son's condition, and to hide its deception behind a smoke screen of propaganda that there was hope as long as those who suffered from ALS stuck to the program. My son, steadfast in courage and conviction, felt he had to resign. He knew his decision not to participate in the program would stir the emotional pot heating inside his loved ones, but he had to do what was best for him. "It isn't healthy," he said, "for the family to think BNI offers me hope." By now, Lou Gehrig's disease was like a fire spreading through Nick's body. The program was fuel for the fire. "There's no way in the world I'm going to take a drug to prolong the crippling process of my body." he insisted. It was painful to see how his decision affected others, but I had to trust each knew in his own heart that Nick's life decisions were his own to choose.

The tremor in Nick's right leg was a more frequent and bothersome occurrence. He never knew when it would start, and several times it happened while he was driving. For the safety of others, he stopped driving. It was another loss and another change as his body weakened. In order to go somewhere, someone now had to drive Nick to his destination. Another diminishment. His friends were right there to get him around, and more than happy to visit Nick at home when the staircase at his brother's apartment proved to be impossible for Nick to climb. Nick recognized each new symbol of decline. His speech, like his walking became more laborious. He had to drag his voice up out of dead muscle the way he had to lug around his legs that now felt like they were weighted down by sand. Yet his green eyes still sparkled, and his wavy red hair still crowned the head of a very handsome young man.

Carol Loving

After months of demanding that my son jump though hoops made of red tape to prove he was dying of Lou Gehrig's syndrome, to prove he was not someone attempting to defraud the government out of money, an appointment was made for Nick to verify his condition to a social security doctor. The appointment was Tuesday, the eighth of February. Seldom does it rain in Phoenix, but on his appointment day, the rain came down in constant, heavy sheets. The busy streets were flooded and were dotted with accidents. We got off to a rough start, because the car battery died after we left our place when we stopped to pick up Drew on the way to the doctor's office. Luckily, someone was able to jump-start the car battery, and soon we were on our way across town to the appointed place.

When we arrived at our destination, I dropped Nick and Drew off as close to the entry of the building as possible before parking the car. However, there was no escaping the rain. Drenched though we were, we made it inside and took the elevator up to the floor where the doctor's office was located - all the way at the end of a very, very long corridor. For Nick, the distance down the hall was halfway around the world. But he made it, lumbering forward on limbs that resisted him, and we entered the doctor's examination area.

Nick sat on the edge of the examination table resting his body. Only four months had passed since we learned about the condition, but the extent of damage to his muscular system was frightening to think of. Muscle loss reduced body heat and for the first time in his life, Nick was susceptible to variable temperatures of the ambient air around him. The examination room was air-conditioned and with his shirt off, Nick shivered unceasingly from the cold.

My Son, My Sorrow

The young, idealistic doctor soon entered the room and gently performed the routine exam every doctor did to test Nick's muscle strength. Through out the examination, he listened with great care to every word my son said. He understood the difficulty of speaking with voice muscles that are deteriorating along with the rest of the body. Like Nick, the doctor had a good sense of humor and the two of them connected right away.

Below the surface of Nick's skin, threads of quivering electrical impulses ran askew. It was especially notable along his chest and shoulder area. Nick could no longer extend his fingers outward. His hands had lost too much muscle and his fingers rolled up in his palms creating a problem with dexterity. Regardless of all that was happening to his body, Nick was still a master of dignity and in control of his life. However, the aggressive progression of the disease didn't give us any time to waste. It was important to live every moment to the fullest. Cherish what we had. The doctor was so moved by the tragic future of my son that by the end of the physical examination, he acted upon compassion and impulse and embraced Nick. I saw tears well up in his eyes.

Nick and I felt a mixture of sadness and respect for the young man who examined him, because the doctor's feelings for Nick were real. He was fragile and he was human in the face of Lou Gehrig's syndrome. He understood the prognosis of the condition. He knew the helplessness that was going to come Nick's way. It was becoming very rare for me to walk away from a doctor with respect, but I had respect for this one. And Nick did too. Nick and I felt that he must have been working for social security, because he had too much integrity to lose himself in a system that exploited the dying patient and made the doctor rich. In his own unassuming way, he was the most beneficial doctor Nick would encounter in his battle with ALS, the master of death.

Meanwhile, our family battled with the sorrow we all felt. Drew wanted, like the rest of us, to give Nick as much joy as he could. He got a couple of tickets to a Suns' game scheduled for February eighteenth. Good seats behind the Suns' bench. It took months to get the tickets. But, by February, Nick couldn't go to a basketball game. He couldn't walk the distance it required, and he couldn't handle the steps inside the stadium. "I'm really sorry Drew," he said to his twin, "I just can't make it. I'm not ready to resort to a wheelchair to see a game, and I just can't make it by foot."

Drew had to accept the decision despite the pain Nick's words caused in his heart. Nick wanted me to go instead of him. "You have a good time for me," he said. I had never been to a game, and I accepted his gift. "I'll listen to the game on the radio," Nick said.

The afternoon of the game, as we were about to leave the apartment, something on the television caught our attention. Suddenly the hand of death moved in catching all three of us. A news blip showed Dr. Kevorkian and a photograph of someone with Lou Gehrig's syndrome, whom the doctor had helped to die. We froze in place before we could break away from the numb sensation we all experienced as we saw the images on the screen.

We believed in what Dr. Kevorkian was doing and wished he were in Arizona rather than Michigan. When life was no longer livable, it would give us great comfort to know

My Son, My Sorrow

Nick could call on him for help. He could not prevent Nick from being rendered totally helpless by the deadly syndrome of ALS, but he could stop the tragedy of an excruciatingly painful death. There is nothing moral or ethical about a medical system where people are forced to live by artificial means against their individual will. Dr. Kevorkian offered compassion to people caught up in the struggle of death. Caught up in the midst of spiraling and tragic suffering. We lauded Kevorkian's courage to do what is right in a world where everything had gone wrong. But what was the sense of talking about Dr. Kevorkian when he was worlds away? How did anyone get in touch with him anyway? I had no idea. None of us did.

Drew and I went to the game, but we could not forget the story we'd seen. However, we pressed the sight to the back of our minds and tried to have the good time for Nick we'd promised him.

More time inched by.

We never heard from Nick's stepfather, and I debated whether I should make a second call. I knew it would be good for Nick to see Paul before he died, before the extent of Lou Gehrig's syndrome became any worse. That convinced me to make a second call. I was surprised to hear Paul had stopped by our place on the one day that we were not home, Christmas. He said that he knocked on our door and no one was home. Paul left a note, but I seldom use the front door and never found any note. He said he had plans to be in Phoenix again and gave me a date to expect him. I conveyed his words to my son, who glowed with the joy of love to know Paul was going to come to see him. But when that date finally arrived, instead of one filled with meaning as it should have been, my son sat, waiting in our apartment, until we realized Paul just wasn't going to show. He didn't call.

As Nick's body became more and more wasted, daily life became increasingly burdensome. The paralysis now crept up the length of his fingers and hands, stripping away the everyday use of the appendages we all take for granted with each and every movement we make. The death march was advancing up his limbs to leave rigid, shaky feet below his ankles. His legs tremored when suspended in mid air. Respiratory activity, an involuntary action of the human body, was shallow. It required extra effort for Nick to breathe in deeply, or to take in an adequate amount of oxygen into his lungs. The saddest thing of all was the deterioration in his throat, which continued attacking his limited ability to speak and made swallowing food a hazardous task rather than the pleasure it should be.

Most of Nick's walking was now limited to our home. It was quite laborious. It taunted his ability to maintain the balance it took to ambulate. Nick still got out when someone came by and took him for a drive in the desert or up north for the afternoon. But he spent more time resting now. He would play sports on his Sega. With his thumbs, he could participate in football and basketball and box in the ring with the all-time boxers of the century.

Nick's wonderful, spiritual ability to rebound began to completely unravel. Friends started to shy away and only his closest buddies came by on a regular basis to visit and challenge him at Sega sports. Life was pretty much sedentary. The other activities he had to pass his day were television and radio. I suggested reading, but it hurt his eyes and he quickly got a headache as a result. Despite it all, Nick still had reason to hold his head up with pride. He was waging a courageous fight.

As April, May and June came in turn, Nick watched spring show the first sunstruck signs of summer. Nick's life was perishing just as the earth was being reborn. After falling too many times while trying to walk unaided, he had finally accepted the cane his Uncle Rick offered him. Six months had passed since he learned his body was under attack by Lou Gehrig's syndrome. Six months of drastic change. Six months to look back over the days of his youth. Six months for Nick to search for reasons as to why it was happening. Questions flooded his agonized thoughts. Was it the poverty and lack of nutrition in his diet after his father abandoned him? Was it something he had been exposed to in Taiwan? Was it the blow he received on his neck back in 1990? Was it the night he braved sub-freezing temperatures in the snow in 1992, when he could not find his way back to the highway? Was it any of the chemicals he worked with in various jobs he'd held over the course of his life? What? What was it?

One night as we sat together on his bedside, we began to fit the pieces of the puzzle together in a way we thought made some sense. The number one reported cause of Lou Gehrig's syndrome was a blow, a severe blow to the body. A blow that shatters the electrochemical balance between the nerves that send impulses of life to the muscle and chemical that feeds the nerves. "There are two incidents that stick in my mind." Nick recalled. "Remember, at the beginning of 1990, when I received that soft tissue injury to my neck?"

"That summer when you turned twenty-three, when you began putting on weight for no known reason," I said.

He nodded, "And then at the beginning of 1992, I spent the night in the wilderness, under a billion stars in the freezing snow. Alone, yet not alone."

"That summer, you turned twenty-five," I said. Again, he nodded.

"Remember, I laughed that I was starting to feel old. I began to slur my words. That was the beginning of 1993, and the rest is history," he said sadly. "After that I lost the weight."

So, it was probably the trauma to the neck at the concert that started the end of his life. But was it his highly accelerated body chemistry that made the illness receptive? Was this the key that set his destiny in motion? Whatever the reason behind it all, he was dying. And I who would have done anything, given anything to stop the onslaught, could only sit beside him and comfort him as best I knew how.

But it was not just his death sentence which gave us pain. Frustration and anger began to team up to knock dignity outside of the ring of his experience as Nick faced one after another crippling effect of the disease. As if that wasn't enough, beyond the curse of his medical condition, the government played the waiting game with the social security disability due him. It was a game of power which adversely affected people's lives. There was a time when Nick thought he would use his money to travel. To go to Europe to see the world before he died. But by April twentieth, when Nick finally got his check, he was in no shape to head off and see the world. His life was becoming limited to the circumference of our home. With his money, I bought Nick a color television for his room. Though Nick had insisted on keeping his own room in order, it was becoming harder, and the dust was mounting. I insisted he let me thoroughly clean his room before setting up his television and Sega. It was exhausting, but I loved doing it. At least it was a way to show the depth of my feelings.

Nick observed most of my efforts from the couch in the living room and was moved to show his love for me. He managed to get up off the couch by rocking back and forth to give him the momentum to hoist his weak body up. Finally, he stood. Then he had to lug one leg after another to get his feet to move forward as he fought to maintain his balance. He walked a tightrope of determination as his body stuttered and bounded, a jutting tremor in his right leg. I held back tears as he drew close and looked down into my eyes. Then he put his arms around me with an embrace that spoke of eternal gratitude, and a higher understanding of what we meant to each other. It was all the thanks I would ever need from my son. With admiration in his eyes, Nick said, "I love you." We savored the moment. We knew something else: Love was our greatest power. It would have to serve us well.

At the end of the month, I bought a stereo for Nick. Both his television and his stereo operated by remote controls that Nick kept on the bed beside him. I knew how much these small items of independence meant to him. He talked of getting a dog to keep him company, but when I wanted to buy one for him he refused. "You've done enough, Mom. Anyway, I don't want to make more work for you."

For a long time, he had wanted one last fishing trip. I wanted to finance it for him, but he insisted on waiting for his money. Now the money was here. Nick and his friend Charlie reserved a houseboat on one of the lakes up north for the end of May. But by the time Charlie took Nick to get a fishing license, Nick's body had weakened even more. Even with the cane, he could hardly lift his feet, weighted by shoes, off the ground.

To watch him assert so much energy just to walk out the door with a cane for support brought a mixture of joy and sadness to me. Joy to know that as badly off as he was, he still had the heart to get out into the world God created. And sadness to see the effort it took. During the drive, Nick turned his face towards the sun to enjoy its warmth and took in the sights and sounds of the natural scenes he had once so enjoyed. Although he could barely hold himself up, the pride he felt when they purchased the license was infectious. The two friends laughed about the planned outing with carefree spirits.

However, on their way back home, those spirits shut off. Nick had to empty his bladder, badly. Unfortunately, his bladder was as weak as the rest of his body and the need to urinate was an urgent matter. At home, we kept the urinal at his bedside all the time. Charlie couldn't understand the urgency of Nick's request to stop the car, "Can't you wait until we get back to the apartment?" Charlie insisted "We're only a few blocks away."

"There isn't time. You have to stop." Nick begged. Charlie stopped the car in an apartment building parking lot and jumped out. He ran around the side and threw open Nick's door, and helped him out just in time for Nick to pee on the ground.

"It made me a nervous wreck to see Nick humiliated," Charlie later whispered to me.

My Son, My Sorrow

Although he was rapidly weakening, Nick could still manage to get into the tub to shower everyday. But his arms felt too heavy for him to raise them above his shoulders in order to shampoo his hair. Nick had an answer to the problem. He wanted me to shave off his beautiful mane of Irish red hair. We decided to have a head-shaving party during a Suns' play-off game. Several of Nick's friends stopped by and everyone took a turn at shaving away the stubble I left behind after cutting his hair close to his scalp. I saved his beautiful hair in a bag. But later that night when I stole into his bedroom to observe him sleeping, tears rose to my eyes. Nick's emaciated body and shaved head made him look like someone who had been in a concentration camp. Though my mind knew his diagnosis, for the first time, I saw my son look like someone who was going to die.

As his decline accelerated, I wanted everyone in our family to have the opportunity to be with Nick before he got any worse. I again contacted his grandmother, Baba. She arrived Friday night talking. She had it in her mind that she had come to Phoenix to vacation with her grandson. Take him to restaurants. Go places. Do things. She had no concept of Nick's reality. Baba was shocked when she first saw Nick and the condition he was in. She watched him, barely able to get to his feet, hunched over like an old man, dependent on a cane, with movement slow and speech labored. Nick's grandmother could not cope with his illness, and this made Nick even more self-conscious. Finally, I arranged for her to leave.

It was time for the fishing trip, but after watching Nick day by day, the entire idea had become a knot in my stomach. Originally, the trip was planned for Nick, Charlie, Drew and

Charlie's dad. However, I found out that Charlie's dad was not
going. Three strapping young men were going in his place. I
could feel trouble move in as they began to gather at our place.
Like Baba they were completely unconscious of the actuality
of Nick's physical limitations. I wanted Nick to go. I wanted
him to be out in the boat fishing where he had loved to be. But
I shuddered thinking of what might happen. Drew and the
three other young men all Nick's age, filled the living room
with their energy the morning of the planned trip. It was not
their faults. Nevertheless, I hated them. I saw disappointment
edged up on Nick's face as he watched everyone horsing
around.

Nick couldn't get a word in edgewise because everyone was so absorbed in their own youthful spirits It was heartbreaking.

"Let's pick up some beer at the store."

"Yeah, lots."

I frowned. It would be dark when they arrived at the
lake, making it all the more impossible for Nick to get around.
Nick looked more and more uncomfortable in the company of
those who had lost track of the reason for the fishing trip. He
told everyone to go on without him and went to his room for
the night.

Drew, who had been standing near his twin brother,
suddenly felt the crashing reality of Nick's deterioration. He
broke down and sobbed uncontrollably. Drew was furious
about what the ALS was doing to his twin brother. "I hate it. I
hate to stand by and watch you and I can't do anything."

I knew and felt all he was feeling. To be robbed of the
person we loved inch by inch was completely unbearable. This

was one of those times. The others, finally seeing Nick could not go, began making excuses. No one went on the fishing trip.

That evening pretty much closed the door on visitation from anyone other than family members. Nick continued to decline. The cane he once used so agilely Nick now leaned on completely to prevent himself from falling as he tried to get around. Every sound of him falling clamored inside my heart. I felt the pain with every blow from the table and the walls and the floors he fell on. Yet Nick fought on. And though the shadows grew, once in a while, for a few precious moments, the old Nick's sunny spirit shone through.

With summer's arrival, Nick lost more muscle and mobility. Nick's fingers stayed curled most of the time, but there was still enough muscle to extend his hand around a can of soda or beer, as he watched baseball on the television with his brothers or his uncle. His thumbs grew weaker; and it became more difficult to play the Sega games that called for rapid dexterity, such as boxing or football. It was difficult for him to make it to the bathroom and back, and he had to surrender completely his independence in preparing his meals. His body spasmed with tremors whenever he stood on his feet, which made stepping in and out of the tub a danger. Nick now fell to the ground regardless of the cane, but he refused to let me help him.

As the disease's symptoms grew all-consuming, Nick isolated himself in his room. He slept mostly during the day and stayed awake at night. One of his only pleasures by this time was watching sporting events and drinking a few beers. Yet beer made him much weaker and affected his already slurred speech. I wanted to shout, *Stop Drinking!* But how could I take this away too? Sometimes he would cry out, taking his anger out on me. Cursing me, damning me, and wailing. His voice carried through the apartment complex in the late hours of the night, and certainly someone must have thought I was inflicting pain upon him. The truth was I was in pain too. I was as helpless as Nick to resolve the insidious dissolution of his body. At times, he threatened to kill himself, to leave to stay with his brother or go to a nursing home. Yet I knew he was aware that if he entrusted himself to anyone else's care, it would drive me out of my mind.

Afterward, he always apologized for his moments of madness, and I always understood the emotional agony that drove him over the brink. I recognized his misery and sorrow. He was my son, becoming helpless before my eyes. If I were in his situation, I would want to close the final chapter of my life, too. But I argued that there was still so much love and laughter he could give to his brothers and to me. He could communicate, discuss matters and assert his control over his daily routine. Nevertheless, bouts of depression were inescapable. The best I could do when he sank into depression was to leave him alone. It was difficult, not to be able to comfort him, especially when the periods of despair lasted longer and longer.

In July, Nick became so lost in his melancholy that he shut himself off from contact for seven days. I brought his meals to him, emptied the jug, brought him beer and bore the brunt of anger as his strength diminished. I worried about his mind. I feared he would lose his sanity, and that I would soon follow.

In hope of some magic solution, I went out and bought a beautiful black and tan dachshund puppy, only six weeks old,

My Son, My Sorrow

in a desperate hope to reach him. When Nick first saw the dog, he rebuffed the innocent puppy, who was no bigger than my hand. Nick seemed not to want to care for anything, lest it too be taken from him. But the lovable puppy stood his ground, and the next day Nick took him into his heart. The puppy, who Nick named Norm, was not the answer to the unrelenting stripping away of Nick's life. The stripping away of his mobility, his speech, and his dignity. The anger and bouts with depression did not end with Norm. But the animal's presence definitely helped my son wade through the anguish of the present.

August arrived, and Drew and Nick had their twenty-seventh birthday. It was a tragic day for both of them. Nick cried long and hard as he shared the event from the side of his bed with his twin brother. "No way in the world do I want to see another birthday," Nick said. "There won't be a living muscle left on my body by that time. Something has to be done to prevent a fate worse than death."

By September, Nick only got off his bed to get his failing body to the bathroom. To shower now required a bath bench plus the extreme determination of my own will to assist his rigid, spastic body in and out of the tub.

As Nick was forced to endure his increasing hell, the remnants of his once optimistic spirit failed. He expelled his rage and anger by screaming obscenities, day or night, for all the tenants to hear. The cruel and highly insidious means of death seared his body and the dynamics of his mind, and forced his soul into a well of stagnation.

I suffered my son's hell. I had given him life, now I was forced to ask God to give me the means to assist my son in ending it. But how on earth was I going to end the suffering of this rare and terminal condition doctors refused to address with honesty, civility and compassion? The prescribed method of treatment for ALS was to allow it to 'run its course.' Thus, Nick could expect to suffer until he choked to death on his own saliva or until his lungs collapsed. He was no different than a dying rat in a cage, left unattended to experience every moment of suffering a mad doctor could eke out of him. All Nick could do if he remained alive was watch his body die inch by inch.

The extent of muscle death that had taken place already made him look like he was a living corpse, and in a way he was. Common sense and human mercy could not be found in the army of doctors. "Why is the world afraid of dying?" he kept asking.

Nick was boxed in a corner and I was tied to the wall, forced to watch him suffer.

6

Enough is Enough

My son's growing depression did not stem from his crippling disease; the depression was due to the fact that there was no way out of the suffering attached to Lou Gehrig's syndrome. There was no out because society is not mature enough to accept death as a natural part of life in the given order. Yet for my son, the end was welcome. He had a terminal condition. This was a fact. He had no choices. He had no liberties to set him free. Thus, anger wrapped in frustration permeated with agony in his waking moments and his dreams. He was dead. He was dying. But no one would let him go.

As the months of summer ran their course, Nick grew weaker day by day, and more despondent about the forecast of a future which was not a future. I stood staunchly beside him as he was forced to endure the process of becoming a completely helpless thing rather than a vital human being. Banished friends called on the phone; however, Nick had to struggle now to say even a few words. Most times he felt it was useless. As Nick lay confined to his bed watching television, the beer he sipped brought memories of the past over and over. Camaraderie, friends, all the joys of good times would be no more. Family still visited. But once that person left the room to return to his own world, Nick was left behind to struggle in the quicksand.

He stubbornly refused a wheelchair, and this I understood. But increasing falls were the price to pay for each battle he waged to remain afoot. The sound of each fall filled my ears with the pain and the agony Nick was experiencing. His misery was an absolute torment for me to endure. When his body fell, he landed on tables or against doors and always on the floor. Every blow was an assault on my soul. The sound of his slow-moving helpless body hitting the floor also meant he had to struggle to get up and make it back to his bed.

Each fall ended in a stubborn refusal to have me help him up. Each fall released further glutamate toxicity to neurons assigned to animate the body's muscles. Each fall was a crack of the whip which did further damage. Each fall was a slap in the face of dignity. Afterward, he insisted I keep the door to his room closed so he could brood alone. At these times, Nick even banished Norm from the room.

Nick was swiftly passing through the threshold of independent living and was becoming a crippled, dying human being with skin clinging to the bone where flesh had once been. His fingers had begun to curl up into his palms to create a pathetic sight. Nevertheless, summoning his indomitable will, he could still use the combined effort of two mutant hands to lift an aluminum can to his lips. He could still feed himself the soft meals I fixed for him. His occasional game on the Sega had become more difficult as his thumbs stiffened, but he used all his effort to continue playing. Passive games of baseball, fishing and golf replaced the active ones at which he had once excelled. His feet were stiff and arched, the spasms came regularly. He couldn't walk to the bathroom without the assistance of his cane and me.

Now I was his nurse, companion and servant. I had to adapt my ear to understand words he struggled to speak. I rejoiced in my heart when he was content, and I was crushed by the weight of his madness when he churned in the agony of depression.

The weight I bore on my shoulders was great. My son required more and more of my time as his ability to care for himself diminished further. I had to be on call and one step ahead in anticipating his needs. I had to be there for him in ways that were not required by other members of the family.

There was little respite for me now. Except isolated times when Nick had company. The simple act of drinking two light beers with his brothers or uncle as they watched sporting events together was a blessing for Nick. It was also a blessing for me to see him cling to his independent will as the syndrome robbed him of his strength and restricted his activity. Family would come, see Nick at his best, then leave everything behind when the visit ended while Nick remained. All he had left were his memories of yesterday, and the tears that he shed as anger, frustration and damnation invaded his mind and soul. He could not keep these feelings from surfacing as the pain and suffering took over his existence.

Carol Loving

All the while, the more control Nick lost over his life as autumn encroached, the more control he was compelled to assert over me. The tables turned in the relationship. He was no longer the son who looked out for the welfare of his mother. As our roles changed, Nick's frustration and anger increased. Soon Nick had become the desperate elder of the family, the master of the house whom I was obliged to serve. I was the prisoner at the whipping post when his rampant rage burst through. I let him yell at me and damn me to hell for not giving him a gun. I let him spit anger at me like a flame thrower. I let him pierce my armor of motherhood with riveting bullets of pain when I misunderstood what he was saying. It was my job to mop up after the storm of darkness dumped depression on top of the maelstrom. As usual, Nick was quick to apologize to me when the spell of grief passed. I always assured him I understood the agony that had come upon him. Death was not easy, especially the way the doctors were allowing him to die. He was a puppet whose strings were being stripped away. Soon there would be nothing to animate his motionless figure. My son had every right to be angry at the things that tormented him. What tormented him most was the fact that he could not die. He hated the authorities which allowed him to suffer instead of helping him to die. Doctors understood the prognosis and what it would do, but they did nothing. They didn't care. Death was Nick's problem, my problem, not theirs.

A year had passed since the fateful diagnosis. It was the worst year of Nick's life. It had also been the worst heartache I had ever known as a mother. Caring for my son's life and his death were entrusted in my hands, and I was duty bound to my Father in heaven to be of faithful service to my son to the end. I was responsible to provide for his body, his mind, his soul. But it was a heavy cross to bear.

In searching for ways to lessen his pain, I found out that the effective use of marijuana to ease suffering was very beneficial. Along with decreasing Nick's pain, it prevented the buildup in his mouth of saliva, which would otherwise drool down the side of his mouth and add further to his indignity. Unfortunately, the doctors wouldn't give it to patients. Our family was able to locate a source. Pot also helped to reduce the muscle spasms Nick dealt with every day. It stimulated Nick's appetite and helped him sleep. With his hands crippled to the point of helplessness, I loaded his small pipe and put it in his hand so he could gain relief. It also relaxed his troubled spirit. Smoking pot was good exercise for his incapacitated lungs. It was comforting for the soul. Once in a while, weary and depressed, I too smoked. It was good for both of us. Smoking a peace pipe together after a bout of agonized pain coupled with depression and anger, was a calming way to forget the torment and to escape to a place where we could express how much we loved each other. I thanked God I was alive and able to help my son make it through the dying days of his life. I prayed to God every day for the strength to keep going.

Finally, Nick and I both realized we were coming to a crossroads. I would have to assist my son to pass over the final thoroughfare. At this point, I had no idea how I was going to do it without a doctor to provide me with the means to peacefully shut down all systems and let him go. Move on to the next world. But I knew I had to find the help, or I would have to resort to something drastic when he could endure no more, such as smothering my son to deliver him from his suffering. Now was not the moment. It was coming though, and at locomotive speed. Meanwhile, Nick and I were faced with a system that didn't seem to give a damn. Those in power seemed to be saying, let the people suffer, let them be tormented. We would have to depend on ourselves to seek out the method and have the courage to stop the torture and torment.

Meanwhile, I had to assist him as best I could. Then, as if endurance of such agony was not enough, another twist of fate. The mindless, as well as heartless female who became my boss through a corporate takeover of the property I handled as a resident manager, walked into my office Wednesday morning, October 12th. She said I was fired. She had planned to get rid of me a year before, but backed off because of the sudden and shocking news of Nick's medical condition. I knew she and the company wanted me gone, but I didn't think they would kick me out on the street with a dying son to care for. They did. Their only concession, because of his condition, was that I was given thirty days to vacate the apartment rather than the usual three days.

The loss was a shattering blow for Nick to take as he lay helpless in bed. He immediately offered half his government check to cover our living expenses now that we were forced to leave what had been my home for three and a half years. Though this newest dramatic change in our lives enveloped me in immediate shock, I soon realized the loss of employment was a blessing in disguise. Nick needed my assistance twenty-fours a day, and I needed to serve him without the stress the job placed on me. I believed God and the Angels assigned to Nick's death were in full charge of our lives; it was

My Son, My Sorrow

up to me to figure out what was expected of me as my son entered the worst phase of his crippling death.

As if in answer to my prayers, the next day I found a check in the mail for one thousand dollars. Where did it come from? With the stress of my son's fatal illness weighing heavy on every aspect of my life over the past year, I had unknowingly overpaid a thousand dollars on a loan I was paying off. The bank discovered my error and returned the money. The money was a blessing to receive, and it provided us with the money to move. One year to the day that we learned of his diagnosis, I began searching for a new apartment we could afford in central Phoenix. After canvassing all the possibilities, despite being given the monetary means, I began to worry if anything decent was out there for us. Everything I saw was a dump. Then, just when I was about to give up, I picked up the newspaper and my eye caught an advertisement telling about a two bedroom apartment near Sunnyslope. The price was one we could afford.

The following day was ushered in by heavy rains, but I had to go there quickly. Before anyone else took the apartment, I rushed over and found it to be more than I dreamed possible. It was large and open, filled with windows to let the sunlight in. There was a large, pleasant bedroom for Nick, a small bedroom for me, and a comfortable living room. It even had a doggy door and backyard for Norm. I put down the money immediately. Now I was sure I had been liberated from my job so I could prepare my son for the end of his life.

I cashed Nick's government checks against my account and gave him the money to keep for whatever he needed.

Carol Loving

Suddenly, there was a problem. Bank officials said I could not make any more transactions with his checks. The financial institution wanted his checks deposited directly into my account, which I refused. There had to be a better way. On the twenty-fifth of October, I put a pen in my son's talon-like hand so he could scrawl his name across a living will, a power of attorney, and a medical power of attorney in the presence of a notary public whom I brought to the apartment. It was a necessary move my son and I had to make for his own protection. However, it was also another critical acknowledgement that Nick was helpless. "I feel like I have signed my life away," he said, as my own heart broke.

Every day now saw a worsening of Nick's condition. I watched the flesh being stripped away from my son's hands and forearms, leaving his bones covered in a thin layer of skin. It was the same with his feet and calves. His neck, shoulders, hips. It was agony for me to be unable to do anything to stop the rapacious destruction of my son's life, and it was worse for my son to suffer the execution of his body by inches. As he struggled to maintain his dignity, Nick raged anew. Anything I said or did could cause an eruption to take place. Knowing how possessive Nick felt about the place we were living—the last line to his youth and joy—I began to dread moving day. I knew something bad was going to happen, because I lived every minute of the paralyzing death he was going through. I understood how he was clinging to the past.

The first person to offer to help on moving day was Charlie, Nick's closest friend. He had only seen Nick once or twice since their failed fishing trip at the end of May. Nick was much worse now than he was at that time. I knew Nick hid the worst so Charlie didn't suspect how insidiously the disease

118

was taking over Nick's body, mind and soul. When Charlie arrived that day and saw Nick, he became upset with the reality of his very best friend dying.

I told Charlie that Nick was in charge of the move because he needed to have as much control as possible over all things that affected his life. Unfortunately, an argument immediately erupted. Nick had decided he wanted his belongings moved last. Charlie wanted to take out the larger pieces of furniture in Nick's room first. I tried to stop him, but Charlie wouldn't listen. Nervously, he jetted back into Nick's room and started randomly picking up tables.

Nick set his anger loose on me and his friend. "You think because I'm dying I don't know what I want, damn it! Charlie, you're an idiot. Now do what I told you to do!" Nick yelled, which was a terrible blunder when all Charlie was trying to do was help someone he loved.

But Charlie was wrong, too. Charlie failed to see many things surrounding the dying process. He failed to understand that though Nick's physical skills were failing, his feelings were, if anything, more acute. He was striking out because it tormented him deep inside to have Charlie help out when it was always Nick who helped his mother. Because our present home represented to him the life and future he'd once dreamed of. It tortured Nick to be helpless and vulnerable where his strong, healthy, best friend, took charge and unknowingly disrupted the fragile plans that had already been arranged. It became really ugly and was rocketing out of control.

Charlie wanted Nick to quietly sit in a chair. "I have to move the bed while I have my truck," Charlie insisted. I couldn't stop the misguided energy flying around the room.

Carol Loving

Angry with me and Charlie, Nick rolled his body off the side of the bed onto the floor and yelled at Charlie, "Take the fucking bed and get out!"

What do you do or say when someone tries to help and destroys something in the process? Doesn't it depend on the circumstance, the people and the wisdom one is able to discern? The pain in Nick's heart, the stress on his physically debilitated being thrown out of his home, were not comprehensible to Charlie. Nor were Nick's angry words.

Charlie did not understand that his room and the bed were Nick's life. They were the only things which accommodated his dying body. Charlie should have listened to Nick instead of charging into the chamber of death and recklessly throwing his weight around. But Nick's terminal condition hit Charlie so damned hard that he just couldn't cope or bear the change in his friend. He wasn't the only one. We all made fools of ourselves on any given day in face of the tragic circumstances. All I could do as he left was thank Charlie for the effort he put forth. I knew, that in time, he would look back on this day and probably cry when he understood the all-consuming pain and angry helplessness his friend was enduring.

It grew dark. I was grateful when Uncle Rick and Drew came by the apartment and tried to elevate Nick's mood. "Let us drive you to the new place," they said. Nick was still on the floor with legs stretched out before him. His back was pressed up against the wall to keep from slumping over. The very sight of Nick sitting on the floor upset everyone, but Nick refused to communicate with anyone and refused to have anyone help him up. "I'm not going anywhere," he insisted.

My Son, My Sorrow

We packed all the boxes and bags of household items and loaded them in our cars. Taking turns we drove to the new place, unloaded and returned. Our friend Del showed up with his truck. He helped us move more belongings, including Nick's weight set, which was collecting dust on the patio outside. Another load off.

This time, Drew stayed behind with Nick, but he couldn't get his brother to respond to anything he said or did. Drew grew increasingly frustrated. He hated what the deadly disease had done to Nick, but couldn't imagine the humiliation Nick was experiencing as his body melded to the floor. No one could imagine what it was like to be confined to a worthless body, surrounded by healthy, vital people. That is why no one understood moving day, but me. For the first time that day they heard Nick's anger, his cursing and his dead silence. When spoken to they heard, 'Fuck you!' at everything they said. Nick shut them out and refused to interact as he had done with me since his illness had begun its spiraling descent.

At last, the place was cleared of our belongings. The sun set on what was a long and strenuous day. My brother and Del drove to our new place while Drew and I remained in the apartment trying to coax Nick into leaving. "Why don't you just leave me here," he said brokenly. We had possession of the apartment for twelve more days.

"I would never leave you behind. I'll wait it out with you. Two corpses." I tried to kid him.

"Maybe we'll get a cut rate," Nick joked, at last. We all laughed. It broke the desperation.

With his twin coaxing and nudging him, Nick allowed Drew to put shoes on Nick's feet and help him into an upright position. With his cane in his left hand and his right hand securely cupped on top of my right shoulder, we left the apartment. I was his legs as he leaned his weight on me and trudged on his shoe-heavy feet. I helped him maintain his balance as his weak, stiff, jostling body traveled the length of the small quarters, struggled over the front door jam, and hobbled down the sidewalk to the open door of my car.

It was equally a struggle to get from the car to our new home. But, once inside his new surroundings, Nick saw that I had everything in his room set up for his convenience. It was a perfect arrangement for him and for Norm, who had proved to be a loyal friend as well as a happy, obedient member of the family.

Nick and Drew, Del and Uncle Rick visited with Nick as I went to work putting things away in apartment. Finally, Rick and Drew left. Del remained for a while, and the three of us watched television until Del finally had to say good night.

Nick looked around, suddenly pleased with his new home. "I'm really sorry for the way I acted today," he apologized. I told my son I understood the profound suffering he endured and the loss of control over his body that haunted each moment of his life.

When Del came by a few days later to see how we were doing, Nick was in good spirits and the two of them had a good visit. Del had known Nick for more than twenty years. He had watched Nick grow into a fine young man. It brought sorrow into his heart to see Nick becoming a shadow of the person he had been.

Del came out to the living room to see me for a few minutes. "Stay there," I said, and went back. I helped Nick to the bathroom and onto the toilet. A few minutes later, Nick called for my help to get him off. But Nick wanted to risk getting back to his room by himself. I went back into the living room where Del and I started talking when we heard a loud noise. My heart dropped within me. I knew Nick had fallen. I wasn't allowed to run to assist him and God forbid I should have Del help him to his feet. I gently encouraged Del out the door before I went to see how Nick was doing.

Nick was in the hall. He'd managed to get himself seated upright with his back against the wall for support. He smiled at me when I looked down at him. His smile told me I'd done well. I had not embarrassed him.

However, we quickly found ourselves with a very serious problem. I could not get Nick off the floor. No matter how hard I tried, the dead weight of his body was more than I could hoist. In a few moments his happy mood vanished. Nick became infuriated with me. He got his body to fall forward so he could get on his belly. Then he used the last vestiges of strength he had in his arms to drag his body across the floor to the bed. But I had to help him by wrapping my arms around his torso, hoisting him up so he could get his arms to fall on the bed and then maneuvering him the rest of the way up off the floor. Once Nick was back up on his bed and in control once again, I was banished from the room.

7

A Strand of Pearls

The greatest burden of my life was before me. My past was a series of tragedies strung together like a strand of pearls around my neck. Pearls born of pain. A necklace to grant me strength and essentially to prepare me. I had to nurse him to his grave. I would be required to do more than I ever thought possible as the road to great suffering opened for me and my son. Thank God I believed there was a light at the end of the long journey and Nick would eventually ascend to a better realm. But now I had to accept my earthly burden. My son was going to die. Before that peaceful end would come, the scenario of Nick's demise would almost shatter his family. The despair would explode. Never would we be more estranged than as we would become when the force of Lou Gehrig's disease crumbled Nick into someone less than human. Nick would become a pitiful sight. It would make those who loved him turn away from the painful vision evoked by his decline. They would turn away from a painful world that belonged exclusively to Nick and me. Through our family's tragic experience, all my children would learn why there is a dire need for euthanasia in our world.

In a very fundamental way, everyone in the family was about to undergo death. Nicholas John and each of us would become part of the process at one time or another. Pain and sorrow would swell in the heart of each sibling through the process of impending demise. But, the love in the hearts of my children would never end. Something each already comprehended, it was something that would eventually be known in his or her heart.

One day I received a call from an organization for victims of Lou Gehrig's disease and their family members. I went to several monthly meetings and saw things that made my soul cry out in protest. The group was primarily family members, but a few ravaged by the killer disease also showed up in wheelchairs. I saw pain and sorrow and agony and misery in the eyes of the suffering. I saw people who cared about their loved ones and sat numb, silent, and terrorized by the disease. I saw people scouring for power and control over the group. I saw the mask of hypocrites and their fear of death. Those afraid to consider their own death, let alone cope with the gruesome death by Lou Gehrig's syndrome.

I saw a parade of ALS victims over a period of time. Victims affected by the disorder in various ways. For one elderly women, all muscle was intact except in the extremity of the neck. She could not speak or swallow. She consumed only thick fluids through a straw. She constantly kept a handkerchief to her lips to catch the saliva drooling from her mouth. A man close to sixty was affected in the shoulders. He couldn't lift his arms above his head. He was collecting disability, and had been for several years. He had more physical strength in his body than I had in mine. One old woman spun around on a go-cart to conserve her energy. She had a stronger hand grip than my son, and eventually found out she had been misdiagnosed. A women close to forty was slowly, very slowly, wearing down.

I saw more. I saw a completely motionless human being with an expressionless face and an almost transparent sheath of skin clinging to his skeletal form. He was a flaccid figure in a wheelchair. He had a plastic devise attached to a hole in the base of his neck so a machine could pump air into his lungs. He was a wealthy man who had been attached to a breathing machine for twenty years. His attendants said he communicated by blinking his eye. I found it hard to believe anybody had the courage to look into his eyes. My heart went out to the man who had passed from an animated human being into an inanimate object. I could not reason why anyone would want to be a virtually dead creature thing. People at the support group said hello to the lifeless form in the wheelchair as though he was healthy and fine, like there wasn't anything out of the ordinary. Some actually told the speechless figure entombed in his chair that he was looking good.

Around me I saw many poor souls strapped in wheelchairs, unable to keep their heavy heads erect on necks without muscle. They were unable to prevent a stream of saliva from drooling out of their mouths and down their chins into their laps. Unable to lift dead arms up from their sides. Unable to feed themselves. Unable to speak a few basic words. Unable to do anything at all on their own. Some had haunting looks that cried for mercy.

Carol Loving

Some had eyes filled with tears. In one woman's face, I saw the looks of dread and fear. The look of someone mistreated.

No one spoke about death at the meetings, which I thought was totally unrealistic. After all, ALS is a devastating and deadly disease with a fatal end. However, people who were supposed to be caretakers were traumatized by the prognosis of the disease, and were afraid to speak of the suffering or the death sentence it created for the victim. These people were foreign to me. I couldn't bear the level of collective denial attached to the group.

Nevertheless, being in a group gave me an opportunity to release some of my feelings about the heartache attached to the tragedy unfolding in my home. It allowed me to speak of the disease to those who understood what Lou Gehrig's did to the body.

I also shared my group experiences with Nick, who refused to go there. He told me, "I have no intention of being dressed up like a puppet to be gawked at by a group of people who don't know me or give a damn about my life." I respected his words; however, by going to the meetings, I could pick up what information was available. I could discern with a careful eye the progression and meaning of Nick's symptoms and illness. I could comfort those in need.

The group was supposed to provide help to the Lou Gehrig's victims and their families by making available medical equipment, information on care, and some treatments. But aside from soliciting money, I found little help available. By September, it was a difficult task for Nick to get his body from a supine position to an upright position. He thought an electric bed would be of benefit, and asked me to ask the group to provide us with one. We got a rapid promise, but little action. We got nothing but dialogue about why the group could not find a bed for Nick, who only got weaker with each passing month. They did have a lift chair they wanted us to have, but that did not fulfill our need. It was not what Nick needed. Nick needed help getting from his back to sitting upright on the side of the bed.

I stressed the urgency to the organization of my son's need to obtain the bed we requested. Excuses, Excuses and empty promises. And a very strong desire to give us a lift chair touted to be the greatest thing in the world. Like a fool, I let them send the chair to our place. I couldn't believe my eyes when it was ushered in through the door. The chair was a monstrosity. I should have said no right then and there.

It arrived while Nick was napping, and I wasn't going to have anyone disturb him. So the monstrosity sat in the living room. It was so big it needed a room all to itself. It was Halloween orange in color. The chair was a joke. It spoke loud and clear that mankind was adrift in its ability to cope with and understand the process of dying. The chair represented the collective consciousness of the group. It existed, yet did no good.

The giant chair remained in the living room until one weekend when Drew came to stay with Nick. He thought it would be a good gesture to put it in Nick's room, so Nick could make use of it. He insisted on doing it regardless of what Nick and I said. When he couldn't get the obtrusive object the size of a tank through the doorway to Nick's room, he removed the steel feet from the base of the chair and succeeded in his deed.

With all the work he put into it to aid his dying brother, how could Nick not show gratitude? Nick was too kind. It was a great effort to get him into the chair. Drew put the controls in his brother's withered hands. Nick's crooked, bony thumbs tested them out. He said he would watch the football game from the chair while I took Drew back home. I was nervous about it, but Nick said he was fine.

It took thirty minutes before I got back to our place. The minute I opened the door, I could hear the state of panic my son was in. He had elevated the chair to get him to his feet and then lost control of everything. His cane fell to the floor. He couldn't get the controls attached to the chair in his hands. "I needed you and you weren't there to help me." He was in a cold sweat. His body shivered and spasmed as he tried to keep his balance in the awkward, upright position the chair had put him in.

I helped my son back to his bed as he cursed the chair. I cursed the group that brought it into our lives. I cursed Drew, whom I loved, as well. Like Charlie, he couldn't stop at 'no' and listen to Nick. The chair remained in Nick's room because I did not have the physical strength to move it. At least it allowed people something more than the floor to sleep on when they stayed overnight to keep Nick company.

I went to another group meeting so I could vent my frustrations to the people who knew what it was like to lose someone they loved to a terminal condition that the rest of the world did not know about. Only that night, I didn't speak on the comfortable level to which the group was accustomed. Infuriated, my voice rose as I shocked them into silence by shouting the truth. I spelled out in detail the suffering we experienced. Tears spilled from quiet eyes. I vented my anger about the medical community and the insurance scam I saw as a blight on the American people. I damned the doctors for being apathetic towards human suffering and dictating the rights of patients and their families. "By not stepping in to save Lou Gehrig's victims from the inevitable protracted suffering, doctors are the perpetrators of outright sin!" Silence fell on the room as I sat down.

That night when I went home, I sat on my bed thinking. Lou Gehrig's disease was killing more than my son. It was killing our family as well. It became ever more difficult for those who loved him to spend time with Nick because the pain of seeing him grow increasingly helpless day by day was more than a heart could bear. A visit was greeted with good cheer from Nick, who looked forward to the company. Yet a few minutes of joy could be painful in many ways, and a visit at best was just a moment of diversion. If it hurt to be with Nick, a sibling or uncle or friend could escape the pain and go home. Out of sight, out of mind. I was becoming disgruntled with my family, because I was the pack animal who carried the weight of the burden. The heavier the load became, the more Nick and I were left alone to manage the emotional baggage of dying. I was becoming an emotional wreck after more than a year of watching my son disintegrate.

I felt we were losing everything that makes life worthwhile to the insidious syndrome that could continue for years. I cooked Nick's meals and took care of his personal hygiene. Those two tasks alone took hours each and every day. I prepared his meals from scratch. He was limited in the foods he could swallow and I spent a lot of time in the kitchen preparing his choice of the day, mashed or finely cut up. I washed his hair and kept it short by giving him regular cuts. I brushed his teeth. Shaved his face. Clipped his finger and toe nails. Washed him from head to toe and dried him too. I supplied him with fluids all day and emptied his urinal every hour. I cleaned his pipe and loaded his bowl with marijuana so he could get some relief from pain, rest his spirit and continue to cope with each day.

I needed support, and perhaps some assistance from my children and my brother. But not one of them was able to handle the kaleidoscopic array of duties Nick required on all levels in a twenty-four hour period. None of them had the strength or the fortitude that drove me forward. The world weighed heavy perched on top of my shoulders and I had to keep it spinning. I could never rest. Sometimes, overwhelmed by burdens, and sorrow, I felt God expected too much of me. Yet still, I humbled myself to his will.

At times, I acted like a steamroller with family who couldn't cope. There were times when I hated my brother. I hated my children. I hated everyone, because Nick and I suffered like two people shackled to the rack.

Everyone in the family was at their emotional worst, because it only got harder and harder to watch the deadly force of Lou Gehrig's syndrome turn Nick into a helpless creature. The family was a smashed clay pot with its bits and pieces of suffering scattered everywhere. But our love for Nick was the glue to reassemble the pieces back together. I stood alone to aid Nick with his needs, but everyone was united in sorrow and offered Nick compassion. Everyone in the family was angry with the system that dictated his death. It was tyranny the way that he was forced to suffer. All he wanted was his freedom. Where were his personal choices? Where were his personal liberties? Where were his rights? All agreed Nick had every reason to die a dignified death. And we all felt it was the civic and moral duty of the medical community to facilitate his final comfort.

Thoughts of impending death affected the entire family. It was agonizing to know we were losing Nick to Lou Gehrig's disease. Even more heartbreaking, he was forced to suffer in an unspeakable manner, and we suffered as we watched him. Agonizing questions went round and round in our frantic thoughts. What will we have to do? Give him a gun? Shoot him up with heroin? Put a pillow over his face and smother him? We were as helpless as Nick to end the madness and torment that increased with each passing day.

And always we were acutely aware that things were going to get worse before they got better. The strain on the family would increase until only an act of divine intervention could remove the cloak of torment from all of our hearts and set destiny onto a smooth track. It was obvious that I was the one assigned to serve as keeper of the gate, the only one who could help him bring an end to the pain and suffering he could no longer endure. The question was how?

Part II
The Final Approach

Nick Loving in
school photo
at age 11.

The Loving family before Nick became ill. Standing, left to right: Drew
and Nick Loving. Seated, are their sisters.

PHOTO BY JODY LYNN STUDIO

Luke, Carol, and Nick Loving in happier times, before Nick's diagnosis.

Nick was an exceptional, robust boy who excelled at sports.

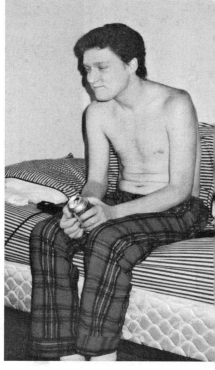

Nick tried to maintain his usual, upbeat demeanor, but two years after his diagnosis his physical deterioration became more and more apparent.

Luke and his mother,
Carol Loving,
embraced as the family
said goodbye to Nick.

Carol Loving and her son, Drew, Nick's fraternal twin brother, embraced at Carol's home after Drew said goodbye to Nick.

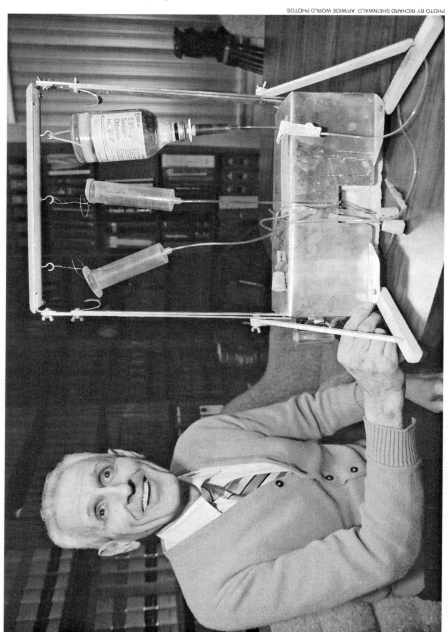

Dr. Kevorkian with his "suicide machine."

Dr. Kevorkian's van is moved from outside the Oakland County, Michigan Sheriff's Office. Nick Loving's body was found inside after Dr. Kevorkian notified officers.

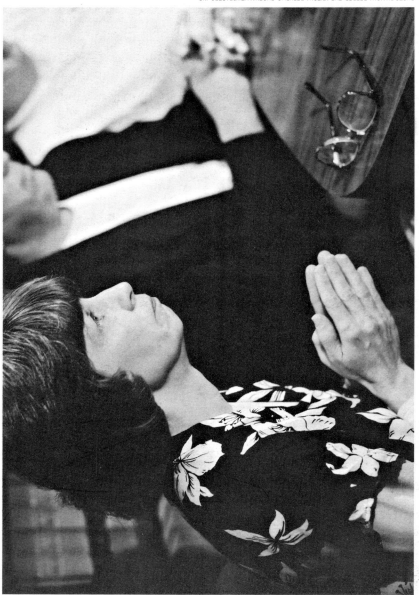

Carol at a news conference in Southfield, Michigan the day after Nick took his life.

Carol Loving leaning against the memorabilia wall she created for Nick's wake.

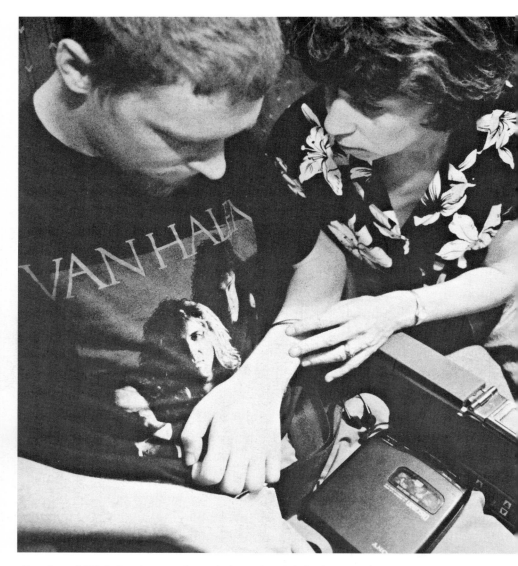

Carol and Nick Loving on board their fateful flight to Michigan.

8

Losing Ground

Our new apartment was larger and much brighter than our old living quarters, but it was also colder and Nick had become acutely sensitive to the temperature of his surroundings as a result of extensive muscle loss. I bought an electric heater for the mattress and Nick kept it on low all the time. I bought him heavy pajamas to keep his legs warm for the hours he sat on the side of the bed, but when Nick lay back down the pajama bottoms hampered free movement by twisting about his hips and waist as he turned over. We kept extra thick socks on his feet at all times. How hard it was to see Nick grow weaker day by day. Yet, despite the sadness, sacrifices and hardships, I found myself clinging to the present because the future offered even less. Bad as it was, I desperately wanted to hold on to Nick before I could hold on no longer. I wanted time to stop.

Nick fought to maintain his ebbing independence. Each struggle demanded fortitude and perseverance. Though his mobility was becoming more and more limited, he devised a workable method to ambulate back and forth to the kitchen for a shampoo. Starting at the side of his bed, Nick rocked until he had momentum to stand. Then he put his right hand on top of my right shoulder for support, manipulated his cane with his left hand, and in tandem, we made the long slow trek to the kitchen. A journey which took me only seconds, took him fifteen minutes and exhausted him too. All the while his body was jostled by tremors. Afterwards, we would make the return venture back to the bedside. Our method of hobbling along also enabled Nick to continue his trips to the bathroom. In fact, it was easier to do our tandem trot to the bathroom than it was to actually get Nick seated on the toilet. Because the bathroom was very small I had to be extremely careful with the linoleum surface below his sock covered feet. With the right maneuvers of my small frame, I positioned Nick with his back to the toilet and his fingers wrapped around the bar of the towel rack on the wall in front of him. I braced him on the left side as well as I could and Nick let his fingers unwrap from the bar. Then his body would fall back onto the toilet. I knew it hurt to hit the toilet, but what mattered to Nick was that he wasn't forced to use the bed pan. It was difficult to get him back up on his feet, but stubborn determination can defy the laws of human impossibilities.

The most exhausting activity in Nick's routine provided him with the greatest pleasure. That was a shower. Getting him on the toilet was easy compared to the task of getting him seated on a bath bench in the tub which was more narrow than the tub in our previous quarters. That made even less room for the bath bench. It was a mighty struggle to get Nick's atrophied body seated. It required patience on both our parts.

My Son, My Sorrow

Especially when we maneuvered his stiff trembling legs over the side of the tub, with the toilet in our way. Every time we did it, I wished we had a drain in the middle of the bathroom floor like homes in Taiwan. It would have made showers more accessible for him. I soaped the wash cloth and let Nick do what he could for himself, which was less each time. Nevertheless, he always said it felt soothing, cleansing, and refreshing. Unfortunately, it was another wrestling match to get him out and back on his feet again, but we never failed.

Grooming took hours. I brushed Nick's teeth while he sat on the side of the bed. It sounds simple, but it wasn't. It was difficult for Nick to spit the water out and easy for him to choke. I had to be careful as I moved the toothbrush around in his mouth. His jaw was weak, so I supported it in my left hand as I brushed. Nick, always fastidious about himself, swirled mouthwash several times a day to combat the stale breath of illness. Each day I cleaned his ears, massaged his scalp, combed his hair, and shaved his thin, worn face. When clean and in good spirits, he still was a fine looking young man, but I could see the mask of death lurking beneath the surface of his skin, clinging to his skull.

His dog, Norman, was Nick's constant and faithful companion. He wanted to participate in all of Nick's limited activities. In the months that Norman had been a part of our lives, Nick became weaker and less able to play while Norm had become bigger and stronger. Strong enough to overpower Nick, but so gentle that he slept under the cover in the cradle of Nick's legs or in the pocket of his arm. He brought joy into Nick's life. But when depression got the best of Nick, Norm also suffered Nick's anger and isolation. Whenever Nick demanded I close his door, Norm was no more welcome to remain in the room than I was. And the dog would lie pressed up against the door waiting to return.

Nick's bed was flush against the wall. We used a bolster to support his back when he was going to be seated for several hours at a time. It was lightweight and Nick could still remove it from his bed by himself, but I usually did. Beside the head of his bed was a small low table for tissues, mouthwash, remote controls, etc. The reach from his bedside was close and conveniently low to compensate for the restricted range of motion in Nick's upper body and arms. A small wastebasket was kept beside the bed. We kept it half full all the time because it made a good cradle for the urinal. A large window above the head of the bed brought the outside world to Nick. Hummingbirds frequently came into view and their song sometimes lulled him into dozing off.

Bitter as it was my losing job, it and the move had come at the right time as had my loss of employment. I needed to devote all my time to my son, who required more and more from me as the ALS syndrome coursed through his body, robbing him of energy.

We were slowly adjusting to both the inevitable reality that he was fatally ill, and that we were not going to get any merciful help from the medical community when his life became unbearable. We had to prepare to help him pass. The society in which we live made no provisions for the needs of those whose lives were filled only with pain and suffering.

Nick could have gotten a gun months ago from one of his friends, but he didn't want to blow his brains out and leave me with that image for the rest of my life. He didn't want to do that to our family. He wanted to die when his life was no longer bearable. He needed the knowledge that there would be a limit to the agony he would have to endure. "But I don't want to leave a bloody mess behind," he said passionately. *And he shouldn't have to*, I thought just as passionately. It was hard to begin to let go emotionally. Equally as hard for Nick as it was for me.

On the other hand, it was impossible to believe what a year had done to Nick physically and mentally. The change was frightening. We could only imagine what a few more months or another year would bring.

Before his life came to an end, though, we were given these few precious moments together, dwindling sands left in the hourglass of Nick's life. In this microcosm of time, pure and pristine, we were free to love before we relinquished each other. There was good to be had in each day, for me anyway.

Though exceptional love came to the surface through Nick's long struggle with ALS, there was always present the reality of encroaching death. My son became preoccupied with it as he lay trapped in his bed. Death was destiny. Death was mercy. But more important than his own mortality? Yes. It drove him mad to think of his mind further trapped in lifelessness. The idea of being alive in a body rendered completely immobile, with no way to verbalize his thoughts, exist without purpose, and be a burden to others made no sense at all to Nick. I loved sitting beside Nick, laughing with him, holding on to him, crying with him, sharing the exceptional bond we had, the exceptional

Carol Loving

love between mother and son I didn't want to lose. Love was enriching, but it wasn't the solution to the problem. I had to prepare myself in spirit and mind to assist my son to his death.

We walked a tightrope between happiness and despair. Nevertheless, because of it, Nick and I made the most of every moment we shared. Despite the wasting away and the crippling of his body, we had a love quintessential in nature as well as an exchange of communication which allowed a splendid understanding of the other's thoughts, feelings, and beliefs. In addition to the hours we were together accomplishing the daily tasks of grooming and hygiene, we were together watching sporting events or movies or television shows. We listened to music or we talked about everything from past to present. On numerous occasions, we discussed his need to move on, and how we would approach it. We agreed when the time came I had to take the reins of destiny and become the executioner to free him from a body that was going to lose all mobility and all speech.

His body was turning into the body of an old man, requiring round-the-clock care. His fingers were bony and awkward and curled up in his palms. He had to put his two fists together on the sides of a plastic cup or aluminum can in order to lift it to his mouth. Although he could sit up on the side of the bed, he sat hunched over because of the muscle loss he suffered. It took a lot of his strength to speak, and I had to train my ear to listen correctly. His speech was a challenge for everyone, and Nick became easily thwarted when asked to repeat himself again and again.

142

My Son, My Sorrow

Psychologically, it was heart-wrenching for me to see my son losing his life, his spirit and his will to live. His mind was still vibrant. His body was becoming worthless. I know Nick thrived upon challenge and motion. Now, his motion was slow and exhausting, not to mention frustrating. Which was worse, the crippling that attacked him inch by inch or the mental anguish attached to the loss? For Nick, one did not exist without the other. As for me, it was all too painful to accept. I did whatever I could to make his existence easier. I didn't know what steps to take to end his suffering, and pushed thoughts of his death to the back of my mind as I went about my everyday tasks. But Nick thought about his death all day and most of the night. It was all he had to look forward to. From the beginning, he struggled with the idea of suicide. Part of him wanted to end his life when he first learned what was ahead so he would never be rendered helpless. Another part of him fought that notion because he did not want to leave his family with the memory of his suicide. Now he was becoming a helpless cripple and wanted his rightful death. I wanted that for him too. I knew life was a burden for him. And yet, I still wanted to care for him. And I struggled with the thought of having him no more. I wasn't ready to relinquish our bond. I could still love him and touch him and laugh and cry with him. We could joke, get angry, and drive each other mad as we made it through each day. Though it was unbearable for me to witness the slow torment of my son's existence, how could I live without him? I was in agony. I wanted God to take him from me, but I still wanted to hold onto the loving son I brought into this world.

However, as the days passed and the ALS did more damage, Nick got more depressed. Then the scope of his thoughts changed from the contemplation of his death to a new problem: how to die.

I agreed with my son that no one should have to suffer the ravages of ALS. But, I didn't know how to end the suffering and that made it harder for me to let go. The reality of Nick's deteriorating state loomed before me. I knew my son's remaining physical strength was going to dwindle, and his will to see even one more day was going to come to an end. He was living now to share what he could with me and his siblings. I had to trust God and allow him to direct me and help me find a way, when Nick felt he could bear no more, to end his suffering in a civilized and dignified manner.

Meanwhile, the amount of control my son had already lost over his body was having a mirror effect on the control he maintained over his emotional stability. The anger, agony, and frustration ALS created as it progressed, crippling his life, grew in proportion to the dwindling control he had over his body. The more incapacitated he became, the more anger came to the surface. The more helpless he became, the more helpless I was to aid him.

Early on, Nick's good days outweighed the bad days. That was changing. The bad days were edging up, ready to take the lead over the good ones. Sometimes, I bore it stoically, but at others it wore me out to suffer through his outrageous fits of madness, to be a sponge for his frustration. Then, I wanted to cry out, *I'm wounded too. I hurt too.* His torture was mine. His torment resided in my heart and mind. I witnessed the misery and suffering that consumed him as the syndrome rapaciously took everything from him.

My Son, My Sorrow

What made it even more difficult and less understandable was that there wasn't a medical doctor anywhere who observed or watched over him as Nick lost his life to the incurable, irreversible process that was enfeebling him. Not a medical doctor anywhere saw the extent of the suffering he endured. With this in mind, could I possibly get a doctor to help us end his life when it became senseless and intolerable? I doubted it. The thought kept recurring. I had to help Nick die, but I promised myself I never would do it when he was in a fit of rage demanding that his torment be over. A final decision would be made when his rational senses governed his emotions so that I could be sure I was doing what he really wanted.

But as the days passed and Nick experienced more loss of control, more frustration, it fueled the anger inside. His life and death, his personal liberties were tethered to the dictates of the establishment. The establishment would hold him prisoner as long as it could. He had every right in the world to be angry. Rules and laws dictated that he must exist as he lay ever more lifeless in bed.

All he could do was think how awful the next day would be. And, the next week. And, the next month. The thought of losing anymore of himself than he already had tormented and tortured him. He was dying. Suffering. Now there were only bad days and good moments. Nick's body, in effect, was turning to stone, and the weight of his grief turned me motionless alongside him.

Thanksgiving was quite different than last year when Nick still could host family and friends. This year only Drew shared Nick's favorite family holiday. Dinner would take place at the side of his bed. I was in charge of the kitchen and prepared all the favorites of the day while Nick and his brother played basketball on Nick's Sega, an activity Nick rarely enjoyed anymore because of the stress inflicted on his thumbs. They listened to music, watched the football game, and drank a couple of beers. For the day, Drew replaced me as Nick's companion, which made it his obligation to keep the urinal empty for his brother. He also had to load Nick's bowl with marijuana to decrease the pain and so Nick could work up a holiday appetite. But, most important, to stem the saliva which would otherwise build up, causing Nick to drool.

   Just as last year, we vowed there would be no tears shed. It was to be a time of joy and gratitude for all we shared together in the short lifetime Nick was here on earth with us. Indeed, it was a day of fond memories, high spirits and laughter in spite of the circumstances. We all knew it was the last Thanksgiving. It had to be the best. It was also the first and only Thanksgiving for Nick and Norm to share. Drew and I sat on the floor balancing our plates. Nick ate from the small table on wheels I rolled to his bedside for his meals. Norm sat on the bed as he always did when Nick ate. And, at Nick's suggestion, we gave Norm his own Thanksgiving plate of food. I set it down in front of him. Norm's dream come true; a plate of people food. He wagged his tail back and forth as he gazed at Nick and me.

   Drew tried to help his brother when he was with us, but he didn't grasp the fact that the urinal had to be emptied right away or the accumulation of fluid would become too heavy for Nick's crippled hand to lift. Drew didn't empty it immediately. I still found myself checking in every hour to take care of the matter. It was added stress for me, and I was critical of Drew for being so lax, but Nick acted like a forgiving father toward his children when I would scrap or grumble or purse my lips to indicate that Drew wasn't holding up his end of the bargain. Even in the middle of the night, with Drew asleep smack dab in the middle of the bedroom floor, I was still the one who got up from my bed to take care of the urinal.

With a word or just a look, Nick expressed his gratitude. He felt fortunate to have me as a loving caretaker as Lou Gehrig's disease took over his life. As much as I hated what the deadly disease was doing to him, God made me strong enough to bear the burden and provide my son with the best care possible. I was grateful to my Creator that I was able to help my son. Of course, I still wondered why our lives had been brought to this junction, but I was steadfast in my resolve to remain by his side to the very end. I had been designated to support my son psychologically, spiritually, and emotionally. To prepare him for life in the next world while I cared for his physical needs in this one. Now to our life-long bond was added this special tie.

The Christmas holiday was ushered in by heavy rains, a welcome change from the parched weather Phoenix offered year round. Four weeks had passed between Thanksgiving and December 25, and the continued ravaging of Nick's body had made him even weaker and me more distraught. I cooked another turkey because the meat was tender and that was crucial for Nick to be able to chew it. Though only a month had gone by, eating was no longer something to look forward to because Nick found it so difficult to swallow. But he still looked forward to having Christmas with his family. Drew and

Carol Loving

Luke spent the holiday with us. Nick was moved to tears when he first saw his younger brother, whom he had not seen in seven months. "I'm so glad to see you. Luke, you seem to be turning your life around."

Being with Hannah would have made Nick's last Christmas on earth complete. But we did not know where she was. Her life was in turmoil. Nick expressed the sentiments of us all when he opined, "I've never been so worried about her. Let's pray for her welfare."

Nevertheless, nothing could stop the flow of love that moved through the house on this unique day. We cherished the opportunity to have one last Christmas together. Nick spent his time sitting on the side of his bed or lying down because now the energy it took for him to sit up for long periods of time was severely limited. However, Nick was content just being in the company of Norm and his brothers. Though we gave each other little of material worth, I was happy to count my blessings and remained grateful to know that inside our hearts, we were rich in the spirit that sustained the soul. At dinner I prayed, "Our Lord made it through this world of heartache and strife. May the spirit he left behind for the world and her people provide us with the strength to move forward and face our sorrow."

New Year's Eve fell on a Saturday. Nick and I planned to share a nice tender steak for dinner early in the evening. It was a good day for Nick even though he now had to drink all his fluids with a straw. There were sporting events, music, and the relaxation that came from us both drinking a couple of beers. Around six o'clock, when I asked Nick, who was listening to his stereo, if he wanted me to start dinner, he asked me, "Mom, will you get me two more beers?" I started to protest.

He said, "It's okay. I can handle it. I'm not going to slip into a funk." I didn't want him to drink any more, but I also did not want to interfere with his request on his last New Year's Eve. So I got the beers for him.

To my distress, everything in the world toppled by the weight of two beers added to two beers. Nick had to use the urinal and, by misfortune, his hand knocked it out of reach. He tried his best, but the object was impossible to secure. He called for me. I was in the kitchen and it took me a moment to hear his call above the music. By the time I got to him it was too late. I walked into his room to find him peeing on the floor from the bedside. He couldn't help it. His bladder could not hold the urine. He had no choice. His disabled body was out of control.

"Why can't you get in here when I need you?" he asked, angrily. I knew he was disgusted with me, because he was frustrated with the loss of dignity attached to losing control over his own body. Staring at his tortured face, I knew we were in for a night of hell.

As anger churned into a bout with mania, Nick leaned his body forward causing him to fall off the bed. To watch him fall without any way to protect himself against the impact was more than my heart could take. I ran to his side and tried to buffer his fall, but that was only fuel for the fire. He was infuriated that I tried to help him.

"Damn you for letting my life reach this point. Look at me!" he cried out. "Don't turn away. Look. I hate what this damn disease is doing to me. It's consuming me and I hate the entire medical community for its control over my life. Most of all, I hate you for letting me become a slave confined and shackled by my own flesh."

Writhing on the floor, Nick screamed out his torment. I gazed down at my crippled son. He looked back at me with lost eyes and I at him. My son was no longer a vital human being. He was a helpless member of a barbaric and cruel society.

"Leave this room," he demanded. I refused. "Leave!" he yelled up at me.

I stood my ground and yelled back at him, "No! You don't really want to be left alone. I know it and so do you."

His eyes were distraught with the look of a caged animal. His soul was being strangled by a wicked death grip. Reflecting the classic torment of a person confined against his will, he dragged his useless body about the floor, cursing me for letting him live. Then he tried to drag himself into the urine. "I'm an animal, not a man and the worst of it all is once I'm dead, who will ever know I was alive?" he screamed. I managed to cover the area with towels before he rolled his body on the spot. He thrashed trying to free himself of the straight jacket his body had become. He lost his boxer shorts by dragging his body on the carpet and lay sprawled out on the cold floor naked, except for the socks on his feet. I stayed close to my son as the wrath of his anger choked him.

I watched horrified as saliva flowed from his mouth onto the floor as he sunk his face into the carpet. The jerking motion of electrospasms tormented his body, and he was chilled to the bone, causing him to shiver uncontrollably. "Please let me cover you," I sobbed. He refused.

My Son, My Sorrow

It was two and a half hours before my son returned from the edge of madness. I would not leave him all the while. He was exhausted from the journey. His voice was parched and raw. "Mom, please help me back to bed," he rasped. His body was dead weight, but I gritted my teeth and hardened my will. The task of getting him back to the bed took nearly half an hour. My son was naked and cold, dehydrated and dirty, helpless and hopeless. When he was finally under the coverlet, I gave him a bowl of marijuana to smoke to dry out his mouth and relax his spirit. I lovingly cleaned him and got him into fresh underwear and pajamas. I gave him fluids to replenish him and told him I loved him.

I sat on the bed while Nick told me how sorry he was for everything he put me through. "It doesn't matter, Nick, it's alright," I comforted him. His body was now the true meaning of purgatory. I understood that. It was more pain than a mother should have to bear.

He needed to die before life became even worse for him. He had the right to be raging mad at the world as he was being sucked down into the black hole society creates for those who are dying in pain and torture. Once again, we shared our feelings. Just the fact that each of us could express his feelings, even of torment and rage, and know that the other would always understand, picked up our spirits.

Then we had our steak dinner. Afterward, we took a memorable journey through Nick's life with the aid of photographs we had accumulated.

We then spoke of his death, not as a tragedy, but as an accomplished certainty that would bring relief to my son. Nick chose the photo we should display for his wake. He told me he wanted cremation, and that his ashes should be scattered on one of his favorite places, Squaw Peak. "I don't want a funeral," Nick said. "I must have hiked Squaw Peak a hundred times. I love it up there. You can see forever." He told me to get prices and begin making the arrangements for the cremation.

Finally, we made it to midnight and the new year. Nick leaned his head on my shoulder, saying, "No one could have possibly cared or given me as much love as you have over the past year."

"No one could possibly deserve it more," I replied, and meant it with all my heart.

9

Cumulative Suffering

In mid-January, another fragment of Nick's independence had to be relinquished. The trip to the kitchen was no longer possible. It was way too far. All attempts at ambulation had to now be reserved for the treacherous journey to the bathroom. Nick was so much weaker. His hands were sad extensions that hung from bony wrists like a couple of weights. Yet Nick fought the helplessness. He was able to hook his fingers around the handle of the all important urinal. He could still feed himself, though only mashed and strained food, with a spoon. I knew it wouldn't be long before he would lose the ability to do even that. But I tried not to think of it. I tried to live not only one day, but one moment at a time.

Back in October, at Nick's request, I had asked the ALS Association to help us find a hospital bed for my son. They assured me they would. It was three months later and still nothing. All we got were pat answers and a chair we didn't want. "I've called all over town to find you a bed. There's nothing available," the woman said when I called. I tried to retain a civil tongue by not reminding her of their promises, promises which came to nothing while Nick suffered.

I went to January's ALS meeting, because the guest speaker was a representative from a local Hospice. Perhaps they could help. I asked the speaker, Joy Davis if her organization could help us find a bed. I described Nick's deteriorating condition, emotionally and physically, and pleaded, "We're desperate. Isn't there something your organization can do to help?" Davis said she would speak to the Hospice doctor, and if nothing else, he would at least make a house call to determine our needs.

She added, "I'll definitely get you a bed" she promised, "even if I have to get one from my church."

On my own, I contacted the Muscular Dystrophy Association, Easter Seals and other places, begging for help, but no matter who I called, I came up with nothing. I had to stop. I was too emotionally drained. A friend said she would make some calls for us. Five days later, she let me know of an organization she found which would give Nick a bed. I would have to arrange for a pick-up, but before I sought a truck and manpower, I called the ALS chapter to inform them of the organization with medical beds for loan. I couldn't believe it when the woman told me she had just found a bed for Nick, only minutes before my call.

In our small apartment, space was tight, and besides, it was senseless to keep what we did not use. I wanted the ALS chapter to pick up the lift chair. They hemmed and hawed. Luckily, we heard of someone else who wanted the chair and arranged to have them pick it up. The father and son came to our place on the twenty-eighth of January. We talked, and they were sympathetic to our situation and offered to help me go and get the hospital bed I had been promised. I was grateful for the kindness of these strangers. We made the pick-up. It was Wednesday, a day that marked a new low for Nick. His hands could no longer lift even a spoonful of food. One more loss of self-control. The anger that accompanied this low was as strong as his hands were weak. Norm and I were banned from the room. The disassembled bed took up space in the living room until that Friday when my youngest son helped me assemble it.

Luke came down that day after work. Nick was still a rock of isolation, but he agreed to let us into his private world of hell to provide for the change in his beds. The electric bed we had been given was a popular model used in the seventies. It was a good model, one that lowered the frame far enough for a patient to firmly set his feet on the ground when leaving the bed. When Nick first asked for a bed, prior to our move, it seemed like the bed would be of great assistance. But the intervening months had weakened him too much. When he lay down on it, he found that the mattress was as soft as a marshmallow and prevented him from lying on his stomach comfortably. And, it impeded his ability to turn over on his back. In order for Nick to sleep that night, I had to remove the hospital mattress and replace it with Nick's regular mattress which was a good foot shorter than the frame. And, with a regular mattress on the frame, the back of the bed could not be elevated. Another disappointment.

The next day, February 4th, Nick continued to isolate himself. He was frustrated by the new bed and still depressed and despondent that he could no longer feed himself. "I can't take it anymore. For the love of God, this is Madness! Sheer Madness!" he cried.

Finally, Nick allowed me to feed him something that afternoon. Having to be spoon fed was quite tense, and my son barred eye contact as he tried to eat the mashed potatoes I put into his mouth while he sat hunched over like a man of ninety. I winced as I saw him hardly able to control the weight of his own head. His throat was as crippled as his hands and feet, and the rest of his body revealed thin bones. We were both on edge as I continued to slowly feed him. Then, despite my caution, I said something wrong. I did something wrong. I caused the dam to break. Once again, I was banned from the room.

Several house later, I could hear the stereo playing. Over the noise of the music came a loud thud. I knew Nick was on the floor. The weight of his world pinned me down and pressed hot tears from my eyes. I knew I had to go to him, but when I opened his door, I was plunged into shock and screamed.

How on earth he did it, I'll never know, except by sheer will and determination. He had rolled his helpless body around on the floor, disconnected the phone wire and secured it to the foot of the bed. The wire was looped over the frame of the bed with the other end wrapped around my son's neck, and he had elevated the bed to its maximum level. A home-made gallows rigged to hang himself. Choke himself at the push of a button. But the bed would only go so high, and it didn't bring his nightmare to an end. He had failed.

My heart was breaking as I grabbed the controls from him and lowered the bed. Begrudgingly, he let me remove the cord from his neck. I gently placed his head down on the floor. "Let me help you get back on the bed," I begged. He refused.

"Get out. Get out!" he yelled. The ban on visitation continued until the sun went down. Only then, did he let me come back in to help him with his struggle to get up off the cold floor.

It was truly the lost weekend for my son. It wasn't until Monday that I was allowed to clean his room and the patches of urine that soaked the carpet either where the urinal fell or where Nick had urinated while laying on the floor.

All at once, it seemed overwhelming. I had the room to clean and I had my son to clean and feed. To make matters worse, the Hospice doctor whom we had been waiting for weeks to contact us called that morning. "I'm nearby," he offered, "and I want to stop in to see Nick."

"Look," I told him, "We had one of the worst week-ends of my life. It would be best to re-schedule for another time." Reluctantly, he agreed to postpone his visit.

Nothing improved. Each minute was unbearable for Nick as the week unfolded. His body was now failing rapidly. Creeping paralysis sucked the life out of him. Since he could not turn over or change position, his immobility prevented him from even getting relief from the simple act of sleeping. At times, he screamed like a madman held captive in a pit full of snakes. At others, he was as silent as if a mummy.

By that Thursday, Nick and I were on the brink of exhaustion as his illness closed in on his soul like a coffin. That day, he reached the brink of insanity and once again his body fell to the floor. Like a lunatic in a straight jacket, he waged another battle with his enemy. He wailed deliriously, crying, "Kill Me! Kill Me!" Among shrieks and howls of damnation, I went to my son and pleaded with him to let me help him get back in bed. He looked up at me with madness in his eyes. There was drool slobbering from his mouth. "You have to get me a gun, and now," he begged. He demanded. The truth is, if I had a gun that night I would have ended his suffering. It was insane to go on. I probably would have shot my son in the head and turned the gun on me for having done the deed. But, of course, I had no gun.

What was I to do? How could I end his misery? Desperate, I put my hand over his nose and mouth, but he broke for air after the physical urge to breathe became the master of his body. In the end, we were both crazy with despair, frustration and pain.

A few days later, someone mentioned a group to me called the Hemlock Society. I had no idea what the organization was, but I found a number for the local chapter and had information sent to me. When I read their literature, which detailed how they offered advice and help on dying to those suffering from terminal illnesses, I called the chapter and heard there was a meeting February 11th. Though I was afraid it was just another organization that wanted money, I went there. I found a scant group of people concerned with the battle that existed between death and doctors. I filtered fact from opinion and left with a book on self-deliverance for the dying and something else. I left the meeting with a possible lead to ending Nick's despair. Someone gave me an address they thought was Dr. Jack Kevorkian's.

In the past, we had seen the ill-famed doctor on television, but didn't know how to contact him. I clutched the paper, but felt there was little hope. Even if it was actually his address, I doubted that he'd help. On the other hand, I had to hope. I felt that the doctor could be our last resort.

On Valentine's Day, the Hospice doctor finally made it to our place to evaluate Nick's medical condition. A year had passed since we went to see the doctor for the exam required by Social Security. Nick had long fought the idea of Hospice entering our home, but he desperately wanted something, anything, to help him sleep. For that reason he allowed the Hospice doctor he see him. "Please," Nick begged, "I've been up for days. I have to sleep." We emphasized how lying in bed without movement created pressure build-up, as well as physical and mental stress.

"If Nick has to lie immobile in his bed, at least help him sleep. That's all I ask," I pleaded.

In truth, besides aid in getting some rest, Nick wanted real help. He wanted a doctor to see and commiserate on the reality of his situation. He couldn't walk. He could hardly talk. He had trouble swallowing both solid food and liquids. He couldn't feed himself. It was becoming senseless to pretend there was reason to go on. He couldn't contribute to the family he loved or to society. His state of helplessness was a mandate for compassion by the medical profession. The doctor knew what the future held for my son. Moreover, he knew, just as we did, that the torment that was Nick's life could continue far longer than the six month period that was supposed to indicate a need for Hospice. The doctor knew that Nick's heart could keep on pumping for a long time regardless of what happened to the rest of his body over the course of this year. But he only said, "I'll report my findings to the Board." There was so much red tape involved—even in prescribing medication. The requirements of institutionalized medicine took precedence over my son's broken condition and distraught state of mind.

The next day, Barbara Baron, a heavyset Hospice nurse with a brusque manner, came to our home to start the official ball rolling with an avalanche of paperwork. Her job was to fill out forms and request equipment. Walker, bedside commode, bath bench, all of which I repeatedly stated were either being taken care of or were not necessary. My words made no impression on her. She ordered the equipment anyway. It arrived that evening only to take up space in the living room. But, no prescriptions to help Nick get some sleep. "They're not going to help," Nick said, disillusioned.

Thursday, a tall, thin Hospice social worker, her hair pinned back in a bun, entered like a whirlwind. She was in charge of reams of paperwork and threw her confidence around like a military sergeant. Nick had no more interest in seeing her than he had in seeing the nurse. But she didn't let his needs rule her behavior, and she walked right in on him, ignoring his right to privacy while he was urinating. "I have his best interest in mind," she insisted. At least, that was the way she put it.

"All I want you to do is go," Nick pleaded. Still nothing from the doctor to help him sleep.

Baron came back on Friday to tell me who would be assigned to my son's case. The Hospice plan was to have someone make a home visit each day of the work week from then on. A nursing assistant on Mondays, Wednesdays and Fridays; an R.N. on Tuesdays; and a social worker on Thursdays. "This is unrealistic," I said. My words fell on deaf ears.

My Son, My Sorrow

Baron phoned the druggist to say the doctor would call in a prescription for Nick. "Something to help him sleep, I think you requested." I said nothing. The medication was delivered to our door early that evening. It was in liquid form. It didn't do a thing, even when we doubled the recommended dosage. We felt cheated, belittled, angry. Nick was right. They were not going to help. The mask of death hung over our home, laughed in our face, and taunted our sanity, but Hospice looked the other way. Between the combined efforts of a doctor, a nurse, and a social worker, no one brought comfort to my son.

The weekend passed. Monday. Still nothing.

On Tuesday, the registered nurse assigned to Nick's case knocked at the door. She was slovenly in appearance and looked like a bag lady. She spoke like a tyrant. She entered our domain convinced she knew everything. She was brash, ignorant, and had no listening skills. I cried out. "Nick received no benefit from the prescription even when I gave him more than the prescribed dosage, and he needs sleep. He has to sleep." I demanded that she tell the doctor to give my son something strong to help him get some rest. She left and called later that evening to say the doctor said to double up on the prescription. I was outraged. What was wrong with Hospice? Did they want to make light of my son's dying days? Taunt our sanity? It only added to the madness.

Nick's sleepless torture continued. Now sleepless nights piled up like a tower, driving Nick into lunacy. It was the twenty-third of February. By that night Nick could not bear it any more. He screamed "I have to get off my back." The burning pressure on his shoulders and hips was excruciating. Hard as Nick tried, he couldn't get his worthless hands to cling to the edge of the mattress to help him rock his body and pull himself over to his side. And he wouldn't let me help. Frustrated beyond reason, he hit the stereo remote button beside him and filled the silent night with loud, rocking rhythm. Next came a round of vengeful yelling as the torment that enveloped him grated and shredded his soul. I cried with his pain and knew he would end up on the floor again.

It was past 1:00 A.M. I was just as angry and frustrated as Nick. I was fed up with the world which allowed his suffering to continue unbridled and for no reason. The sounds of moaning and groaning came from his room, and I knew he was on the floor. When I walked in, I saw to my despair that he tried to hang himself again, but the gallows would not strangle the life out of him. He didn't want me to free him from the cord. But I did, against his will. "I hate you," Nick screamed. It was ten days since Hospice had entered our home, and they had done nothing but worsen our agony. The doctor still had not provided Nick with anything to help him sleep. I called Hospice's emergency number and demanded they send over two strong men to lift the dead weight of my son off the floor.

The man who answered said, "We'll send the nurse on call." That nurse just happened to be the same one that was in our home on Tuesday. I was livid. At them. At myself. Even at Nick. When I hung up, I told Nick, "You'd better do everything possible to help me get you back on your bed because if you don't, that stupid excuse for a nurse is going to come into our home again and see you naked on the floor. She is even going to put her hands on you." The idea was well beneath his dignity. Nick came to his senses, and the adrenaline in my

My Son, My Sorrow

body enabled me to lift what was equivalent to a six foot bag of wet sand off the floor and onto the bed. It was a twenty minute struggle to get him there and once seated on the side of his bed, I gave him water to replenish the fluid he lost. Then I gave him a bowl of marijuana to diminish his pain. We talked as I took care to clean him, cover his privates in clean boxer shorts, return him to his dignity and calm him down.

I made another call to Hospice. "Don't bother to come out to our place. I took care of the matter." It was too late. The nurse was already on her way. Despite my attempts to stop her, the slovenly nurse showed up at our door about two in the morning. Stepping outside, I lambasted her along with the entire medical profession. "As far as I am concerned, the system feeds off the sick like a cancer." I demanded they do something out of respect for the dying and give my son something to help him sleep.

"The doctor doesn't want to prescribe something stronger than he already has because he fears a stronger medication might be fatal," she said, nonchalantly.

I felt hysteria creep up my throat. "Heaven forbid, you should grant my son's only wish! Nick is dying. What does it take for Hospice to understand? My son is suffering." My words fell on deaf ears. "You mean what Hospice essentially is saying is that it is better for Nick to continue to be in agony than it is for him to be at peace."

It was ridiculous for me to think I could get Hospice to help us in our dilemma with death. It is my belief that the medical profession harbors an aversion to death. A denial of death. It exploits the process of death. It prohibits death. In addition, death is not as profitable as continued suffering to the medical industry. It was obvious Hospice was not there to fulfill my son's needs. Hospice had the control button in its hand. The game was played by Hospice's rules. It didn't matter if the court belonged to us. It didn't matter if it was my son's death. Not to them. Only to us. We alone would have to find some means to end his torment.

10

Desperate Measures

The rest of February was even more disastrous. Nick slipped rapidly into a state of almost total incapacity. The day was fast coming when he would not be able to move at all. We both saw the signs. I had to find a means to end the paralyzing process of death Nick was going through before that time. But everywhere I looked for help I faced a closed door. *Final Exit*, the book I'd gotten from the Hemlock Society, suggested using a combination of Seconal, a barbiturate, and alcohol to induce death.

I involved family and friends in a dragnet hunt for the drug. We scoured the city. We contacted people we heard had connections. We sought doctors and nurses, but they all turned away from our pleas like we were a family of lepers. Their excuses were always the same. They were sympathetic, but they had professional lives to protect. It was possible to find the right drug. It was whispered that it was readily available deep in Mexico, but I had neither the means, the time, nor the will to go there to explore.

For hours at a time, I searched the city. Nothing. In the seventies, when I was young, Seconal could be found anywhere by anyone. They were known as Reds on the streets. This was the nineties, and the streets offered all sorts of soul destroying drugs, but Seconal was not out there.

According to the book, if the barbiturate Seconal and second choice, Nembutal, were impossible to get, Valium and Darvon were recommended as back up drugs. We had to be careful not to use the wrong drugs or the wrong amounts of the recommended drugs, and the ingestion of the drug was to be combined with alcohol. One thing I did not want to do was fail in my attempt to end my son's life. As a means of insurance against failure, the book recommended the additional use of a plastic bag over the head of the loved one. The very idea of putting a plastic bag over my son's head to end his life on earth repulsed me. Nick said, "I don't care, I just want to be able to die when I can't stand it any more." How he was able to attain death was not as important to him as bringing his suffering to an end.

The quest to secure Valium or Darvon was just as fruitless as my search for Seconal. I drove family and friends crazy begging them for help. But they were as unsuccessful as I was. The law and the medical profession stood in positions of authority over my son, over his pain ridden life and destiny in what amounted to most cruel and unusual punishment. "As long as the government can inflict and prolong the suffering of the dying, how can we say we are a nation of freedom and personal liberties?" I asked. "Where is my son's freedom to leave this world? Where is his liberty?"

My Son, My Sorrow

The idea that if I aided him I would suffer the iron hand of the law once my son was released from bondage was an added burden for Nick. It tortured him to think of his mother arrested and locked up with the scum of the earth. It wasn't just. No more just than the torment he was forced to endure. The idea of what the law could do no longer bothered me. I had to keep searching. The problem, the real problem was finding the means to successfully help Nick end his life. If the law wanted to punish me for doing what was right, so be it. However, the stress on Nick's mind concerning what the law would do forced him to reconsider the idea of a gun. I said, "You don't have the strength anymore, Nick."

"I'll succeed," he vowed. "You just get me one." Yet, as much as he wanted the mercy of a bullet, when he was more rational, he confessed that he didn't want to leave us with the devastating effects that such a death was bound to have on all of us.

No one wanted Nick to die at the barrel of a gun. He deserved better than a violent end to a tragic and devastating disease. But, the drug hunt never turned up any drugs. I was disappointed with everyone. I was disappointed in myself. One evening, I began to reconsider the plastic bag method to end my son's life. At this point, he was helpless without me. Powerless without me. I had to come through for him. I had to help him to die. At that moment, I remembered hiding the address for Dr. Kevorkian that I had been given. But even if it was the correct address, it seemed like such a long shot. It did not seem realistic at all. We knew nothing about the doctor. How could Nick allow himself to think that Dr. Death, as the media referred to him, would come to his rescue?

Carol Loving

Nick and I rode the seesaw of emotions. Up and down. Down and up. Life was tolerable at best and miserable most of the time. Worst of all, Nick was suffering more each day. I continued searching for the drugs he needed. I begged and pleaded with friends to help me and I turned over in my mind repeatedly how to end my son's life. I had yet to complete my mission and Nick was becoming more helpless. By this time, his moods had utter control over me, control over my ability to function as a mother, friend and personal servant. As low as my son would go, so too would I fall. Unable to function, just like my son. Suffering every moment as ALS robbed us both of life.

However, during this period of despair, we had one of our heart-to-heart connections. We had a long discussion about his need to die. "I understand," Nick said softly, "how hard it is for you to let go, but I don't want to go on anymore." My son tactfully told me to look beyond my personal sorrow and stop procrastinating. "Please, let go," he begged. We sat side by side on the edge of his bed, my hands always touching him, and after he spoke, we put our heads together. Tears rolled down my cheeks. I looked into his eyes. I realized through the intermingling of our spirits that he was right.

"It *is* me," I said insightfully. "I am the one who is still clinging to the thought of some miraculous reprieve but I have to let you go." We looked at each other quietly for a moment, reflecting on my sudden moment of awareness.

Yet there appeared to be no way we could undertake the end ourselves, as both of us had hoped. Could the answer to our dilemma be Dr. Kevorkian? His name kept rummaging around in my brain and yet...

My Son, My Sorrow

My thoughts ricocheted back and forth. If Dr. Kevorkian stepped in, it would take the burden of assisting my son to his death off my shoulders and remove Nick's worries over the possibility of his mother ending up in jail once he was gone. It could be the solution, but could we believe he would help? Dr. Kevorkian couldn't come to Phoenix. How would I get Nick to Michigan? Was I just avoiding what I had to do myself? I had to believe there was a way to end my son's suffering other than placing a plastic bag over his head. But, maybe that was the only answer to this problem we faced. The bag was right there in the living room, on the lid of the bedside commode. It was neither too large nor too small and it was clear, transparent. But more than the idea of the law stepping in to further denigrate the passing of my son, I believed it was beneath human dignity to have my son go to his death with a plastic bag over his head.

Meanwhile, the hospice experience was barely tolerable for either one of us. Nick and I agreed that the sorry excuse for a nurse assigned to Nick's case would have to be replaced. I notified them and the next one was another unbelievable character, Robin Levin, a blond-haired minx, a mixture of innocence and ignorance. She was laughable in her condescending attitude toward Nick, whom she treated as a two year old child. When Nick asked her to try to get him another mattress, she opened her blue eyes wide and seemed to have no idea how to fulfill the simple request. "All it takes is for you to phone them," I said, shaking my head. It would have been there possibly by that night. After waiting five days, I finally called the main office myself only to find out she had never made the request. I was promised they would page her and we would have a mattress that day.

Of course, Hospice still would not provide us with anything to end Nick's life. In fact, it took a real battle to have a mild muscle relaxer added to Nick's other prescription so he could get several hours of sleep at night. Nevertheless, that, along with the mattress, were the only reasons to have Hospice in our lives. Otherwise, it was an intrusion into our privacy, not to mention the sorrow it caused. One day when my desperation seemed to have reached a zenith and I felt completely undone, I communicated Nick's desire to die and his attempts to kill himself as a result of his life being ravaged by ALS to the hospice worker. I might as well have been speaking in a foreign tongue. The young nurse looked upon Nick as an irritable child, not a dying young man deserving a peaceful end. Death was everywhere, but Hospice was afraid to face it.

Hospice wanted Nick to take Prozac to counter the depression brought on by his helplessness, as if depression were the problem and ALS was the side effect. Out of desperation, Nick relented to the idea of taking an antidepressant. I think he wanted to try the antidepressant for my benefit. A few minutes after he took one he said, "It makes me feel like I'm on speed." He didn't like it at all, but he wanted to use a quantity of them with a bottle of alcohol and the plastic bag. "Maybe that would work," he whispered to me. To thwart any such attempts, they gave him one at a time and checked to see he wasn't holding them in his cheek. As if he could spit the pills out and hoard them. If only...

When on the drug, he became jumpy, feeling like he had to get up and walk around. But, of course, he couldn't. He was a clam enclosed in a shell. His mind raced as a reaction to the drug. But even that was a frustrating process. He couldn't rattle off at the mouth like the nurse who was free to prattle with her health intact. For him, each word was an effort and the effect of the drug further complicated his already limited powers of speech. Nick and I damned Hospice for its ludicrous approach to Lou Gehrig's disease and its inept approach to meet his personal needs. He was dying. His psyche was as fragile as fine china. Yet, to Hospice, he was just one more person who could be poked and prodded on his deathbed.

Never in my life could I have ever believed I would see my son dying little by little. He now looked like a living corpse. His skin pale and thin. His eyes dark and hollowed out. His body was useless, confined to bed. His hands were bony dead weights. Only his mind remained intact, and it was tormented by the plight of his body. His heart begged for mercy. *What is the matter with the medical profession that this should be allowed to go on?* I asked myself over and over again. Soon my son would not be able to move a muscle. Were we supposed to acquiesce to Hospice's answers to my son's total helplessness? In our tortured thoughts, what the Hospice members needed was a shot of reality. A good bolt of gut-wrenching suffering to adjust their idealistic but unrealistic perspective of what it is to suffer and how hard it is to die.

Nevertheless, I held on tightly to the little aid they had provided. As stunted in the area of meeting the needs of the dying as Hospice was, I fought the urge to dismiss them from our lives. Hospice had a record of Nick's recent medical history. When we resolved our problem of how to handle his demise, I planned to report his death to the Hospice doctor rather than placing a call to the police. Then, it would be the Hospice doctor's duty to decide if the police should be called. I hoped there was the possibility of the Hospice doctor looking the other way and reporting Nick's death as the result of ALS. That was a lot to expect from a staunch opponent of euthanasia. But, how could I expect to be rational when I was backed into a corner, forced to end the life of my son? If the Hospice doctor wanted to draw the police into the matter and have me arrested for assisted suicide, he would have to live with his own decision and conscience.

We were no closer to finding the means by which I could help Nick die. Each time we thought of a method, we followed it only to reach a dead end. But for whatever reasons, one idea kept recurring. One was still open.

Approaching Dr. Kevorkian with a letter was now a serious consideration. Since we couldn't gain access to any other means of bringing Nick a merciful death, it made sense to bring Nick's dilemma to the good doctor's attention in one last attempt to get help. Nick and I agreed on this. The problem was getting the letter written.

I procrastinated while February's end had us riding an emotional roller coaster. This one took us to summits and plummeted us all the way down, dumping us in a heap, until it was impossible to separate the two suffering souls fused in one mission. Nick would tell me to write the letter when all was peaceful. But anything could aggravate the madness. When depression tripped the circuits, contacting Dr. Kevorkian went up in smoke. One moment it was "write the letter." Another moment it was "don't waste time chasing rainbows." Then it was back to "you have to do it."

My Son, My Sorrow

By the first day of March, I was stuck in my own emotional paralysis. I felt like a failure and a disappointment to my son. I had to help him. On Saturday, the fourth of March, after I raised hell with Hospice, the doctor finally broke down and prescribed one milligram of Valium for Nick. We had a reasonably good day, and after I fed Nick his dinner, I sat down on the bed beside him and helped him with an after-dinner smoke. I loaded his bowl and placed the small pipe in his palm. He slowly got it to his mouth. I lit the bowl, and he drew in the smoke. When Nick felt peaceful and was no longer suffering pain, we engaged in a heart, mind and soul communication about the urgency to move forward with what we needed to do.

"The time has come," my son said. My heart skipped a beat. With tenderness and care, Nick told me he loved me and didn't want to leave me but his fate had led him down a path to this point, and there was no turning back. He was so right. The weight of his words pulled tears from my soul.

I looked into my son's eyes. "You mean now?" I said slowly.

"Yes, now," Nick replied. "I can't stand it much longer."

The words were spoken. I vowed he wouldn't live to see the summer. "I'll get your medical records sent to Dr. Kevorkian, but I won't stop searching for a way to accomplish it ourselves." We wanted to make sure that we made every effort to find a solution.

Whatever happened as a result of breaking the law would happen. I believed God knew what he was about, and I really couldn't envision myself in prison. Nevertheless, I prayed that Dr. Kevorkian was going to help us.

A few nights later, a flicker of light appeared. Dr. Kevorkian appeared right before my son. Not in the form of a vision. The doctor appeared on television on the late, late show. Tired, I went to sleep while Nick watched an interview with the doctor who had been bold enough over the past five years to help twenty-one terminally ill people end their suffering. Nick was able to assess for himself the man the country called Dr. Death. When I got up in the middle of the night to go to the bathroom, Nick caught my attention. For the first time, he said with conviction in his heart and voice, "Mom, we have to get to Dr. Kevorkian somehow—and now." That night, in Nick's mind, the idea of Dr. Kevorkian assisting him had become more than just a pipe dream. Yet for me, it still wasn't a reality. And, in my mind, the act of writing that letter would signify the end. I still couldn't bring myself to do it.

11

Our Helpless Family

As Lou Gehrig's disease continued destroying Nick's body, it was also choking the life out of our family. We stood helpless to the power that turned muscle into dust and transformed Nick into a pitiful figure of despair. Nick was the heart of the family and each beat of his suffering sent ripples of shock waves through the rest of us who watched Nick's deterioration.

I didn't know where Hannah was, and I prayed she would resurface soon to spend time with Nick before it was all over. Hannah loved her brother, and I knew it was her life being in disarray that was keeping her away. To my dismay, Drew had stopped his weekly visits when the new year replaced the old one. Now he came only once in a while, because he could no longer bear to watch his twin brother shrivel up into a decrepit old man. Even the always optimistic Luke who came by regularly with a smile on his face usually left with tears running down his cheeks. My brother Rick was still drinking to numb the pain inside that came from having to witness what the deadly chemical syndrome did to his nephew.

I was grateful to the Lord that my spirit was strong enough to care for my beloved son. No one else in the family had the medical background, knowledge, patience, or level of commitment it took to provide the things I was able to provide for Nick. But it was a draining task that left me with only my instincts to cope with the weaknesses of others. Nick, alone, was the center of my focus. It was my job to protect him from being hurt by those he loved, as well as to provide him with shelter and food and other necessities such as shopping, cooking and constant cleaning. Not to mention the personal grooming that had to be done. Sometimes it reminded me of the period after his birth, when as an infant, I was responsible for his very existence. I was as protective of my son as a mother elephant with an injured calf. When they hurt him, I turned on my family and lashed out at them.

During this period, Drew became an emotional and physical drain on me. I understood that he needed to know I loved him too. However, this need often took selfish forms. For instance, he rarely took a bus to our place. I was his chauffeur. An extra responsibility on my already long list of responsibilities. And it took me away from Nick who might have desperately needed my help at any given moment. Drew seemed to have no idea what I was going through as the mother of the family. I considered his actions irresponsible in the crisis we were living through, although, one night, he proved to be a saving grace.

That evening, I withdrew after serving Nick his dinner, so that the two brothers could have some privacy. As I sat in the kitchen reading, I suddenly heard someone choking. I ran for the bedroom to see Drew using the Heimlich maneuver on Nick, who was choking on a piece of meat.

But most of the time, Drew was immersed in his own concerns. He never relieved me of any workload, and his demands added to what was already an impossible overload. He no longer visited Nick every week and his excuse was he didn't have time. *He didn't have time.* His words struck me like physical pain. Of course, I knew he couldn't bear to see his twin dying. I knew Drew was suffering and tried to comfort him, but it was Nick's immense suffering on which I believed we all had to focus. This made me even less sensitive and sympathetic to Drew.

Even Nick, who always saw the best in his brother, was very disheartened with his twin as week after week followed without a visit. Nick jokingly began calling Drew "the phantom twin," but I could see the hurt in Nick's eyes when he said it. Nevertheless, Nick understood the psychological trauma Drew was experiencing and forgave his brother.

My brother Rick was incapable of dealing with the condition that was devouring Nick's body. But putting up with his drinking was more than I could take in the wake of the dying that was draining my life. My brother had succumbed to his weakness while I could not succumb to mine. I didn't want him around, but I never stopped him from entering the door to see his nephew. How could I, when I knew he loved Nick so much? But each time he came and I smelled liquor on his breath, I yelled at him to stop drinking. I loved my brother and I hated my brother. I needed him to be straight and sober so I could release the tension and sorrow that clothed me like a shroud of death. He was not there for me.

Nick was annoyed with his uncle. Rick acted like an idiot every time he drank beer. He repeated things over and over, and there was no way for Nick to turn him off. Even if Nick had the strength of mountains, he would not be able to shut him up because Uncle Rick was beyond the realm of reason. He brought up memories of shooting hoops and playing guitars and how great it was in the past when Nick was a vessel of power and strength. Talk like that only made the present more depressing. Worst of all, when Uncle Rick was drunk he didn't have the wherewithal to discern the few words Nick spoke to him. He either asked Nick to repeat himself one too many times or he pretended he understood what Nick said and tried to fake his way around it. Nick wanted his uncle to get a grip on reality before his end came so that they could say the things to each other that needed to be said.

Hannah's absence still weighed heavily on Nick's heart. Nick was discouraged that his sister had never been able to take control of her life. However, he still loved her and hoped she would grow into her own person and know happiness. He worried over the fate of Hannah's children and was sorry he would not be around to continue the role of uncle to them. He wanted to see Hannah, to talk to her about her future, but we didn't know how to contact her.

Then, suddenly, my youngest son matured beyond his years. Luke began a job right up the street from our place. He came by every workday to see his brother. Sometimes Nick was asleep when he came and Luke simply sat in Nick's room until it was time to go back to work. It was good he stopped by so frequently. It helped fill the void left by Drew's absence. Luke had also taken on the responsibility of a wife and was ready to prove his worth. Nick admired the growth in his little brother, but worried at how young Luke was, and about how only a short time before he had been caught up in bad company and fast times. Nick wished he could be there to counsel Luke. Time would tell, and time was something Nick did not have. Whatever was to be, Nick was content to rekindle their brotherly love.

Aside from his active mind, Nick had become a helpless figure lying on his back in bed all day and night. I was a helpless figure walking around on two feet. I had no appetite, and sometimes several days went by before I was able to force anything down. I was just as crippled emotionally as Nick was physically. Like a spring wound too tight, I felt I could snap at any given moment. I really needed support and encouragement from my family, but I got none. Everyone was too paralyzed by his or her own pain to be of any assistance to me. I was the blood that ran in my son's veins, but Lou Gehrig's syndrome was ruling both our lives. Nick and I were one. As he died, I died. When he was gone, a part of me would be gone from this earth forever, leaving an empty and hollow place within me as long as I lived.

As painful as the past seventeen months had been for each member of the family, one thing was certain in everyone's mind. Nick had the right to die when life became unbearable, and it was inherently evil of those in authority to force him to live on like this. No one in the family wanted to see Nick's awful condition reach its present state, let alone continue. Despite our feelings, the powers that be had us and Nick in chains. We were forced to watch Nick suffer.

It was the evening of Saturday, March 11th, an especially difficult but introspective day for Nick. The letter had yet to be written. Nick told me, "You have to at least try. I'll give Dr. Kevorkian ten days to respond." If the doctor was not the avenue to mercy, we agreed to use a combination of alcohol, anti-depressants that we had been hoarding, and a plastic bag to bring an end to Nick's long trail of suffering. The image of a plastic bag over my son's head to end this already degrading terminal condition still made me choke with anxiety and anger. It just wasn't right. My son deserved so much more in the way of dignity. However, if Dr. Kevorkian couldn't or wouldn't step in and release me from this great burden, I had to prepare my mind to accept what I had to do myself to help my son.

Nick and I had another long discussion that evening. He reiterated his reasons for deciding the time had come. Once again, I asked God why Nick had to die instead of me. Especially by such a horrible means. But I was thankful to God to be entrusted to assist my most beloved son out of the cradle of this world and into the glory of the next. "I agree to do what is necessary," I told Nick. "Soon, I promise you. No delays."

I lived now to serve Nick in every manner possible. I lived to laugh with him, talk to him, touch him, believe in him, know him, share secrets and jokes with him. Reminisce about the past and envision the kingdom yet to come. I left my son in good spirits that night. Saying good night, I tried to make him as comfortable as possible as he remained awake to watch television. I could not help thinking, *This is our last month together. These are our last memories together. We have made it through the past year, and now it is clearly time to move forward.*

My Son, My Sorrow

That same night, I woke out of a light sleep to the sound of rock music blasting through the bedroom wall. It was after midnight. I had no idea what debilitating act of frustration set him off this time. It could have been a number of things. Most likely, it had to do with the urinal and his inability to sit up to use it. If that was not the case, he could have knocked it out of his reach once he was up on the side of his bed. It may have been this. It may have been that. Whatever it was, it happened. Another siege of madness came. I lay frozen on my bed. Dread in my bones. Tears spilled from my eyes. I prayed he didn't end up on the floor again. I felt too weak to manage the dead weight of his body. The music went on for over an hour and then it stopped. The foreboding silence that followed was spattered with angry howls of a caged animal begging to be set free.

Once the ranting ended, I struggled to make out the sounds from his room. Finally, I realized the muffled sounds barely perceptible to my ears were coming from the floor. My heart sank. I left my bed. I found my son, for the third time, with his head hanging from a neck gripped by a phone cord. A sorrowful sight. Another fruitless attempt.

I removed the cord that left a deep impression around his neck and begged him to return to his senses, but the distant look in his torpid eyes revealed that he was outside the realm of reason. "I can't bear another minute," he yelled. He demanded to end it now or he was going to a nursing home. I refused to end his plight when he was in a deranged state of mind. I wasn't going to do it when either of us was engaged in a frenzy of lunacy. I begged him to listen to reason. But, he had plunged over the edge. He was being pulled down again into the dark waters of madness.

Nothing either one of us said could change the mind of the other. My son was so besieged with suffering and the need to die that he demanded I call Hospice and have someone come and take him away. Then he told me, "I would rather die like a dried up rat in the corner of a dirty nursing home than spend one more minute of my life with you, you coward."

He refused to let me touch him. He yelled at me and forced me to keep my distance as he moved around the floor like a slug. I couldn't bear to see him drag his useless body on the cold floor. With no way to assist him through his siege of madness, I complied with my son's demands and picked up the phone. Hopeless, I gave Hospice a call. I explained the situation and was told a nurse would be on her way. I knew in his heart this was not what my son wanted, but I was powerless to stop it. As powerless as my son was to pick up his body and walk out the door.

The rage went on even after the call was made. Nick was a madman on the floor, and he wasn't going to stop damning the life out of me until the fire went out. He was so compelled to leave the prison cell of his bedroom that with some superhuman will, he crawled and dragged his body out of his room. Out of his boxers. And, much to my dismay, he lugged his body forward through the living room and into the kitchen. All the way to the back door where he remained naked, helpless, and cold laying on the linoleum floor. He would not let me near him. He would not let me cover him. He would not let me help him in any way.

My Son, My Sorrow

Norm howled over Nick's behavior and stayed close to his master, nudging him with his nose, licking him, and looking to me for answers. I was as worn down as Nick and could do nothing except stand close to my son. As close as he would allow until someone came to the door to help.

It seemed to take forever, but a tall, blond nurse in a white suit eventually showed up. We had never seen her before. She approached Nick with respect in her voice and he responded to her. "Get me out of this house," he demanded, "and away from her."

In a calm voice she responded, "You can be taken to the nursing home downtown if that's what you want."

"Yes, take me there," he insisted.

"If that's what you want, I'll arrange it." She looked at Nick with concern. "You look so cold, Nick. May I cover your body now?" Nick consented.

She covered my son with a blanket I provided; then she started a round of phone calls. She tried to get in touch with Nick's doctor, but she could not get his phone number. She called a medical transport service. They said they would come, but we waited well over an hour before anyone arrived. During the time we waited, I explained Nick's medical background and the crisis that unfolded after midnight which led to my calling for Hospice to intervene. Nick remained silent, still lying on the cold kitchen floor. Norm remained beside him. Periodically, the nurse knelt beside Nick and said something encouraging to him.

I knew in his heart, Nick didn't want to go into a nursing home. This was just one more example of how everything could change in an instant because his frustration level was so sensitive. The slightest frustration could cause him to explode. The pain and heartache attached to dying mounted minute by minute. The agony and regret at all he had lost—mobility, independence, life, and love—tortured him night and day. The prospect of tomorrow was worse than today. All good reasons to have the heart and mind revolt.

But this present explosion, the one that rocked him off his bed and tormented his mind, was by far the most volatile yet, as each month of the new year stripped him of more and more human dignity and self worth. Now my son's anger with the world would take him to where no dying person wants to go—a home for those no one wants.

When the transportation service showed up at our door, I was exhausted and Nick was silent. He stared straight ahead. Several large young men brought in a gurney. Their presence consumed all the available space in the kitchen. My heart dropped as the young men, intent on helping, utilized their joint strength to get my son up off the floor and onto the gurney. Nick had used up the little energy he had to drag himself to the kitchen. Now he lay completely helpless.

Norm didn't know what was going on and continued howling. He didn't want Nick taken away. I picked him up to see his master, and Nick said goodbye to his little companion but said nothing to me. Then he was whisked out of our home by the attendants. I watched from the door as they slipped my son into the back of a van. It made me sick to see him taken away. Out of my reach. Out of my protection. I was hollow. Numb. I thanked the nurse for her compassion and sincerity and said I would be down at the nursing home within the hour.

My Son, My Sorrow

Once I was alone, I got dressed, made a large cup of coffee, and sat down with Norm on Nick's electric bed. The bed had been in his room for only five weeks. A period accented by grief so deep and shadowed with frustration, so bitter that there was hardly any calm to break up the anger and madness that dominated our lives. We knew what we had to do. Yet we stumbled and huddled like rats in a rainstorm when madness sprung from Nick like a tornado. We had to synchronize our emotions and get the job done. The drama of the past seventeen months played out before my eyes. I sat crying at the events that pulled my son down into an unyielding spiral of death. None of this suffering had any meaning attached to it.

I was empty inside. An empty hole. I looked at my watch and realized it was five o'clock in the morning. Nick had been taken away around four. I had no idea what I was doing or what I was going to do. I only knew I had to get my exhausted body downtown. I had to get to my son. After I found him, then I could figure out how to get him out of the institution and back home in his bed so we could carry out our plans. Nick was totally disabled and vulnerable. And now, he was subject to the power and pressure of the doctor and his staff of nurses who do only what the doctors tell them to do. They had the advantage. It was a long drive down the streets of Phoenix that were not yet heavy with traffic. By the time I arrived at my destination, the sun already spoke of another day on the horizon.

As I got out of my car, I asked myself how I was going to be able to cope with the medical mindset and autocracy once I walked into their locked chambers. Now that

Carol Loving

Nick was in the nursing home, what were they going to do to him? Certainly, the doctor would have a plan that would work against us. Something that would keep us separated. Was I paranoid? Was I crazy? Was I being unrealistic? They wanted him to live. I wanted him to die. All I could do at this point was rely on my instincts and powers of observation. My son was in an institution, and I had to get past locked doors to see him. I knew the staff was waiting for me to arrive to sign the reams of paperwork required so that they could be in control. But I was only interested in seeing my son and tending to his concerns.

12

They Call It Respite

I quickly found my son's room. Nick was in the first bed; the other lay empty. The very moment our eyes met they locked in the embrace of love and trust that has always held us together. And the very first thing Nick said was, "Ma, get me out of here!"

"Without a doubt, I will," I promised. He was vulnerable, fragile. In the short time he'd been there, Nick had gotten a bitter taste of what it was like to be in a nursing home. He began to tell me about the bug-eyed nurse who forced Tylenol down his throat and caused him to choke. I wanted to choke her. There was no need for Tylenol. And it was unacceptable to force any type of medication on anyone. Not to mention down the constricted throat of a dying man.

The back of the bed was elevated too high, and Nick had slipped down, slumped, unable to move and looking terribly uncomfortable. I leveled the bed and managed to move him up the length of the mattress by a few inches. Then I cranked the bed down to a slight fifteen degrees.

Carol Loving

Nick's lips were parched; he was obviously dehydrated. After the nurse had forced the Tylenol down his throat, she had put a glass of water on the table next to his bed. "She expected me to take it from there," Nick said. We laughed at her stupidity. I offered him sips of water through a straw, which I bent so he could drink. Nick drank very slowly, but drained the cup.

Then Nick said, "It's so hot in here." There were beads of perspiration on his forehead. I walked over to the windows which were shut tight. When I tried one of the levers, I found that the window actually opened. I opened one wide enough to allow clean air and oxygen into the room.

Standing beside my son, I held his hand as we talked. After an hour of sharing together, he told me, "Mom, on second thought, I wouldn't mind staying a couple of days as long as the nurses and attendants don't leave me in here for hours at a time and come in when I buzz them. You know Mom, I wouldn't mind if I didn't absolutely need them." My eyes filled with tears.

I remained with my son until he closed his eyes and fell into a light but restful sleep. I lowered the bed and when I felt satisfied that Nick was going to be okay for the next few hours, I left his side and signed the ridiculous number of papers they insisted on. I drove back home to see if it were possible to calm my mind and get things ready for Nick's coming home.

Exhausted, I finally laid down, but couldn't sleep. Hours later, I still laid there, sleepless and drained. I was drawn to Nick's room like a magnet. I got up. I felt empty without him. I felt like my soul had been stretched out to dry in the desert sun. Nick was gone. I was alone. This moment of separation was a forecast for all those moments in the future. I cried until I could cry no more, and then I went into Nick's room and frantically began straightening it up. I started with the bed. Shaking, I removed the telephone cord that I had been forbidden to touch. I spent the entire morning doing a thorough cleaning. The chemicals I used to clean the room helped disguise the obnoxious smell of urine in the carpet, but it remained a real problem. Since the carpet was wet, I had to draw last night's urine out it before I could proceed. I cried off and on as I ran the vacuum, and then got down on my hands and knees to rub in the solution. Yet I took comfort in what I was doing. I was preparing the room for my son's return. However short that homecoming might be.

During the course of the day, I picked up the large empty plastic bag that lay on the lid of the bedside commode which had been taking up space in the living room for a month. Through my mind shot an image that set my stomach churning. I saw myself placing the bag over my son's head. I pictured my son and I gazing at each other through the clear plastic, until the space inside the bag fogged up with the final breaths of his life.

For a while, I sat down holding the bag in my hands and staring at it. Then I put it away and continued cleaning. At noon I had a small bite of food, took a long, long shower, and drove back downtown to see my son.

A sitter had been assigned to Nick for twenty-four hours, because the Hospice had placed him on what the medical profession called a suicide watch. Nick was not going to commit suicide. There was no way he could. He was flat on his back in a hospital bed. Bed rails up. Helpless. That was the physical reality. Nevertheless, a young man had been assigned to sit in his room with him as he slept.

To my surprise, that turned out to be good. Of all the people in the world they might have chosen, Robert was the right person for Nick to discover when he woke up. He was about the same age as Nick and he was an extremely good listener. For the first time, Nick spilled his woes to a stranger, as best as he could articulate them. Robert, in turn, told Nick he couldn't image how awful it must be to be trapped inside a body dying from Lou Gehrig's disease. He certainly understood why Nick did not want to carry on any longer.

When I entered Nick's room, Robert left us to our privacy. Nick was like a well overflowing. "I'm so relieved to have someone listen to me and be honest with me, instead of giving me a lot of meaningless platitudes and crap." He had nothing but words of respect for Robert, who Nick said was not pretentious and full of answers. Robert did not pretend to understand the well of suffering attached to what Nick was feeling about his impending death, but he was compassionate and kind.

I noticed that the blinds on the windows were shut again. I walked over and opened them and looked out. There was an attractive courtyard with plenty of vegetation outside, and since I had brought my son's cane with me, I asked him if he wanted to move to the other bed. He did. With the skill and mutual trust involved in the undertaking of our well-honed ambulatory act, I got Nick to the other side of the room where he sat on the edge of the bed.

My Son, My Sorrow

For a while we were engrossed in conversation. Then a red-haired and attractive nurse walked into the room. She saw Nick seated on the bed opposite the one assigned to him with his legs dangling over the side. This flustered her. "Are you sure you should be doing that?" she asked, a little alarmed.

"I'm very sure," Nick smiled. "It won't kill me, believe me." I caught a glimpse of the old Nick.

"Okay, if you say so," she replied, lightly.

Doctor's orders included turning Nick every two hours to prevent pressure build-up on certain areas of his body. I asked Nick if they had been doing so. "No," he shook his head. "They feed me, they ask me for information, they put down things in my chart, but that's it. They all seem too busy to turn me."

"Typical," I shook my head, remembering my own nursing experience of what goes undone in nursing homes. Charts get all the attention. Charts are more important than people dying behind closed doors. Before I left my son for the second time, I helped groom him. Dying though he was, when I left, Nick had a refreshed glow and was looking forward to my return that evening.

By the time I returned home after my third visit to the nursing home in less than twenty-four hours, night had fallen over Phoenix and I was weary. I had left my son in good spirits. That was all I had to carry me through to the next day. I felt completely exhausted, physically and mentally, and went to sleep on Nick's bed with Norm curled up beside me. I woke up at dawn and did nothing for hours, nothing except drink coffee and think about the crisis and tragedy that dominated our lives. Thoughts careened through my mind. How extremely difficult it was to die. Not just the process of the terminal condition itself, but the overwhelming power those in authority have to take advantage of the dying and turn what should be a peaceful experience into a hellish one. The clock was ticking and time was passing. So many things to get done. But, for the moment, all I could do was try to steady the inner workings of my anguished mind.

Back at the nursing home, I found Nick in the company of a scruffy old woman volunteer who talked on and on about nothing. Nick was happy to see me. As much as we intimated we wanted our privacy, the crude woman would not leave us alone.

Nick whispered that he had to go to the bathroom. He would not consent to a bedpan. We assumed our treacherous tandem position to reach the bathroom despite her presence. She got all nervous and flustered. "You can't do that," she screeched. "You'll fall and hurt yourself and it will be all your fault for being stupid." Her voice was the sound of nails drawn across the blackboard. If I could have turned her to dust with the power of my mind, I would have, as long as I got my son safely to the toilet. We just ignored her, and continued our trek.

Finally, we managed to get into the bathroom. But I found that rather than having the toilet on our right, as it was at home, this toilet was to the left. On such formerly insignificant things, Nick's and my present stability could crumble. I began to tremble, because the gravity our bodies exerted in our tandem gait made it difficult for me to shift my weight in the opposite direction. In our home, there was a safety bar directly in front of the toilet, which Nick desperately needed to hold onto. Here, one was angled on the wall beside the toilet instead.

My Son, My Sorrow

I couldn't reach it. Our ability to adapt to the new surroundings was tense and nerve-racking for both of us. But in the end, somehow, I managed to change directions without Nick using the bar. We did it!

I left Nick to his privacy in the bathroom. The woman, whom I pierced with hot anger flashing from my eyes, finally left the room. I was taut like a rubber band. Solitude was my savior when she left.

It was short-lived. A balding male nurse came in, stared at me, and did busywork, tending to one thing or another. Then he left only to come back again and again. Time passed. Nick remained in the bathroom. The male nurse stuck his head in again for the umpteenth time and began to show concern over the fact that Nick had been in the bathroom for so long. "I'm going to check on him," he insisted. I protested. But I had a battle on my hands.

"Nick will alert me when he's ready," I objected. The nurse shook his head. He was convinced he knew better and made a move toward the bathroom door. I countered his move to invade my son's privacy, ran over and took hold of the door myself. To keep him at bay, I pulled it ajar. "Are you okay?" I called. That was it. I disgraced Nick. I humiliated him in my attempt to protect him. Nick was angry. Nick's eyes shot through me like spears.

"When I'm ready, I'll call you. Get out!" he said furiously. The male nurse left the room, and I waited by the door for Nick's call. A few minutes later I heard it, but when I walked in, I felt the full force of Nick's rage. It only made him more angry with me as I nervously struggled to get his deadweight body up off the toilet that sat too high off the ground to give me any leverage. Somehow, I managed to defy gravity. We focused our anger and aggravation into the energy it took to get his decrepit body moving.

As we left the bathroom, that stupid woman appeared out of nowhere, flapping her lips with condescending prattle. Her behavior ruptured the volcano building up in Nick, who furiously threw his disgust in her face. He yelled, "Get her out!" She stubbornly remained and defied him.

I yelled at her to "leave us alone." Finally, she did. I maneuvered my son back to his bed. Nick was pissed with me and the world.

"I want you to leave," he told me. Nick wouldn't look at me or soften to my pleas. I left with a broken heart, angry at myself for not respecting his privacy and at Hospice for allowing idiots in his room—especially when the damn suicide watch had ended at six in the morning.

All I could do after I left my son and returned to our home was retreat to his room and seek solace for my war-torn soul. I couldn't function. I couldn't eat. I couldn't move my body from his bed. I felt like I was dying inside, and I lay there curled up and hugging myself.

Then, out of the blue, my daughter Hannah walked into Nick's room. I could utter only a few words before I started to cry. Hannah tore off her jacket, came over and threw her arms around me. She understood the import of pain and suffering. She held and rocked me gently in her arms. I told her where Nick was, and that she could visit him. She promised she would that night.

Later, when I returned to the nursing home, Nick still didn't want to have anything to do with me. The young nurse, who he usually had kind words for, pestered him and disturbed his privacy. He even yelled at her, "Leave me alone." She left, but soon came back bringing two other nurses. They could not understand the volume of his anger. How could they? They were not dying from a neuromuscular disease. Not one of them was confined to a lifeless body.

I returned home more down-trodden than ever. I lay down in Nick's bed for a second night, but this time I was drawn into a deep, restful sleep.

When I awoke, I looked up and saw light coming into the room. It was Tuesday morning. I took my time as I agonized over my thoughts, sipped coffee and took care of the chores that had to be done around the apartment. Hoping to put a smile on his face, I cooked some of Nick's favorite vegetables to take to him.

I drove back to the hospital, and was surprised to see Hannah on the spare bed across from Nick when I walked into his room. She had spent the night with Nick. I was glad she was with her brother. Nick was still irritated with me because of the bathroom incident, so I had no choice but to respect his wishes and leave him with his sister.

As I walked to the entrance, I found out from the talkative receptionist that the administrators at Hospice were in a whirlwind of turmoil over Nick's bills. He was not covered by any form of medical insurance, and, therefore, was not qualified to stay at the Hospice nursing facility. "If he stays, you are responsible for the bills," she told me.

She also let me know that something else was abuzz. While the doctor was at the institution that morning, he had tried to persuade Nick to take Prozac again to counter Nick's riveting battles with depression. What the doctor actually wanted to do with Nick was have him placed in another facility to undergo an extensive psychological observation. The staff was working on this.

When I heard this, I thought, *There isn't an institution that will take him without insurance.* And even if there was, I wasn't about to let Nick be shuttled off to some institution. In this dark time, we were each other's strength. No one was going to separate us.

However, it was frightening to observe the medical staff moving in that direction. The administrators were doing everything to try to counter the insurance stumbling block. *Good. Fine. Let them stay busy.* I was glad I had Nick's medical power of attorney. The administrators thought they were putting their best foot forward with the idiotic drive to get Nick into a mental institution while reinforcing their own convictions that they were doing what was best for my son. I let them entertain themselves. I let them think they were doing a good job. They weren't going to keep my son. Nick was going home. He was going home to die. I don't know how I remained so calm while a mad plan was being enacted to try to have my son placed into a mental institution. If that happened, Nick and I would both go insane, permanently insane. But it wasn't going to happen.

I returned to see Nick again Tuesday night and brought Norm, who showered Nick with licks. Hannah was with her brother. She had not seen Nick since May, when Nick still had the freedom to walk about, though slowly, with the aid of a cane through the apartment. At that time, he could speak

My Son, My Sorrow

with far less strenuous effort and have his beautiful niece crawl up on his lap for a bundle of hugs and kisses he could still give. I knew how shocking the change in Nick was to Hannah and understood the disturbed look in her eyes.

This time, Nick was glad to see me and that warmed my heart. I stayed only a short while as I didn't want to take time away from the two siblings, who despite the place and Nick's condition, were obviously enjoying each other's company. I was glad Nick was no longer angry. Hannah's visit was doing him a world of good. I left Nick with his sister and took Norm back home.

On Wednesday, Hannah was there once again when I went to the nursing home in the morning, and I was quite surprised when Nick told me, " I want Hannah to move in with us." I knew he was overcome by the joy of seeing his sister again, and had forgotten for a moment what the next weeks would bring and how limited our space was. I said we could talk about it later. We then discussed the absence of medical insurance and how the money attached to his stay was now our financial burden. It was his decision when he wanted to return home. Nick wanted to stay another day.

The young nurses, who despite his moodiness, were taken with Nick, had supplied him with a VCR and John Wayne movies. Nick looked like he was enjoying the attention he was getting from the pretty women who entered his room. They were all about his age. Vital. Full of life. Unfortunately, all had been primed to suggest he take Prozac. No one could force him to take it. Prozac wasn't going to put the muscle back on his bones or help him die. But the sweet, innocent girls with so little experience in life charmed him into taking one after his sister left. He still hated the effect. He said it made him feel like a zombie. "I'll be dead soon, but I'm not willing to feel that way before-hand," Nick told me.

Thereafter, I left to take care of errands and pick up groceries. When I returned to the apartment, the smell of urine was worse than ever. I had used the carpet cleaner and the deodorizer. The windows were already wide open in every room, yet the smell was overwhelming. Like a cat's litterbox left unattended. I set a fan in Nick's room to dry the carpet and move the air outside. In the three months we had been wrestling with urine in the carpet, this was the worst it ever was.

I returned to see Nick early that evening, and he wasn't happy with me when I told him about the carpet. I asked him if he would stay one more day, so I could try to reduce the odor that now permeated every square inch of space in his room. I knew by the look on his face that I had let my son down again, something which I was culpable of from the beginning the tragedy began to unfold. Shrinking away, I went home.

I went to see Nick the next morning. He felt weak and simply wanted to rest. His body ached. "I need to be back home in my own bed in my own familiar surroundings," Nick told me. I apologized for the extra day it would take to get him back. "Mom," he said pleadingly, "I need to die."

After I left Nick, I went home and worked with fans and chemicals. By the end of the day the smell was toned down, but clearly there. It was a losing battle. Retreating to the comfort of Nick's bed, I thought about my son's last words to me. Suddenly, I realized I had forgotten about contacting Dr. Kevorkian. I had completely forgotten about the only doctor who might actually end Nick's agony, and the letter Nick wanted me to write. The notion was so profound that a flutter of certainty entered my heart. I actually believed, at that moment, the doctor would help. I called the nursing home early that evening and told them to let Nick know I was too tired to make it down. "I'll be there in the morning to pick him up. And I want to take his medical records home with me."

I called the Hospice again early Friday morning to remind the nurses that I needed Nick's medical records. For the first time in a long while, I felt energized. I went shopping and did some other chores I'd been putting off. It was noon before I arrived at Nick's bedside.

When I got there, I looked him directly in the eye and said, "I've drafted the letter to Dr. Kevorkian you asked me to write. I'm getting your records from the nurses' station to send with the letter. As soon as we get home we can discuss the matter." I had given him something to turn over in his mind.

Shortly thereafter, the transportation team came rolling into the room with a gurney. Without giving Nick time to acclimate himself, they clumsily moved Nick from the bed to the large steel table on wheels and whisked him out of this room. The healthy young men rolled him down the hall as if they were in a race. As they passed the nurses' station, the young nurses waved and called tearful goodbyes. Sad to see Nick leave because he had captivated their hearts.

I stopped at the front desk. No one had copies of his records ready. I had to remain behind and wait for them as the transportation vehicle took off. It was certain that Nick was going to end up in the driveway waiting for me to arrive, but I wasn't about to leave without his records. I finally got them in

hand and drove home to find exactly the situation I'd anticipated. With some effort, we got Nick inside.

It was then that Nick and I learned the young men had
forgotten Nick's cane. Fortunately, we had another one. But
unlike the one left behind, this cane failed to provide him with
a good grip, and his hands had deteriorated so much.
Nevertheless, we were forced to use it. Nick and I resumed our
two-man shuffle. The team watched us as we struggled to
move forward without falling and held their breaths as we
made the turn around the side of the bed so Nick could drop
his rigid body down on the mattress.

Norm, who was sleeping on the floor next to the bed,
awoke and leaped high into the air with joy when he saw Nick
had returned. When Nick was seated on the side of the bed,
Norm made his way up beside his master. One young member
of the team was terribly saddened at the plight of my son. He
bent down to put his arm around Nick as he said goodbye.
Norm misunderstood the action and snapped warningly to the
stranger to keep his distance.

The transportation team left. Then we learned that
Hospice not only discharged Nick without his cane, they sent
him home without his urinal. Inexcusable. No urinal to relieve
his bladder pushed Nick's frustration button, and I received a
verbal licking for things gone awry. We improvised for the
moment, and then I drove all the way back downtown to the
nursing home to retrieve both the urinal and the cane.

When I finally got back, I opened the door to his room
to find Nick watching television and smiling at me. He was
glad to be home and sorry I had to pick up the slack when others were irresponsible. Nick asked me if I would get him a

couple of light beers. Agreeing, I drove to the store, got them, and returned a short while later.

Then Nick and I settled down to talk about Dr. Kevorkian. We agreed we both now felt contacting him was the thing to do. "If we fail to get a response from him in ten days, I will honor my word," I promised, "and assist you without delay."

Nick mouthed a soft "thank you."

It was late Friday afternoon. The plan was to mail Nick's request for mercy to Dr. Kevorkian, on Monday, the 20th, by overnight express. As we were about to call our discussion to an end so Nick could rest, a Chinese film with English subtitles came on the television. "Mom, look, it's China! Let's watch for a while," Nick suggested. So Nick and I were transported to China for two hours. It was a poignant recapturing of a memorable experience shared by the two of us when Nick was vital and looking forward to a wonderful future. Now, Nick was flat on his back with his head turned toward the television. He was helpless. I was on the floor beside him. Just as helpless. Yet, for that short period, we were as we had been, and our spirits were together.

We made it through the weekend. Monday, a prayer went out from me on behalf of my son. I prayed it was our Father's will that Nick receive the blessings of euthanasia. *My son deserves to die at the hand of someone determined to help the dying from the shackles of terminal suffering. After all the suffering he's been put through, it just has to be. Please, please, grant this plea.*

A few days went by, and Nick worsened. His body seemed to have turned to lead. It was nearly impossible for Nick to move even his head without direct assistance from me.

Carol Loving

I had to be there to meet his every need. Assisting him was nearly impossible, but I never failed him. Nevertheless, he saw my struggle. Once again, the frustration inside him exploded. His anger touched my nerves and seared the fibers of my soul. He demanded, "We have to end it now!"

No matter how he lashed me with his tongue, I countered, "We have to hold to our commitment to wait ten full days to hear from Dr. Kevorkian."

Part III

Departures

13

The Good Doctor

Each day that passed as April approached was a test of our ability to cope. Yet, somehow we made it through Tuesday and Wednesday. That Thursday, Nick was quietly watching television. The lights were out and we were both ready to call it a night. I was sitting on my bed lost in thought when the phone rang. It was ten o'clock. Tired, I was inclined to ignore a call at bedtime. But when I heard it continue to ring, I went into the living room, walked to my desk and picked up the phone. I felt the weight of my son's burden lifted off my shoulders as soon as I heard the voice on the other end of the phone. It was Dr. Kevorkian. "Oh, my God," was all I could utter as I slowly sat down to listen to what he had to say. Nick could hear my side of the conversation from his room, and he hung on to every word with a prayer ever present in his heart. *Ask, and you shall receive, my son. Ask, and you shall receive.*

Dr. Kevorkian asked me about Nick's decision to seek his help. "Was it actually Nick's decision to contact me?" he asked. "Was there anyone in the family who talked him into it?"

Carol Loving

"No, no," I insisted.

"Was anyone in the family opposed to it?"

I told him, "Nick wants desperately to die, and we as a family are behind him one hundred percent." I went on, "Nick and I stand on the very precipice of his death. I am ready to end Nick's deplorable suffering with a plastic bag, if you don't help us."

He quickly warned me not to take it on myself. "You'll certainly be arrested if you do," the doctor told me.

Finally, he said the words we'd almost lost hope of hearing. The words no one else in the medical profession had the courage to say. "I'm going to help you," Dr. Kevorkian said.

He wanted to schedule Nick for the first week in May. I nearly choked. It was the 23rd of March. That meant six more weeks of being restrained in a body that was hardly more than a mummy. He said he would call again in a few days and give us a specific date for Nick's departure. I thanked him and put down the receiver. I heard sobbing from the bedroom, great heaving sobs of relief.

I went straight to my son. He was lying flat on his back. His head slightly elevated by a pillow. His bone-thin forearms resting atop his chest. "Nick, Dr. Kevorkian's really going to help us!"

Nick's entire being was enveloped by great sobs. "The doctor, the good doctor," he cried. His deep-throated sobs pulled me to him. I, too, cried tears of joy and profound happiness along with my son. Free. Nick was going to be free. He could die at ease, knowing that I would not have to face the clutches of the law once he was gone. It was impossible for

My Son, My Sorrow

Nick to put his arms around me to embrace me and just as impossible for me to put my arms around him as he lay like an ancient mummy on his back. But, I bent over my son, placed my hands on his upper arms and pressed my face against his face. It was the first and the only good news Nick received in the long downward spiral that robbed him of his vital powers, his liberties and his happiness.

The shock of knowing it was real, knowing that our prayers were going to be answered and we no longer had to resort to desperate measures, knowing the unrelenting agony of the deadly electrochemical syndrome would finally come to an end, permeated our consciousness. It brought me back to that day in October when Nick and I had sat on the bed in the hospital in a state of total disbelief at the prognosis that he had ALS. The news of his sickness had devastated us. But tonight, the news that he would be helped made us cry tears of joy. At last! Nick had control over his destiny. He had control over his life. He had control over his death. He had what fate and the medical tyrants had taken away from him. He had freedom. He was free to die. He was no longer a slave to a system that incarcerated him and sentenced him to the rack to be tortured, stretched to the breaking point until he was forced to scream and beg for mercy like a lunatic set on fire by a cruel and taunting master.

At long last, my beloved son's sorrowful heart knew joy. He was going to carry out his death with dignity and self-worth. After everything in his life had been taken away by a tide that washed up stripping him to the bone, leaving those bones to dissolve into sand, he was going to die according to his wishes. Peace of mind returned to my son. With it came the fortitude to bear six more weeks of what essentially would be time spent wasting away. Time in which he'd be drained of what little strength he had left. Yet, tranquility had come. His spirit was uplifted to know he would soon be free. He had reason to live his remaining time, to close the last chapter of his life on earth.

I was so happy for my son I couldn't contain myself. The blessing of euthanasia was a gift from God. *The good doctor was going to help. The good doctor was going to help.* I wanted to tell my brother Rick the news. We were in the middle of a feud because of his drinking around Nick. He was quite surprised to see me stop by his place. I told him Dr. Kevorkian was going to help his nephew. My brother met the news with a mixture of joy and sorrow. He didn't want Nick to suffer anymore. But the realization that in a short time he would never see Nick again made tears of personal loss come to the surface. The news of Dr. Kevorkian was so unexpected, so unbelievable, and so welcome that the impact actually took days to settle into the consciousness of everyone in the family.

We had been fractured. Now it was time for the family to mend, reunite, and become strong, so Nick could rely on us for the difficult weeks that lay ahead. So Nick could leave this world knowing our family was whole again and one with him.

I next got in touch with Drew. He was glad to learn Dr. Kevorkian was going to help his brother. "It's so right and so just after all Nick's been through," he said. The news was bittersweet for Drew, who found the extent of suffering rendered to the brother he so loved to be more than he could bear and yet, he didn't want to let Nick go. But the news was welcome. And, it provided a wave of relief because Drew realized, as Nick had, there would be an end to his brother's agony.

When I called Luke, the youngest, he cried for Nick's loss before he was able to thank God on Nick's behalf.

Dr. Kevorkian had opened the final door for Nick. He was a stairway to heaven. The man with the key to unlock Nick's faltering body and release his soul to the wonderful world beyond.

The knowledge that Dr. Kevorkian was going to help so empowered Nick that he now wanted to embrace those he loved and say goodbye. Though he had long ago banned everyone except his immediate family, he rescinded the order. "Anyone who wants to come see me is welcome." Welcome. Even the Hospice nurse was welcome to come and chatter away. It didn't matter. He was going to be allowed to die in his own way. He was ready to speak his last words and wishes to all. The very idea of a peaceful deliverance created such tranquility inside him that my son dreamt of going outside the house one more time to indulge in one of his favorite leisure activities: fishing. Of course, it was impossible, but the inspiration was there and so was the desire. Happiness had returned to his heart.

My son was serene. Each day of the remainder of his life, Nick would have to struggle to talk, to eat, to perform the most rudimentary of tasks, even to breathe, but the power to overcome frustration was very strong. Nick was in command of the ship. During these last weeks he would become weaker in body. But, hopefully stronger in spirit. He wanted to conserve every bit of energy possible for the weeks that led to the countdown to his departure, so that he could share his love with those who loved him. Harmony had been restored to our house, and never again would I see my son on the floor in a mad and helpless plea for death. Gratitude would prevent frustration. Tomorrow was on the horizon. No more suffering. No more torment. Each day was one more opportunity to plan and meditate and set aloft his soul. Birth of the eternal was at hand.

Later, I spoke with Dr. Kevorkian again. I also spoke to his assistant, Bruce Whittaker. A date was set. Tuesday, May 9th. We were to fly to Michigan on Monday night and stay at a motel. Departure would take place at dawn the next day at a location yet unknown. First, the doctor would interview Nick on videotape, so that Nick could record his desire to die. Every bit of information I was able to pass along to Nick was the same as giving him silk threads to adorn the Morontia robe he would drape across his shoulders once he passed through the veil of death to stand again.

14

Time to Say Goodbye

The media had been snapping at the heels of Dr. Kevorkian for the five years he had been helping terminally ill people to die. Yet, despite the myriad of articles, he was still somewhat of a mystery man, reclusive and retiring. We didn't know anything about him other than what was reduced to blips and sound bites on national news. Now, that media coverage would include Nick's last journey.

Nick and I had absolutely no idea what the media would say and how the news would unfold, once he became a number on Dr. Kevorkian's list that presently stood at twenty-one. We knew there would be more attention than usual on Nick because of his young age. We felt Nick didn't have any control over how his death would be reported by the media. Or did he? Something weighed heavy in my mind from the moment the words were spoken on New Year's Eve, when Nick was in the dreadful fit that pulled him to the floor in a pitch of madness. "Once I'm dead," he said, "who will even know I was alive?"

Carol Loving

The agony in his voice reverberated inside my heart. We both knew he had been given the potential for greatness in his life. Had the opportunities unfolded for him, he might have made a name for himself in basketball or in business or in music. But his disastrous illness had closed those doors. Nevertheless, I believe life takes many unforeseen and indiscernible turns. There is more going on in the realm of destiny than we will ever realize. So perhaps, I thought, this was the stage on which he was to play his destined role. But how, that was now the question.

Even in his short life, Nick had been loved and admired by so many people around the world. He deserved to have the final word on his life and how he came to die at the hands of Dr. Kevorkian. He deserved special attention. He deserved to be remembered. I had a nagging feeling inside me that there was something I was supposed to do so that Nick would not pass from this world unnoticed. I was apprehensive and confused over what to do, but I was driven to follow my instincts and make Nick's story known.

I decided I would need the media's cooperation. I called the city desk of the *Arizona Republic* and had my call transferred to the medical health department. The man who answered could hardly believe what he was hearing as I spoke about taking my son to Dr. Kevorkian. "I want a reporter to cover the story with absolutely no news breaking until the deliverance of my son to Dr. Kevorkian has been completed," I said to the excited, startled party on the other end of the line.

After a few seconds of silence he replied, "I believe I have the reporter who could arrange to meet with you to talk a little further." I did just that the next day. The reporter and I met at a coffee shop close to my home on Friday morning, the thirty-first of March.

It began as a meeting of two people suspicious of each other. Circumstances had brought us together. What reason did the young reporter, John Kirk, have to believe his trip to the coffee shop to meet someone who claimed she was taking her son to Dr. Kevorkian was a valid encounter with a real story behind it? And, dropped in his lap? What assurance did I have that I could trust the press? Trust that not a word of information would be leaked out prior to Nick's date with destiny? Was I even sure I knew what I was doing? Could I trust my own instincts? Was I so worn down by the crippling death that was engulfing my son and so addled by the suffering in my heart that I had gone over the edge? I was totally impatient with everyone except my dying son. I was frazzled and could barely construct a coherent sentence. I could hardly speak beyond a blither to stranger or friend. Now I was trying to get intimate details across to a stranger.

I tried my best to explain to Mr. Kirk that my son was being dragged into his grave by the debilitating symptoms of Lou Gehrig's disease. "Through the grace of God, he is going to leave his suffering behind. Dr. Kevorkian is going to help him. In my heart, I believe my son deserves to tell his story to your newspaper so he can set the record straight. That is, if he chooses to do so."

I told him, "I haven't talked about this to my son yet because I didn't want to introduce the idea until I knew where the newspaper stood."

He nodded, then said, "We'll need photographs."

I shook my head. "I don't think my son will allow any-one to take pictures of him. It's something he won't allow even his family to do. He doesn't want to be remembered in his emaciated and broken form," I explained. We decided to keep that option open.

By the end of our meeting, we had come to an under-standing. Kirk would take the information back to his editor, and I would talk to Nick to see if he wanted to leave behind for his family and friends a written legacy of his life. If this was something Nick desired, all of the decisions about the cover-age would be left to him. It was Nick who would set the rules and call the shots if he decided to allow the paper into his life.

Sunday, Nick and I watched the news together. Once again, Dr. Kevorkian appeared on the screen. We started talk-ing about Nick's delivery day and the media circus that usually followed such assisted suicides by the doctor. It was a perfect segue to ask my son if he wanted to talk to a reporter. I let him know I had already spoken to someone from the newspaper.

To Nick, telling the public about his life and his death seemed like a good idea. "It's better than having the reporters talk about me after I'm gone. Yes, I'd like the opportunity to talk to the press." He had been forced to suffer, and he had a right to speak his voice on the topic of his own death.

Nick also said he wanted his death to spark debate on the right-to-die issue. "I want to tell people the authorities have no right to tell any of us when and how we can and can-not die. No one has the right to control another person's death, except that person and God."

It was impossible for either of us to envision Nick's talking with the newspaper reporter as meaning anything other than a way for Nick to be remembered. We felt it would be a record of his short life and of how he chose to die in a peaceful, dignified manner of his own choosing. Of how he severed the bonds of suffering created by a dreaded terminal condition. As Nick discussed what he would say, I could tell he was enthusiastic. I was glad I followed the persistent nudging inside me to contact the paper. It was amazing, the sense of leadership and command that ennobled Nick once he was given back control over his destiny. The disease had rendered him helpless, set him on the precipice of death only to taunt him and deny him the plunge into the hereafter. Now empowered by the turn of events, he would die peacefully as God intended. The radiance of a settled soul came to the surface, and the peace Nick felt made him comfortable communicating his feelings to a reporter in the hopes that it might help others facing similar tragedies.

On the first day of April, I made reservations for our encounter with Dr. Kevorkian. I booked two seats with Northwest Airlines on a direct flight to Detroit on Monday, the eighth of May. Reservations helped to add a tangible form to our plans. Rather than seeing it as a terminal point, Nick viewed it as the point of his deliverance. As he lived the pain and difficulties of each day, Nick focused on his day of destiny, May 9th.

That evening, when the lower part of his body slipped off the side of the bed and I had to beg the strength of God to get him back up, there was no upheaval. In the past, that agonizing moment would have been enough to set him off for hours or days of torment and isolation. However, those episodes of madness had come to an end now that Nick knew his deliverance was definite.

Carol Loving

I picked up our tickets that Tuesday. To me, the airline tickets to the state of Michigan were equivalent to gold. To my son, the tickets were a passport to freedom. I told myself it was just a matter of getting through each day that led up to departure time. But I knew it was going to be a race to the end in terms of Nick's dwindling endurance. The more strength Nick lost, the more difficult it would be to take the flight.

Monday I called Hospice. Nick had requested a wheelchair and it had never arrived. Nick was so weak he no longer sat up in the morning. It was strenuous for him to have a conversation. His ability to articulate reflected severe loss of muscle. His head was like a bowling ball attached to an atrophied neck and a thin layer of skin clung to his shallow face. His eyes sank back into the pockets of his skull. His jaw was slack, he could hardly chew or swallow food already mashed. Fluids were hard to get down, too. A trail of dead muscle led from the tips of his fingers all the way up his forearms. Skin clung to the visible bone. All motion had slowed to a tortuous pace. Using the urinal became an indignity. I had to be there to get his body upright and to hold the urinal for him. To make trips to the bathroom easier, I moved his bed closer next to his bedroom door shortly after he returned from the Hospice nursing center.

By Thursday, the fifth of April, Nick's waning strength was close to nil after an agonizing night. In the morning, I helped him struggle to get upright and stable on the side of the bed in order to get the urinal in his hand. While attempting to get the lid away from the top of the urinal, the lid closed. Nick couldn't get it off. He tried to the point of frustration. By the time I was able to help him, it was too late. His bladder let go a stream of urine as he fought with his body falling back on the bed. I shuddered, the day was surely damned.

But he said, soothingly, "It's alright, Mom." I helped him get his body back down on the bed and soaked as much urine out of the carpet as possible. Then I left him to his privacy and to a much needed rest. The nurse was scheduled to come out. I called and left a message for her that the visit was off.

She called back when she got my message. "Nick had a very uncomfortable night and just wants to sleep," I said. Sleep was essential for his well-being.

She retorted spewing rules and orders in a bossy manner. She refused to understand that Nick was dying and weary, worn beyond his endurance. She made it blatantly apparent that it was we who were to serve Hospice, not the other way around. The Hospice center had been involved with Nick for seven weeks. The extent of compassion it offered could be summed up in her response: "If Nick is going to refuse to see me, then Hospice is just going to drop him."

It would be a pleasure, I thought, not uttering a word. But we still had a need for the mattress, and we planned to use the wheelchair to roll him out of here and onto an airplane to fly Nick to his deliverance. I had no intention of telling her that. I simply said, "Nick will see you next week."

I had another meeting with John Kirk, the reporter, on April 10th at the coffee shop. I told him Nick was up for the interview. "But Nick is still dead set against pictures. He simply wants to tell people what Lou Gehrig's disease did to his life. How the doors of denial were slammed in his face by the medical profession. He wants people to know the system has no right to control his death."

John had a new proposal. "I want to go to Michigan with you."

His words took me by surprise. "I'll have to discuss that with Nick."

The request didn't set well with me. And Nick immediately refused. "My death is hardly a Kodak moment," Nick winked, and for an instant the old, witty Nick we all remembered was back.

That Thursday morning the reporter called around eight o'clock and wanted to be at our place in an hour. It was inconvenient for us, but we consented. It was too early, and Nick had had another bad night. He asked me to make him presentable. "I don't want to scare this guy into thinking I'm already a cadaver."

I felt a warm sense of mother's pride as my son talked to John Kirk about his life, matters of importance, family and friends. Nick spoke about ALS and why he wanted to die. My son was open and honest as always. The reporter listened attentively as my son, doing his best to speak clearly, kept up a running dialogue for nearly an hour.

When John left, I walked him to the door. "Nick's quite a guy," he said. "You know, his thoughts and ideas are so meaningful, that as long as he can communicate them he has a reason to hang on a little longer."

The next few days dragged by. We made it to the middle of the month. Three weeks down. Three weeks and a few days to go. Uncle Rick and Nick's brothers had long wished to take Nick outdoors, where he had once loved to be, one last time. But Nick always said no. Except for the day we moved,

My Son, My Sorrow

Nick had not been out of the house for almost a year. Now that he had been afforded the opportunity to die in peace, he consented to letting his Uncle Rick and Luke take him to Del's place in the desert and take care of him.

The very idea struck fear in my heart, but I had no right to interfere. Nick said I could come along too, because he knew I was concerned about him, but I knew there was no way I would be able to cope if I went. Also, it was his farewell party with the guys. On the other hand, it was hard for me to remain behind because Nick required my care.

My thoughts wrestled back and forth as I argued with myself as to what would be best for my son. I struggled with my decision because Nick now depended completely on others to care for him. Someone would have to feed him, and someone would have to help with the urinal. The question was, who was competent? Who could I trust? No one. But Nick argued that he would be okay. He needed this last taste of freedom. I decided it was best to let him go with Norm as his companion and trust he would return home alive.

It was a daunting task to get Nick dressed and into the wheelchair, which proved to be ill-fitted for his debilitated condition. Nevertheless, I could feel his pride in· me for restraining my fears as I tended to him. He knew I was going to be anxious all day and tried to tell me not to worry. But worry I did. Even before he left our property.

My brother, who brought Nick's cane along, refused to give in when I pleaded, "Please put Nick in the front seat." Rick wanted him in the back seat so Nick could lie down if he wanted. He wouldn't listen, and Nick didn't have the strength to argue. Thus, Nick ended up in the back seat with no leg room.

I knew underneath his words that Nick was doing this for the others, and I wished he hadn't. "Please," I said to Rick, "get him home before sundown."

When the sky grew dark and no one returned, I was angry and ready to kill Rick on sight. When they finally got home, a stake was driven through my heart as soon as I opened the door. Nick was slumped over in the wheelchair like a giant banana. His head sat on his chest. His rear end was nearly all the way out of the seat and his spasmodic legs jutted straight out and over the foot plates.

At that moment, as my protective, maternal instinct raged, I could have clawed my brother to death. I knew Uncle Rick's desire to give Nick a good time had been done out of love for his nephew. But at the time, I was too furious to care. "Rick, you'd better leave," I told him, not wanting to say something to him I would regret later. Luke helped me get a silent, brooding Nick out of the wheelchair, out of the cumbersome clothes he wore and onto the side of the bed. Now I could take over from what had turned out to be a disastrous day.

Nick was livid. He was pissed. He was angry. He was on fire. And, for two hours, I heard about his day that was straight out of hell. "They let me spend the entire day in this damned chair!" Unable to move his arms. Unable to do anything. At home, on the side of his bed, he could reach for a Kleenex and get it up to his nose to blow. He could push buttons on his remote pads with his knuckles. He could stroke

My Son, My Sorrow

Norman by his side. At Del's place in the desert, he was a sack of bones, unable to move and barely able to communicate with these people who were supposed to be so close to him. No one noticed Nick was a bomb ready to go off as he watched people he knew all his life look down at him and talk at him like he was a deaf-mute child.

"They were dumb. They were stupid," he cried out. I knew the underlying problem was they were stuck in the past. The passing of time had not crippled or maligned them. But Nick aged a hundred years in the course of this illness. He had been through a metamorphosis of grievous proportion, and they were completely in the dark as to the reality or psychology attached to the process of dying from Lou Gehrig's syndrome. They wanted to celebrate his life with the Nick of the past when Nick was the ghost of the present. It was love at its most dysfunctional. They had no idea what he had given up to satisfy their desire to have him with them just one more time. They even robbed him of his privacy. They stole his dignity. He had to have someone hold the urinal for him. He choked on the food his brother fed him, and was absolutely discouraged when his brother had to dislodge the food from his windpipe because he could not swallow it.

Nick had never known such alienation or estrangement. Looking at them from a body that belonged in the grave, he was heartbroken. Seated helpless in a wheelchair ill equipped to support his body while his old friends walked and talked and took every movement and gesture for granted, Nick soon understood how vulnerable a position he had put himself in on one of the last days of his life. "I hate myself for going," he cried despondently, as he released the frustration and feelings created by the long day.

Yes, Nick's room was a prison cell where he was confined to live out the end of his sentence. But it was also his port of command. From his bed, he could say who should come in his room and who should go out. He could be unencumbered in only his boxers and socks. He had the freedom to blow his nose and to pee in privacy. He had me. I was his faithful servant, who regardless of circumstances, was there to meet his every need. As he released the stress of the day by verbalizing his emotions, I massaged his neck and shoulders, back and arms, seeing the body he no longer had any use for through his eyes. I admired my son for the loving person he was and was glad his painful existence was soon to come to an end. I was so sorry for the agony he experienced during a day that was supposed to be better than it was. But, it had come to an end, and he and Norm shared the rest of the night together where they belonged.

Norm had been with us for nine months. Over that period of time, his master went from scuffling about with the use of a cane to lying flat on his back. Nick went from having enough strength to play with a very small puppy on his bed beside him to having no amount of strength at all. Norm had been through the ups and downs. The small triumphs and the disasters. He had seen it all. Nick's love and laughter. The outrage and the torment. And the torture that came from being encased in a tomb. Norm knew death was in the air. He knew there was significance attached to the very unusual day when Nick left the house with him. He wagged his tail, happy to be home. Norm remained on the bed all the next day, as well.

My Son, My Sorrow

On Monday, April 17th, I talked to the reporter again. John said, "The paper wants to assign a photographer to the story." I reminded him that I had told him the first time we met that Nick did not want to have any pictures taken.

He said, "The paper still wants a photographer on the story, if only to decide which family photographs would be suitable." He spoke highly of the photographer, Gayle Morgan, but the idea of someone taking pictures of my son as he lay dying was not an easy concept for me to discuss with Nick. I stressed that I concurred with my son's desire not to have pictures taken of him as he looked now as a result of the ALS. But the reporter said it would make a better story. I told Nick that the paper wanted a photographer to meet with us. To my surprise, my son consented.

John returned to our home on the afternoon of the nineteenth to interview Nick for a second time. He brought the photographer, Gayle, with him. My brother joined us. He wanted to entrust his favorite picture of Nick to the photographer. It was a picture Nick approved of and one by which he wanted to be remembered because it showed him outdoors, healthy, young and happy.

Luke stopped by, surprised to find the press at our place. After John finished his interview, everyone converged around Nick, who remained upbeat and friendly. Unlike the encounter in the desert, he was comfortable on his own turf. And he didn't have any problem with Gayle being there. She was outgoing, very much a talker, and hit it right off with Nick. I was glad to see Nick so happy, and sorry when everyone left.

Four weeks had passed since my son and I had made our appointment with Dr. Kevorkian. Although they proved to be, in terms of Nick's emotional state, the best weeks since the worst stages of ALS had begun, the physical destruction did not pause for a moment. Though his visitors could not see it, he was like a puppet without the strings to hold him up. His head bobbed atop his shoulders. His hands, his poor crippled hands, were a sad vision to see as his lifeless fingers curled up into the palms. His lower limbs were showing the signs of atrophy. ALS continued to rake across my son's body. Nick now couldn't get off his back without my help. The dead weight of his body was so heavy that I was fearful of the day when I could no longer get him up on the side of the bed for the sake of using the urinal. It was a task he clung to, symbolizing some sense of independence. The agony of anticipating his further deterioration in the remaining time we had to wait made us wish the doctor had decided on an earlier date to provide his service.

As if he felt our need, Dr. Kevorkian called that Friday. He changed Nick's delivery date from Tuesday to Monday. Even this short move forward was welcome. "The procedure will take place in a private home outside of town before dawn," he told me, in a matter-of-fact tone. "And, once again, I want to prepare you for the media which will follow. They'll create a circus-like atmosphere once they arrive on the scene. It won't be nice. I wish I could help you."

I told him our local paper was going to run a right-to-die story on Nick, and they wanted to accompany us. At first, Kevorkian was taken aback by my announcement; however, after I explained there was going to be no news before the fact, he said, "Alright, maybe they can join us. But no one is to say

My Son, My Sorrow

anything to the other members of the press that will be there. My lawyer will be the spokesman."

Unfortunately, the change of dates created some problems as I scrambled to exchange airline tickets and make new reservations. The week that followed was a throwback to the hellish days before Dr. Kevorkian had agreed to help us. Nick's moodiness increased, and the fragility of his patience was mirrored only by the fragility of my own. His ability to get on his feet to go back and forth to the bathroom was further impeded by his lack of balance and control, but we struggled when the need was there regardless of how hazardous and stressful it was for the both of us. Nick insisted we had to. Because of the exaggerated muscle loss that had taken place this year alone, I was fearful that Nick's wrist or his shoulder would become dislodged as we trudged along. I was scared every inch we moved, as we made our way to the bathroom, that we would topple helplessly backward. Somehow we persevered and always made it back to his bed but not without great struggle and spurts of anger. When in the doldrums of that depression, the idea of the press and especially the photographs bothered him. Forlorn, he would wield his waning power by threatening to call the whole thing off.

I was so stressed by this point that I couldn't even put words together to form a coherent sentence. I was coming to the end of my wits right along with my son. For months, I had been functioning on very little sleep. And I had no desire to eat. Each day's energy had to go into the care of my son. At this state in the disease's onslaught, I had to be there day and night to assist him in every action, and often lay all night on the floor beside his bed. If he were calm and able to cope with the moment as we continued to wait for his deliverance day to arrive, I was able to feed off his courage and thus regenerate myself. But, if he poured out his frustration on my shoulders, I crumbled like a falling bridge and had to call on God in order to function. Somehow, I made it through each day.

Dr. Kevorkian called again on Friday, "I just want to confirm our plans and ask how Nick is." I told him we were desperate. He tried to reassure and comfort me. "I'll call tomorrow," he promised.

The next morning when he called, however, Dr. Kevorkian's voice sounded strained. "I want you to bring Nick's driver's license with you to Michigan for identification purposes." He paused. He asked me if I was holding up okay and then he said, "Who else is planning to accompany you?" When I said it was two people from the newspaper, he completely rejected the idea. "The media is untrustworthy. They could interfere. They could stop it. They could inform the police. No, I don't want them there." I wasn't going to argue with the only person courageous enough to help my son. I told Nick about the phone call to try to encourage him, but I was starting to feel like an anti-Kevorkian force was going to burst out of nowhere and rob my son of his freedom to die.

Then, an early-morning call on Sunday from Dr. Kevorkian plunged us into despair. "I have to postpone Nick's departure date." He then apologized. "It's due to a legal matter that has come up. It's something that could not be avoided." The news was numbing, shocking, unraveling. "Please extend my apologies to Nick," he went on. "And don't worry, I'll get back to you on Monday or Tuesday to arrange a new date." He punctuated his conversation with a mild admonishment not to let the newspaper know about the new schedule. His last statement about the press made me wonder if he wasn't really changing Nick's delivery date because of the story we'd promised the reporter.

I was at the point of crumbling.

After five and a half weeks of waiting, the only doctor in the world who would help my son had put us on hold. My worst moment came when I had to tell Nick the plans were off. I tried to soften the news by saying his date with destiny was not cancelled. Just postponed. We were not to worry. "We have to believe," I insisted. "We have to trust. We have to continue to endure."

We waited all day Monday and Tuesday for the call to come in. I was worried sick, and Nick didn't know what to think. Finally, I placed a call in the late evening to Dr. Kevorkian's assistant, Bruce. I woke him up. He told me, "The doctor mentioned Nick just today. I'll contact him tomorrow and have him give you a call."

Dr. Kevorkian called Wednesday. He apologized for the confusion over the telephone date. "I intended to get back with you Monday or Tuesday of next week. Please don't worry. I will call Tuesday, the ninth of May," he said.

"That's the day Nick was originally scheduled. It's getting harder by the hour," I said, beseechingly.

"Don't worry, I'll reschedule Nick."

"You have no idea what we're living through," I begged. "How difficult it is for Nick to make it through an entire day, let alone another week, or however long it's going to take before Nick is finally released from the bondage of his body!"

Once again, Dr. Kevorkian reassured me that he was going to help, and then said goodbye. I was heartsick. My son had come so far only to be disappointed, let down, rejected. "I don't know what to think about this indefinite postponement with Dr. Kevorkian," Nick said.

"It will be alright Nick," I said both for him and myself. "It will be alright. We can trust Dr. Kevorkian."

It was easy to say, but difficult to believe—especially for Nick who had suffered so greatly. With the news of postponement, Nick's mood swings became electrodynamic, subject to his emotional current and the tension of each moment of each day, and able to snap like a dry twig. His body was pulling him further and further into the death-state of ALS, the grave of immobility, the grave of words unspoken. Nick had no time for postponements. And I was worn to a frazzle as I tried every moment to anticipate his needs and interpret his failing speech. Together, we had to rekindle the hope that the day was going to arrive. Nothing had ever come easy in our lives. So why should the end of his life be any different?

When in calm repose, Nick gave credence to the idea of the newspaper following his story. All Nick wanted was the opportunity to explain the reality of ALS to people, to let them know why he was going to Dr. Kevorkian and why he had the right to end his own life. If his story could in any way help the right-to-die movement, that would give all this tragedy some meaning. However, Nick's going to Kevorkian and becoming a semi-celebrity would have more significance to the paper—

since it would bring in a large increase in readers—than to my son. The paper saw their getting an exclusive on the story as something unprecedented. Those involved were on pins and needles waiting to be able to break the story to the public. It had for us the cast of dark humor as they pushed Nick on the subject. But Nick understood. They had deadlines; even though it was Nick's death they were waiting for. When, however, the tides of agitation gripped him, Nick again asserted his control by saying the newspaper coverage was out. "Like Dr. Kevorkian said, they can't be trusted."

I met with the reporter on the fifth of May at the coffee shop and explained to him the present situation with the doctor and how things were going at home. "Nick is refusing to allow the photographer to see him again, John."

"I feel badly about the postponement," John said. Then his face colored, obviously thinking about the double meaning of his words to me. I told him not to feel bad. Nick and I were equally anxious that the deed be done. And like me, he was inclined to think the postponement was because of the paper's involvement.

"Nick wants to manage his own death. And his threats to call it off is a form of control he can still wield over everyone. But he has never gone back on his word in his life, so we'll just have to ride the tide with him," I told John. I said I would let him know of our next departure date, and then left.

By that night, Nick had lost faith in Dr. Kevorkian. "I want you to use the plastic bag without delay."

"Nick, please, Dr. Kevorkian will come through. Let's wait just a little longer. If he doesn't, I promise to do as you ask."

Carol Loving

On Saturday, the sixth of May, Nick's twin brother showed up at the door. He hadn't been to see his brother since April 11th, and I hated him for that. Nick was disheartened with his twin. "Not only didn't you come to see me, you never called," Nick told him, crossly.

"I was very busy," Drew said, sheepishly. I frowned. That was what he always said. Busy. However, I knew that he was feeling despair, and so he preferred denial. I also knew the two brothers needed each other. Strangely enough, if the second date with Nick's destiny had not been cancelled, Nick's twin would have knocked on the door of an empty house. *Funny how things work out*, I thought. I ended up being very glad that Drew had come, and that he could stay until Monday.

It was a good weekend for everyone. Drew faced the truth about Nick and about himself. We somehow retained our faith that the doctor was going to follow through with his word. But, when I got a call from John Kirk on Monday morning, I felt like my trust had been shattered.

The reporter said quietly, "I called you as soon as the news came over the wire. Dr. Kevorkian helped an elderly man to die at dawn this morning."

He had helped another person and not Nick. I could not believe it. I was stunned. All I could say over and over was, "Oh, my God, Oh, my God." I felt so betrayed. Why had Kevorkian helped someone else when Nick needed his help so badly? I put a call through to Kevorkian's assistant, but all I got was a machine. I tried leaving a message, but I was so unraveled by the news that I couldn't speak coherently. A short while later, Nick saw the news with his brother and looked at me with pale, haggard eyes. "Why someone else and not me?"

By nightfall, Nick had lost all faith in Dr. Kevorkian. He wanted me to use the plastic bag on him immediately.

"I can't stand to see you suffer another moment, but we have to wait," I said, with far more confidence than I felt. I put in another call to the doctor. The doctor's assistant, Bruce, called back. He assured me that Dr. Kevorkian was out of harm's way and had every intention of helping Nick. The doctor was going to telephone us within twenty-four hours to set up the arrangements.

He called as promised. "I want to help Nick before this week comes to an end," he said. *Thank God*, I thought. "I'll call back later with a firm date."

My heart beat furiously. I told him, "It is next to impossible for Nick to use the urinal, and he can hardly chew without biting his tongue or choking. We are on the brink of doing it ourselves."

"No, don't do that," Dr. Kevorkian insisted. "Please try to keep your spirits up."

He called again around ten o'clock than night. "I've cleared the way for Saturday, and want you to fly in Friday night." For the first time, he also asked to speak to Nick. His words seemed to comfort my son.

At last, we had a date. I contacted the travel agency about the new change in our plans early Wednesday morning. Another disappointment: it was a no go. All flights for Friday were booked. The best that could be offered was a flight that left Phoenix late Thursday night. It landed in Detroit at six o'clock Friday morning. I relayed the news to Michigan and we waited once again to hear from the doctor.

The phone rang at eight o'clock in the evening. Dr. Kevorkian's voice was strong, but gentle. "I'll help Nick as soon as he arrives. I want you to take a limousine from the airport to the parking lot of a Holiday Inn located a good distance away. When you get there, I'll pick you up and take you to the place donated for the cause. Once you get to the house, I will interview Nick on videotape, have you and Nick sign the consent form, and then release Nick from the bondage of Lou Gehrig's disease."

"Oh God, at last," I cried out. "I don't know how to thank you, Doctor. I never will."

"I understand," he said softly.

Nick could say goodbye to the world and all his suffering Friday morning. At last, Nick would be free. He was finally going to leave this world and, as I had long promised, I had helped him achieve his goal. Never had I been so happy. Never had I been so sad.

15

Flight to Freedom

The tickets were a complicated matter. The last time I had changed our reservations, I had been charged a hundred dollar fine. This time the rules were different, and worse. A change in reservations had to be made seven days in advance. If I had to buy two new tickets, it would cost more than $1,200.00. Far more than the original tickets. Despite the hardship imposed, I was willing to pay if I had to, but I decided to tell the truth about Nick's condition to see if it would help.

"Nick has ALS and is fatally ill," I explained. "He is going to Michigan to see his doctor, who is a specialist. It's the doctor who keeps changing our appointment, which in turn, forces us to change our reservations. Please, we are at the mercy of the doctor and he didn't give us anything but last-minute notice."

I reminded the agent that our reservations carried a red flag notice that Nick was a wheelchair passenger. The travel agent said she would pass the information along to the right person at the upper level, and would let me know the next morning if I had to buy new tickets or simply pay another fine.

On Thursday morning, I got to the travel agency when it opened shortly after seven o'clock. I uttered a heavy sigh of relief, hearing that because the change in our flight plans was based on Nick's medical need, the airline was willing to forego the purchase of new tickets and simply charge us another hundred dollar penalty fee.

I left with the tickets now in hand, and then swung by my brother's place to let him know that tonight was the night he had to drive his nephew and me to the airport. I told myself, "All we have to do is make it through this day and we are on our way!" When I got back home and relayed the news to Nick, his face reflected his relief. Then he asked, "What do you think about the newspaper story?"

"Nick, this is your life and your death. It's up to you to decide if the press should come to Michigan with us."

Without hesitation, he told me to call the reporter. I called and told John, "Everything is a go. We're leaving tonight." I gave him our flight information.

"I wasn't sure if I was going to hear from you again," John said. "I thought Nick closed the door on the idea of having the paper accompany him." He didn't know if he and Gayle were going to be able to make it or not.

I told him it was up to his paper now. "I've done my part, and I have to focus all my thoughts and energy on getting Nick through his last day in Phoenix."

Indeed, my only focus now was Nick. We spent time deciding on the clothes he would wear for his trip. For the sake of comfort, Nick wanted me to dress him just prior to leaving. Then the rest of the transportation arrangements were all worked out. In his usual thoughtful way, Nick had already let those he loved know what it was he was leaving behind for each of them. He made it clear that he wanted those who wished to spend this last evening with him to come to our house for a gathering in his honor. It was not to be a mournful affair, but a celebration.

My son was prepared to take on the responsibility of his own death. He had been ready for a year. Despite my sorrow, I was ready also. God had entrusted me to give life to my son, to raise him and love him, to teach him about the hereafter, to care for him in his hour of need and deliver him without fear or reservation to the world of my son's divine destiny.

Though we both were thoroughly committed, each remaining moment of Nick's life was subject to opposing forces running along a parallel course. Joy was present because freedom was on the horizon. There actually was a light at the end of the tunnel. But the journey to that light meant one more, albeit final, day for Nick confined to a mummy-like body. I knew the sparks of frustration could flair up at any time. The emotional pressure of moving through these traumatic hours in his dead-body existence could lessen the courage of his spirit. I was concerned with the delicate balance his mind needed to pass through this final task.

Nick spent his morning conserving what energy he had. In the early afternoon, I took care of his grooming. He became blustery with me as I tried to trim his mustache.

"Forget it, Mom. It's not important. Let's move on." I did my best not to let my stress pressure him.

Norm remained at his master's side while I made Nick's last home cooked meal. At noon, I fed my son the last meal I prepared for him. He had a special treat planned at the celebration that night.

Drew came by in the early afternoon. This was the twins' last time to be together. Nick and Drew had always loved each other, and it was equally hard on each to be in a position to lose the other. They shared the beginning of life inside my womb and remained companions throughout childhood and their young adult lives. They were as different as night and day, yet, each had supported and appreciated the other. There was nothing like the bond of twins. I know Drew had been smothered by a silent tourniquet of pain from the very beginning of Nick's illness. One that twisted and wrenched the emotions of his heart as each month passed and brought Nick closer to death. He hated seeing it. He hated the helpless way it made him feel. I wished I could relieve his pain, but it was pain only Drew could synthesize and incorporate into the spiritual development of his mind and soul.

Nick knew Drew, like himself, possessed great inner strength. During one of our many discussions, Nick had assured me there was no need for me to worry about his twin. "Drew will grieve, but he is going to be fine." Nick promised.

Luke came by that afternoon. As it was with his brothers, his heart was also filled with the pain and sorrow of our family tragedy. Luke had grown up fatherless except for our few years with Paul. He had always looked to Nick for advice and counsel along the path of life. Now, he would have to face life with only the memories and insights given to him by his older brother.

Del and my brother Rick got there about four o'clock. Rick was sober. Del, Luke, and Rick joined Nick in his room. They wanted to give him all the love and support possible as they listened to some of their favorite music. Everyone wanted to have the honor of holding the pipe to Nick's mouth to help him smoke so that his pain and suffering could be alleviated, if only momentarily. Everyone wanted to make this last gathering joyful and eventful, not realizing it was all too much for Nick to take.

But I saw the dark rings under his eyes. His face pale and haggard from the excitement. Privately, I had to emphasize to each one that they needed to give Nick some one-on-one time. Everyone at his side at once was a terrible drain on his limited energy.

Despite my words, they crowded round him. The intensity of the celebration was affecting Nick's stomach. He whispered to me that he felt like he might have to move his bowels. He was worried about what would happen if this feeling came over him on the plane. I sent everyone out of his room and told them to take a walk.

Nick felt he didn't have the strength left for one more trip to the bathroom. The last two trips were so dangerous, he decided to struggle with the bedside commode. Stress was etched into his face. I was sure it was the emotional strain of the day that gripped at his bowels. Nick insisted he had to go to the bathroom quickly.

We both knew a quick trip was impossible. In great distress, he told me to bring the portable commode into his room. It was a mighty battle for both of us to get his inflexible, spasmodic, and incredibly heavy body from the bed to the lightweight aluminum and plastic structure completely ill-fitted for anyone dying of Lou Gehrig's disease. It was an indignant sight. Nick banned me from the room. I was just as tense as my son and felt ready to burst into splinters from the mounting pressure.

When I left Nick alone, I discovered John Kirk had arrived. He wanted to see Nick. "Absolutely not. No one can go in to see him now," I said. "No one. You have to wait."

Then Nick called me back into his room. "I can't do it. It's the damn commode," Nick said. He was a knot of frustration. The only solution was to get him to the toilet in the bathroom. It seemed impossible for Nick, as weak as he was.

I didn't have the strength or the benefit of leverage to get him off the bedside commode. Yet, somehow, I managed. It was the will to get it done and the anger that raged inside me to defy the world of impossibilities inflicted on Nick that enabled me to raise him to his unstable feet. Nick leaned his entire weight on me and on his cane. We both almost went down. I had to make sure I was able to hold his hand, a hand that once had been able to grip my shoulder for such endeavors. Now it only lay there, under my protection.

Finally, Nick was upright. Now he had to get each foot off the ground to move one inch forward. As long as I could control the weight of his body and maintain my balance while I all but pulled him along, we could make it. We had to make it. And we did.

While he was in the bathroom, the others had returned from their walk. I talked to them again about being

My Son, My Sorrow

more sensitive. "He can't handle all of you at once. I know you want him to feel your love, but you're well and full of energy. He's weak and dying. Please try to understand."

My brother and Del decided it would be best for them to go home so that the apartment would be less crowded. "We'll come back later," Rick said.

It was twilight. The reporter had gone. He never did see Nick. Meanwhile, Gayle arrived and I learned from her that she and John were going to go to Michigan with us. The Phoenix Suns had an early game and Nick had wanted to have pizza for his last meal as he watched the playoff game. Pizza was his favorite food and something he hadn't been able to eat at all these past months. Now he didn't care if his brother had to feed him. Even if Nick could only eat a few bites it would be worth it. One was ordered.

While we waited, Sue Ellen, a friend of mine, came to take Norm to her place while I was away. I called for Norm to follow me to Nick's room and called out, "Norm wants to say goodbye, Nick." But Nick was too stressed to communicate with me or anyone else. He didn't want to see his dog. I let my friend take him and realized as we stood at Nick's closed door that I'd made another mistake under the strain of the situation. I should have let the dog stay until we left. I should have had my friend return for Norman later. Norman seemed to sense Nick was leaving. His eyes filled with the look of panic and distress as Sue Ellen led him away.

Finally, the pizza arrived. It sat in the oven until Nick was ready to see everyone. Slowly, he let people back into his room. The game started. Nick's mood improved as he watched his favorite sport. Though his words were badly garbled, Nick

239

and his brothers traded comments about the team. They helped Nick eat his last meal. To our enjoyment, the Suns put on a good show. One that made a true fan cheer his team to victory. The combination of the playoff game of Nick's favorite team and the presence of those he loved created a successful farewell gathering for Nick.

For a while, I had almost forgotten, amid the camaraderie and love, that it was getting late. "The hour for our departure is nearing," I whispered to my son. Nick let his brothers dress him. Drew called a cab to return home. My brother returned with Del and his car. Gayle, who had left for a short time and came back, snapped last pictures of the family together as tears flowed from everyone who would see Nick no more.

Drew and Nick asked the others to let them share their last moments together in private. When his cab arrived, Drew came from the room sobbing uncontrollably. Nick was sobbing as well, but he didn't want anyone to see him off at the airport. Drew suddenly turned back and embraced his brother. Then Drew and I walked out into the hall where he held me tightly for a few moments, after which he silently strode out the front door. Almost simultaneously, Luke called to me, "Nick has one more thing to say to Drew." I rushed out to get him, but the cab was already rolling down the road. Luke dialed Drew's home phone and in his broken voice, Nick left a message for his twin brother to discover upon his return. "Drew, take care of Mother and always remember I love you."

The hour to leave had come.

Nick's young brother and I got Nick into the wheelchair and rolled him out of the house and into the front seat of his uncle's car. Time was working with us. Nick smiled, looking me in the eyes. Without words, he was telling me he was ready for his flight to freedom. Del took the responsibility of driving Nick and his uncle to the airport. Luke would drive my car back, so he came with me. We arrived at Northwest Airline's drop-off point first. Del's car pulled up at the curb behind us. My brother and Nick's best friend settled Nick into the wheelchair while I got ready to go. But then my brother would not let go of the chair. He broke down in tears. "Rick, please," I said, "for Nick." I forced him to release his hold so that Nick and I could make our way to his long awaited destiny.

I pushed the wheelchair into the terminal moving as rapidly as my feet could take me. The best thing now was activity, movement. That way there would be no time for last minute brooding. As I hurried along, we ran into the newspaper team. They had just arrived. We played it low key with them. Gayle had her camera packed away rather than snapping pictures of us as I wheeled Nick closer to the boarding gate. Soon the flight was ready to board wheelchair passengers ahead of everyone else. Determined, I pushed Nick's chair forward. We still had to get on the plane. And it had to lift up off the ground. This was no time to be deterred. "Jet away into the night sky," I murmured. Then and only then, would it be real for Nick. And, only then, could I relax.

Nevertheless, I was beginning to breathe a little easier. I wheeled Nick through the enclosed ramp that led to the door of the plane, only to run into complications. Airlines have a special wheelchair. A modified, trimmed-down chair designed to move down the narrow pathway in the center of the plane and used to get wheelchair passengers on board. It was not at the door of the plane waiting for us. There was no way Nick could board without it. *Why couldn't they have had it here? Ready and accessible?* Instead, we had to wait while people scrambled around and assured us they would locate one. In the meantime, we had no choice but to remain at the mouth of the plane and watch as other passengers boarded.

At last, the special chair arrived. Most of the passengers had boarded by this time. The two airline employees with the special chair struggled to get my son's uncooperative body from the Hospice wheelchair to the airline chair that bore no sides at all. But at last, the job was done. One of the men took hold of the chair handles and pulled the chair gingerly onto the plane and backed down the aisle of the first class section toward coach. Getting Nick from one wheelchair to another was a problem and a half for the two men. Getting him from the small chair in cramped quarters into a passenger seat was an even heavier task. Poor Nick. He couldn't help at all. He was jostled about by the two total strangers who did their best to get him settled into the passenger seat next to the aisle. My son took it all in good spirits and thanked them. At last, there we were, on the plane ready to fly out of Phoenix.

Within minutes, John and Gayle boarded and much to our surprise, they sat down in the seats directly across the aisle from us. It was as though the first row of coach seats in the plane had been reserved for Nick and his entourage. Nick was in the aisle seat and I was beside him with an empty seat to my left. I buckled in and then assisted Nick. The plane lifted off the ground at 10:40 P.M. "We made it. We finally made it," he said. The moment we had so anxiously waited for had arrived. I felt like Nick and I had escaped from an asylum, and now were flying away from the insanity and madness that had been my son's life for the last year.

Fortunately, the two problems that we considered might arise on the flight did not. Nick was subject to the ambient temperature and we considered the possibility that the cabin might get too cold, but he felt warm enough. "The cabin's very comfortable," he kept reassuring me. We also feared the confinement of the cabin would inhibit the intake of oxygen and might present Nick with a breathing problem. But, that proved not to be the case either. There was plenty of oxygen in the cabin. Another matter of consideration was the need for the urinal in flight. Nick had held back on liquids earlier in the evening. But, we kept it within reach just in case.

During the first half of the flight, Nick gave full reign to Gayle Morgan, allowing her to shoot pictures of him, but he insisted, "I don't want the camera to catch my face." He and Gayle threw quips at each other, they laughed and carried on as the reporter worked quietly on his laptop computer. I enjoyed the empowerment of my son. Finally he was in command of his life after the long trail of agony and suffering that brought us to this juncture. Peace had settled in his mind and joy was present in his heart. Nick listened to his favorite music through his headphones. I changed disks for him and pushed the buttons. However, in as much as it was a night flight, the rest of the passengers wanted to settle in for a few hours of rest.

The photographer was busily moving about, snapping pictures of Nick, the camera flashing in the subdued light of the cabin. I couldn't help but wonder what the passengers thought about the activity generating around Nick. Many had seen how he had been lifted from the airline wheelchair into the passenger's seat. I wondered if any of the passengers or crew had any idea why we were on the plane. Midway through the flight, the reporter switched seats with the photographer and began talking with Nick about his present thoughts. Nick told John that he was absolutely ready to go. Although it was difficult for him to form words to express himself, Nick answered the questions of the sensitive young man who, in only a few encounters, had formed an emotional attachment to my son.

Everything quieted down after John stopped interviewing my son. For the rest of the flight, Nick and I talked quietly with one another. Through the small window of the cabin, we watched the dark of night transfer into the light of dawn. The pastel hues of daybreak graduated into turquoise and orange which eventually rendered the sky a clear blue. It wasn't long before we could see a city below us. The cabin lit up. The captain announced we were landing. People stirred and Gayle was on her feet shooting one frame after another. Nick was a happy person to be landing in Detroit and he decided to allow Gayle to take shots of his face.

We had an understanding with the press that we would separate, and I would call them at their motel after Nick's departure had taken place.

The wheels of the plane touched down. Before long people began the process of filing out. Because it was such an awkward task, we waited for all the passengers to leave before two men undertook getting Nick out. He was very patient as his body slipped and slid and jostled and bumped in the process of moving him from the aisle chair onto the modified chair and then being rolled onto the jetway. Gymnastics again. The two men hoisted Nick up one last time to get him from the airline wheelchair back into his own chair.

Standing behind him, I pushed my son's wheelchair through the terminal. Nick's press team spotted us. We paused for a few words and then I maneuvered the wheelchair away. We could hear Gayle still snapping pictures. Nick was concerned over this. "I don't want any pictures in this wheelchair. I don't want to be remembered that way." I said the photographer was just doing her job. "No one will see them," I promised. "I can veto those shots."

There was a telephone stand halfway to the entrance. I called Bruce to let him know we had arrived. The next step was to get Nick into a car and to our next destination where we would meet with Dr. Kevorkian. I looked around. The airport was large, light and open. It gave one a welcome feeling, but I had no idea where to go once I got off the phone. Fortunately, a smiling young skycap full of kindness came up to us. He took control of the wheelchair. He sped us downstairs and outside where transportation was available. A sedan driver made a beeline in our direction. Along with the driver, the skycap, who was small and agile, used all his inner strength to move Nick's heavy, immobile body.

Nick was touched by the compassion of the skycap. The all-out struggle the young man undertook to assist Nick as gently as possible into the back seat of the sedan helped get Nick one step closer to heaven. He had done a deed greater than he understood. Nick and I were moved to give him a generous tip for being such a kind soul. The wheelchair went into the trunk. The driver got in the car. We sat in the back of a touring car that provided Nick with generous leg room and a very comfortable seat to take us on the next link of our journey.

16

The Long and Winding Road

I sat close to my son, and took his hand in mine. It was a dignified coach which carried us ever closer to the only one willing to extend a compassionate means to end Nick's suffering. My son and I spoke a little, but mostly we took in the beauty of the stately, iced evergreen trees as the car rolled on. The beauty of nature reminded us of the time we lived in Tennessee, from 1975 through 1977. "Those were good times, and we all have good memories of Tennessee," Nick offered. I nodded. The car rolled along down the road with the rest of the traffic. I felt like we were being swept away on the wings of destiny, but within me I felt assured that the angels were in control.

The car continued on down the winding road. It was a postcard-pretty morning, and the scene was quite the contrast to the stark, barren desert from which we'd come. The drive had a remarkable effect on us. We were relaxed and comfortable, taking each moment as it presented itself. The union of our souls was a bond of trust and spirituality. I was about to deliver my son to his Lord and Creator. Our Father entrusted me to give life to my son; now I was faced with delivering him from the entombment of his helpless body to the realm of the next world. I had no fear or reservations about what was coming and neither did my son.

The serenity of nature before our eyes was soothing to our minds and souls. Nick and I were at peace. All words that could be said between us had been said. Our two bent heads together, our thoughts united, we enjoyed the luxury of these last private moments together in silence. I knew deep inside that the bond established between Nick's soul and mine began early in Nick's childhood and evolved into a strong and trusting relationship which would continue beyond the borders of this world. Nick trusted and believed that God was going to free him to live again. We knew this was not the end, but a new beginning, and I was grateful to God that the hour of mercy was truly upon us.

We pulled the car into the vacant parking lot of the Holiday Inn on Telegraph Road, where it had been arranged that we would meet with the good doctor. Even though the driver of the limousine, unlike the kind skycap, was a strong man, moving Nick's body was as difficult as carrying a bag of wet sand, and my son was unable to assist in any way. I felt sorry for our helping hand, because the burly man seemed ill at ease with the task with which he had been burdened. Finally he succeeded and drove off with a look of relief, leaving my son and me alone. While we waited, Nick whispered he had to use the urinal, but there was nowhere to go. It wasn't easy to assist him with his body crunched up in the wheelchair. It was far from private, and Nick had a last moment of frustration we didn't need, a flash of anger that bruised me momentarily. But, like all his angry moments, it was soon gone and forgotten.

We probably waited twenty minutes before I spotted a car that appeared to be slowing down. It pulled off the main road onto the long path on which we waited. I knew instinctively who it was. I alerted Nick, "The doctor is coming." We both watched as the car approached. It was the moment Nick had been waiting for. He was moved to tears when he saw Dr. Kevorkian looking at us from the passenger's window. "Finally, finally, finally," Nick sobbed. Dr. Kevorkian's assistant, Bruce was driving. The car stopped. Dr. Kevorkian got out, looking taller but more fragile than he appeared on television. "I'm so sorry, I didn't think you'd get here before me," he apologized.

I gazed at him. "A few minutes in the parking lot can't compare to the wait of the past seven weeks, let alone the past twelve months Nick has been in need of medical mercy," I responded.

He smiled shyly at us. We had to get Nick into one more car for the final leg of our journey.

Each and every time people lumbered with my son's body, I felt like an army of do-gooders were tramping on my heart. My son was part of me. He was an extension of me. He was locked in a body others were nearly helpless to handle. The vision of Dr. Kevorkian and his assistant making a mammoth effort to get my son into the back seat of a small sedan, my son helpless, yet grateful, was a sight that seared my soul. It was the saddest form of joy I will ever know. This was also the most difficult transfer of Nick's body yet, because there was so little leg room in the back of the tiny car. At last, he was secure. I hopped in beside him, and we headed towards the final destination of my son's journey to freedom.

Bruce drove us to a quiet location in Waterford Township where there were large and expensive homes on big tracts of land. We turned onto a drive that led to Bruce's home. He had offered it before to people in need of dying. Over the front door, as we got closer, I could see a sign tacked on the door that said "Police Entrance." The door had been kicked down by police in the past. "I decided," Bruce said, "I might as well make it an official entry by hanging up a sign."

He pulled the car into the garage. It was cold, damp and crammed full of musty things. My heart sank when Dr. Kevorkian suggested, "Perhaps it's better to do it in the garage." All this way to die in a freezing garage? Had he lost his perspective?

Bruce read my thoughts, "That's a bad idea. Think about my nosy neighbors."

Once we got Nick into the wheelchair, I pushed him into the house and stopped at a bright, open, and warm spot in the living room which had high ceilings and French doors that let in the morning light. In the distance I could hear the sounds of ducks and geese. Nick smiled. I removed the jacket from his shoulders. The doctor and his assistant made one last effort to get my son's deadweight body out of the confining wheelchair and onto the couch, which was positioned beneath a bay window. Nick had been shuttled back and forth from here to there since he'd left his bed in Phoenix. Now, his face lit up as he realized this was his final resting ground. I made sure Nick was comfortably seated on the couch

My Son, My Sorrow

before I took the cumbersome shoes off his feet and took my place beside him. It felt so good, so right to be at the end of our journey.

Dr. Kevorkian sat down and talked to us gently, quietly; his assistant offered us something cold to drink. "A glass of water would be great," Nick said, smiling. I took a straw from my bag and put it in the glass which Nick precariously balanced on his leg with the support of his crippled hands. He leaned his head downward and drank from the straw until there was nothing left. He was refreshed and ready. "Let's go," Nick said. The doctor listened attentively to my son's impaired speech as Nick answered questions about his plea for assistance in ending his life. My son was honest and direct with his reasons. "It is my choice to die and my family stands behind my decision with full and complete support."

The good doctor introduced consent forms to us which required both of our signatures. My son and I read the papers. I put a pen in my son's right claw-like hand, and he moved his wrist across the paper. Then, I too signed it. Nick and I felt very comfortable in the company of the doctor and his assistant who told us this was the first beautiful morning they'd had in weeks.

"Up till now, nothing but a sky of cloudy gray, and today, look," Dr. Kevorkian said as if even he was uplifted by the warmth. The room was filled with sunlight. I felt the definite presence of angels. My son and I were filled with complete calm. I could never in my life be more grateful to another human being than I was to Dr. Kevorkian for extending his compassion and removing the burden of my son's death from the weight of our souls.

Carol Loving

Dr. Kevorkian said he wanted to interview Nick on videotape. "Do you want to be on it?" he asked me. This was Nick's moment, and I bowed to my son's decision which was to have me beside him. The doctor set up the tripod and camera in the living room.

Suddenly, Bruce noticed his neighbor puttering around in his back yard. "That's quite unusual for this time of the morning," he said. It appeared the neighbor was doing his routine landscaping, but Bruce was inclined to think his neighbor suspected that the doctor was aiding another victim.

"Pay him no mind," Dr. Kevorkian said. "We're here for Nick."

The video was a powerful means of capturing the cruelty of Lou Gehrig's disease. Dr. Kevorkian explained, "The tape is for your own protection, as are the papers you signed. I'll send the tape and papers to you once all the hoopla surrounding Nick's death is over." Dr. Kevorkian began asking Nick questions about his medical condition and his request to be released from the bondage of his disease. I was glad Nick wanted me to be with him during the interview, because it was something I could look back on. Our last moments together, preserved on tape.

The doctor asked Nick to demonstrate the range of motion he had with his hands and arms. Although his hands were useless, Nick still had the ability to raise his arms and move them about, albeit with difficulty. Slowly, painfully, my son raised his arms upward from the elbows, a motion which brought his hands up out of his lap. With enormous effort, he moved his arms to his shoulders and spread them out to each side. Dr. Kevorkian asked Nick to demonstrate the movement in his legs.

252

My Son, My Sorrow

For a moment, the sorrow of what had happened to my son overwhelmed me, and I felt hot tears well up in my eyes. As Nick made the effort to extend his legs forward, they began to tremble and jerk uncontrollably. He held them out only momentarily before they fell back to the floor. The faint quality of my son's voice as he spoke his responses was added proof of the muscular deterioration that had taken place in his throat. All of the horrendous degeneration that had taken place in his body, everything Nick had not wanted anyone to see, was being captured on video as testimony as to why my son chose to die. It had to be, and Nick gladly suffered the invasion of his privacy.

Then Dr. Kevorkian began asking Nick more questions. "Whose decision was it to give up your life as it had become through ALS? How did the rest of the family feel about your decision? Why did you not want to continue on with life? Do you understand that you do not have to go through with the delivery if you decide to back out at the last moment?" The doctor kept telling Nick, "If you want to change your mind, you can. You don't have to go through with your plans if you don't want to. You can stop for any reason at the last minute."

Before he turned the camera off, Dr. Kevorkian asked Nick, "Is there anything you would like to say to the world?"

My son replied that he wanted to quote Dr. Martin Luther King, Jr. "Free at last. Free at last. Thank God Almighty, I am free at last." With those words the video came to an end.

The interview was over. History had been recorded. The truth had been told. My son was ready to die. He had long waited for this moment to come, and it was here. *Dear God in heaven, the moment has arrived.*

Nick had been in a seated position for almost twelve consecutive hours. He was weary. He wanted to lie down. I helped him get his body comfortably positioned on the couch and placed a small pillow under his head. My son, whom I loved with all my heart, was ready to be delivered from the prison of his flesh.

There was no reason to wait. I put the CD headphones in place so he could listen to the music he had chosen for this occasion: "Dark Side of the Moon" by Pink Floyd. Dr. Kevorkian put a clear plastic oxygen mask over Nick's nose and mouth. I adjusted it for my son until it was a snug, comfortable fit.

The doctor had already explained to us everything that would happen to Nick as he drew the carbon monoxide into his lungs and it entered his blood stream. The procedure was not going to induce any pain. Inhalation of the gas would cause him to fall asleep. He would pass out of consciousness well before all systems actually shut down, and the life therein contained would then pass out of his body. Attached to the mask was a long clear tube that led to a small canister at my feet. Part way down the tube was a plastic clothespin that sealed off the tubing. Attached to the clothespin was a thin chain with a small plastic ring on the end. I put the ring on the middle finger of my son's right hand. I secured it so that it would not slip off of Nick's fingers which were curled into a bony fist. All he had to do when he was ready was move his right arm away from his body. That would release the flow of gas that would set him free. The tank was open. Dr. Kevorkian leaned toward

My Son, My Sorrow

Nick. "You may trigger the device when you feel comfortable." He paused and then said softly, "Nick, you don't have to do it if you don't want to. Don't worry about hurting anybody's feelings." It was all up to Nick.

My son and I smiled at each other. Rather than feeling sad, there was a great peace between us. For the last time, my beloved son said to me, "I love you, Mom."

For the last time, he heard me say, "I love you, son." I was going to ask him if I could put his hand in mine, when he asked me just that. I took his left hand and gently uncoiled his fingers, cupping the palm of his hand inside the cradle of mine. Music flowed into his ears. With all the strength he had, my son pushed his right arm away from his body. The ring on his finger pulled the clothespin away from the tube and released the flow of carbon monoxide.

Nick drew the gas in with deep, expedient breaths. Noting a crimp was still in the line, I straightened it to allow the flow of gas into his lungs. My eyes held Nick's; his withered hand was pressed in mine as I watched him take in breath after breath. I had no concept of time. I could only feel the attending spiritual support which had brought the two of us to this moment in time, now helping to release his soul. His eyelids fluttered and then closed. Breathing slowed. He was unconscious. Quite unexpectedly, Nick moved his head over to the right. Then came the unraveling of all the pain and torment, as a very long ethereal sigh flowed from my son. Nick's head then moved to the left, and the sigh continued to flow until at last it had completely escaped his lips and left behind a faint smile.

Carol Loving

Dr. Kevorkian watched over Nick during the entire process and was witness to the sigh of relief that poured from my son as he was released from bondage. He looked at me. "No one has ever done that before," he said quietly in an emotional voice.

I looked up at the doctor who had given of himself to help us and told him, "My son is finally happy. He has gone to Heaven."

It was another minute or so before the last of the electrical impulses in Nick's body came to a complete stop. When a pulse was no longer detectable, the doctor turned off the gas and removed the mask. I released my son's hand from mine and set it down. I remained quietly beside my son's body. I was eternally grateful for the service rendered him. So gentle. So peaceful. So necessary. A few moments of compassion for my son who had suffered so much and deserved the grace of death. There were no words to express my gratitude to the good doctor who had not turned Nick away in his hour of need.

17

The Final Phase

My son, the man, was gone. He had been released from his physical bondage. My son, the spirit, was now free. He was given the gift of eternal life.

My responsibility to Nick now was to care for the besieged body he gratefully left behind, the body that originated inside me, which I nurtured as he grew up. It was routine for the doctor to make a call to the police after the passing had taken place to report the body left behind. However, this call would bring the police and the media to the scene where the doctor's lawyer would have to step in on behalf of his client. "I want to spare you from going through the trauma of their invasion. I have something else in mind," Dr. Kevorkian said.

The doctor wanted to drive Nick's body to the Oakland County Sheriff's Department office and then call the medical examiner. By doing this, we could avoid a flood of flashing lights and the snapping of photographs in my face to invade this very private moment. There would be no cameras to exploit the death of my son and no cameras to televise the image of a body bag being hauled away by a crew of indifferent people doing their job, with no knowledge at all about the circumstances of Nick's death. I concurred with this approach.

I had placed my trust in the good doctor from the moment he extended his compassion to my son and I understood his plan of action for the body was for my benefit. However, the neighbor outside had an influence on how we got the body into the Volkswagen parked outside the garage. The doctor's assistant was sure that his neighbor was snooping because "he knew Dr. Kevorkian was there." The doctor and his assistant discussed what to do while I remained on the couch beside my son's body. They decided it would be best to leave the house and get something to eat. It was close to ten o'clock Friday morning. I hadn't eaten since Wednesday. "Is that alright with you?" Dr. Kevorkian asked. I nodded.

And yet, I felt strange leaving Nick's body alone. I gently spread the beautiful blue and white afghan on the back of the couch over the length of my son's body, pulling it up to his neck. Though I was in a state of shock, I felt spiritual forces were guiding me through the experience. As I left the house, I looked back at my son's body stretched out on the couch. There was an aura of peace about him.

To make it look like we were not going to be back for the day, Dr. Kevorkian and his assistant threw a couple of golf bags into the trunk. The neighbor was lingering about out of doors at the border of the two properties. Dr. Kevorkian threw him a cordial wave. The neighbor's eyes were riveted on us as we drove off.

My Son, My Sorrow

We went to a small, dimly lit restaurant some distance from the assistant's home. Still entrenched in the reality of Nick's death, I had no idea where I was. My face must have reflected my shocked condition. As we walked, the doctor bent down and whispered, "Don't be frightened if people come up to me. It isn't about Nick, they want my autograph." He went on, "It happens all the time. The people in the area are in overwhelming support of what I am doing. Only the authorities plague me." I could understand, grateful as I was that he had ended my son's suffering, how he was loved by a multitude of people who felt the doctor was on a mission of mercy. Most of the people in the community had a greater insight into what he was doing than the rest of the country, who only heard about him through media blips. We sat in a booth and before we ordered, just as he warned me, people came up to request autographs of the doctor along with uttering words of praise for what he was doing.

It was good for me to put something in my stomach. Over the duration of Nick's illness I had all but lost my appetite.

During our meal together, I discovered that, like myself, Dr. Kevorkian had a great interest in the Orient. The doctor had knowledge of the Japanese language and an understanding of Chinese characters. I was surprised to see him skillfully master the strokes of his pen as he crafted several Chinese characters on a napkin.

When we returned to Bruce's home, we found the neighbor still outside seemingly tending his yard. Once again, Dr. Kevorkian waved. Bruce left his car outside the garage. We went inside. Although I didn't want anyone to interrupt the sanctity of death by touching the body of my son, I knew it had to be done. I braced myself as the doctor and Bruce struggled to get the body off the couch and into the wheelchair. The hoisting, jostling, and bumping in the effort to move the dead weight didn't clutch my heart as it did when Nick was alive. I wheeled the body out of the house through the garage exit. The van was parked with the rear of the vehicle close to the garage. It was a gargantuan task for Bruce, the slightly built doctor and me to get the heavy body into the van through the open rear door.

Inside, the van had been converted into a comfortable camping van, with a mattress on a raised platform that took up the entire back. We had to lug and lift and pull, but we finally got the body settled. I supported the head with a pillow, as I often had for Nick during the last weeks of his life. I kept the afghan spread over the length of the body. Dr. Kevorkian wanted me to sit up front, but I said, "With all respect, I intend to sit next to the body that belonged to my son until the very moment comes when I have to relinquish it to the authorities."

Finally, we were all ready. Then the unexpected happened. The engine wouldn't turn over. Dr. Kevorkian tried to start it over and over again, but it just wouldn't kick in. Every attempt failed. And there we were with a body in the back of the van. It was the kind of wry humor Nick would have appreciated.

The gas gauge registered empty. The doctor shook his head. "I know there was half of a tank." Finally, Bruce siphoned gas out of his own car and fed it into the gas tank of the old van. The doctor got back in and tried to turn the engine over. The damn thing still wouldn't start. He tried and tried. Then, just as it looked like we were going to have to alter the plan, the tired old engine finally coughed and started. With Bruce in the vehicle in front of us, we followed his sedan as it rolled out of the driveway and onto the road. The neighbor was still out in his yard, close to the property line. He watched us as we drove away. It took a while for the old van to pick up momentum. It was the van Dr. Kevorkian used when he assisted Janet Atkins in 1990, his first act of euthanasia. Thomas Hyde, another ALS victim, was also euthanized in this vehicle. The doctor said the police would probably impound it. My son's euthanasia brought the use of the doctor's mercy vehicle full circle.

As we approached our destination, I moved from beside my son's body up to the front seat of the van. We pulled into the empty driveway of the Oakland County Sheriff's Department in Pontiac. The van came to a halt, and the doctor turned the engine off. We hopped out and briskly made our way across the street until we came to the restaurant where the assistant was waiting for us in the parking lot. Bruce and I remained by his car as Dr. Kevorkian used a public phone to inform the authorities that there was a body in the van parked in their driveway. When he returned, we took the wheelchair and other things that belonged to my son from Bruce's car and put them into the doctor's car, which had been left in the parking lot earlier that day.

It was time to go our separate ways. I hugged the doctor's assistant to express my gratitude for his contribution in aiding my son in a loving act of mercy. I could feel a very warm, empathetic spirit radiate inside him when we embraced. How could I ever repay him for opening up his heart and his house to us? I then got into the doctor's old car, and he drove us to his lawyer's office in Southfield.

Carol Loving

It was somewhere around noon when I was ushered into the lawyer's office. People were especially sympathetic and cordial to me. The receptionist relayed that she had just taken a call by a young lady who had been on the same flight as Nick and me. She had seen the stewards struggle in their efforts to get Nick into the passenger chair. A sight which quickened the sensitivities of her heart. The news of Nick's death prompted her to call the office to say she supported the doctor in the good he was doing. They all wanted to know if I was alright. "I delivered my son to his Father in Heaven, I am fine. I stood by my son and did what was right." As I followed the doctor through the maze of rooms, I somehow got separated from him and found myself alone in an office. Never had I appreciated solitude more.

A few minutes later, Geoffrey Fieger, the doctor's lawyer, came in, expressed his condolences and asked, "Have you brought along your son's driver's license? I need it." He also asked me if I had a picture of Nick. In my distressed state I handed him the two pictures my young son had recently taken, pictures Nick did not want anyone to see.

"If you'll just wait here, I'll get someone to take you to your hotel. I know you need to rest and be alone." I nodded.

Dr. Kevorkian was nowhere around. One of the young secretaries took me in her car to the Holiday Inn on Telegraph Road and registered a room for me under her name. She was kind and escorted me to my room. I assured her I was fine, and she left me to my peace. I know they meant well, but I didn't want people feeling strange around me, and that is how I expected they felt because they learned I helped my son die.

My Son, My Sorrow

How was a stranger to understand that death was the only amelioration to my son's agony? It was not possible. Nevertheless, I was encased in a sheath of tranquility in response to the liberation of my son from his suffering. I was profoundly grateful to have been able to give the selfless gift of a good and proper death to my beloved son. There wasn't anyone in the world who knew what I had been through today or any day that led up to this one. There wasn't anyone who could. All I wanted to do was rest. But, I had one more obligation. I had to call the reporter covering Nick's story.

I stretched out on the bed and called the number John Kirk had given me. I tried to answer the questions he threw at me. He wanted to know everything that happened from the time we left the airport. I tried to communicate the events as they unfolded, but found it difficult to articulate the morning's events in a few simple sentences. I don't know how long the phone call lasted. I simply did my best and tried to be careful not to say anything that might incriminate anyone. "I am not afraid the authorities are going to do anything to me," I explained, but I didn't want to say anything that could be damaging to Dr. Kevorkian or his kind assistant who donated his place for my son's benefit. When I put the phone down, I went to the bathroom and wet a washcloth, then laying down, I placed it on my throbbing forehead.

I turned on the television. After a minute of flipping through the channels, I saw Fieger standing outside his law office. He was getting ready to speak to the press and announce my son's death. It was odd to watch this stranger talk about Nick. He gave very little information, because that was all he had. He mentioned our names, where we were from, and the awful disease that was killing my son. He said the reason the body had been driven to the Medical Examiner's office was so I could be spared the intrusion and circus-like atmosphere the media created. Then Fieger said, "He is not the last. Dr. Kevorkian will not stop what is right. This is not going away." After that, he walked away from the cameras to signal that was all. As I flipped from channel to channel, I found reporters talking about my son on all of them. Suddenly, my heart sank. The picture Fieger took from me was flashed on the screen. The image of my dying son, the one he had not wanted strangers to see, could be seen around the world. It brought me to tears.

My son's photographer came by and took pictures of me while I watched the media sweep on the channels which broadcast news of my son's death. I became saddened as I watched as the truth about my son was altered, presented through a filter of opinions and conjectures by people who had no idea what actually took place. Where it took place. Why it took place. Or even when it took place. Let alone knowledge of who Nick was and how he ended up at the mercy of Dr. Kevorkian. The story changed with the tides and needs of human curiosity, and was exploited by those in search of ratings. I was hit by a barrage of information about Kevorkian's latest victims by local, national, and world-wide broadcasters. It was so distorted. I felt sick. People with hearts dark as coal and completely vacant of compassion publicly denounced the actions of the good doctor and the selfless act of mercy he extended to my son—a young man whipped and chained by a disease which had sucked the life from him.

My Son, My Sorrow

"Enough!" I called out and the photographer turned off the television.

"Would you like me to leave?" she asked. I nodded. At last, I was alone. It was well into the afternoon and I was drained. Sleep was my overwhelming urge, and I sank into bed. I fell into darkness as the swirl of the day, the past twenty-four hours, the months leading up to the new year and those following passed through my dreams. All nineteen months of death. The sun was lost below the horizon when the phone in the hotel room brought me out of a deep sleep.

It was Dr. Kevorkian. "I want you to join me and my lawyer for dinner," he said. "You need to eat something." I was glad the doctor had thought about me because I was too exhausted to care for myself.

At a local restaurant I sat down to dinner with Dr. Kevorkian, Geoffrey Fieger and Fieger's wife. As Dr. Kevorkian relaxed, he began to talk about his mission. In his unguarded moments, I found the doctor to be a person of notable genius with a subtle, innocent, childlike quality interjected into his spontaneity. His commitment to his crusade— that it was right to help people with unbearable terminal conditions—was obvious. He discussed the local political situation and said, "The people are with me. It is only those who do not suffer that make these arbitrary laws to stop what is merciful." He was slight in stature. As he spoke, I noticed he ate not out of indulgence, but frugally, only to nourish himself. Fieger, a large, imposing man with deep convictions of his own, ate to satisfaction. I could see he was very fond of the doctor, and despite the fact that Dr. Kevorkian was old enough to be his father, Fieger was the one who assumed the fatherly role and protected the older man. They appeared to have a good relationship. I was starved and quickly ate the tender steak set before me. Though I wanted to remember every kind word the doctor uttered to me, I found myself losing track of our conversation, thinking only of Nick.

It was late when I got back to my room at the inn, and idly turned on the television. Coverage of the morning's event was still running rampant on the news programs. I had no desire to watch people with absolutely no knowledge of the facts talk about something as momentous and intimate as my son's death as though they actually knew what they were talking about. The tube was a powerful instrument to propagandize, I thought as I turned it off. I went to bed thinking of my son and how good it was to give him his freedom. It didn't take long to fall asleep. I was bone-tired, not only from this very long day of Nick's deliverance, but also from the trauma of the past year.

I woke up Saturday at the crack of dawn, as I always did. The morning sun flooded the windows with light as I prepared for another full day ahead of me before my plane left. I had to identify the body in the morning. I had to meet with the mortician and attend a press conference in the afternoon. I also had to view the body. I still could not seem to call it Nick's body, I noticed, for to me it was only a shell. But still, I wanted to touch him one last time.

I showered, dressed and waited to be picked up by Fieger's law partner, a quiet, restrained man named Michael Schwartz. He arrived shortly and took me from the inn to the medical examiner's office. I was surprised to see Nick's press team there. Schwartz escorted me to a dungeon-like area of the building, with one wall of glass. The officer behind the glass did not intend for me to see the remains of my son. He wanted me to identify the body through a photograph he had. Schwartz spoke up on my behalf. "She wants to identify the actual body." When the dispute was settled, I was permitted to identify the body through the wall of glass. It was evident the body, the one my son once inhabited, had been defiled by an autopsy. I winced. There was no reason for an autopsy. It was an insipid act of retaliation against Dr. Kevorkian and the family of one freed from suffering. Stiffening my will, I straightened my back and refused to flinch or bat an eye as police officers watched me gaze at the lifeless shell laid out on the other side of the wall. Unlike them, I knew Nick had gone to a better place.

As Michael Schwartz and I made our way back to the car, two officers approached me, firing questions. I didn't know what to do or say. That was when I felt the power of the attorney at my side. "She has only a statement to make. No questions," he commanded. His protection was like a cloak about my shoulders. It was like having Superman stand in my defense. No one could touch me.

I gave my short statement. "The good doctor gave something to my son the whole medical profession refused him. He gave my son control over his own destiny."

After that, Schwartz reiterated, "She has been through enough. She isn't going to answer any more questions." The officers then turned to Nick's press team and tried to question them as Schwartz led me away. He took me back to the inn and I returned to my room. Nick, as NUMBER 23 on the five year list established by Dr. Kevorkian, was still the hot topic of the day when I flipped on the television set. Much hype was being fabricated over the fact that we delivered the body to the authorities rather than calling the authorities, as had been done in the past. Reporters were making a big deal out it. "Making something out of nothing. Monkeys, they are," I mumbled, "in the name of news."

I was glad I was hidden away where the press could not find me. Little did I know that there was more to come. A short while later, the official autopsy report was broadcast. It was the news blip of the day and was repeated at short intervals. Proof positive. Nicholas Loving was one hundred percent incapable of any physical movement. Therefore, it was determined by the medical examiner that my son's death was a homicide. "No one is under arrest," they announced, "because there is not enough evidence to make an arrest." I couldn't believe my ears. More propaganda tossed into the ring so more pompous blowhards could have their fifteen minutes of fame. In one day, Nick's long awaited and gratefully received death had been turned into murder. According to the experts, the ones driving the truth into the ground, this was fact.

Later that day, Dr. Kevorkian picked me up at the inn and again drove me to his lawyer's office for a press conference. He said quietly, groping for the right words to comfort me, "There's going to be a gathering Sunday for the survivors of others I've helped, you're very welcome to join us." He was making a kind offer, but I planned to fly back to Phoenix.

While at the lawyer's office, I took care of the proper arrangements for my son's remains. He was to be cremated, as had been his wish. I would receive the ashes in about a week. After the matter of cremation was taken care of, I stayed in

My Son, My Sorrow

Fieger's office alone waiting for the press conference. Fieger eventually came in. He entered like a thespian making a grand entrance on stage, and with a voice amplified by power, punctuated with a pointed finger in my face, he commanded, "Never tell anyone what happened yesterday."

I said, "My son came to Michigan with a team from the *Arizona Republic* and the story of my son's life and death is already being read in the homes of the people all across the state of Arizona." Fieger exploded. He stormed out of his office demanding to have copies of the newspaper faxed over to him. I remained alone until he re-entered with poor quality transmissions of the newspaper I had yet to see. He handed one to me. The print was hard to make out.

Suddenly, he blurted out, "On the couch! You told them he died on a couch in a living room!" He ranted and raved and carried on. He ended by saying, in a manner one uses to reproach a child for inappropriate behavior, that I was ignorant to trust the press.

It was obvious he was angry because Dr. Kevorkian might be compromised, but his attempt to admonish me with accusations of ignorance was really quite childish. I set him off again by telling him Nick's press team was outside. He didn't like that one bit.

"I've prepared a statement for the press." I gave him a copy. His face reddened as he grabbed it up.

He stormed out. A short while later he returned, having had a change of heart. "I actually think it is pretty good and I read it over the phone to Dr. Kevorkian. He was pleased." Fieger had me sign the statement. He planned to have copies made and distributed to the press. I was left alone again.

Carol Loving

Finally it was three o'clock. The lawyers' assistant returned and led me to their conference room. Schwartz, Fieger and I sat down at the end of the conference table surrounded by lights from every angle. A web of cameras and microphones covered the space in front of us, and an equivalent number of people were gathered around with notepads in their hands. Nick's team was in the room. I was glad to see they were included as I requested.

In my prepared statement, I spoke of the disease that took my son's life in a manner of unspeakable cruelty. I spoke of the medical profession that turned its head in pretense that the horror did not exist. I told the silent onlookers, "The promise to help my son die offered by Dr. Kevorkian gave him control over his destiny and actually gave him a reason to live through the seven difficult weeks it took for his final day of deliverance to arrive."

When I finished, the questions began to fly. I didn't expect them to understand the import of what I said. No one understands what it means to die or watch a loved one die from Lou Gehrig's unless they experience it themselves as my son and I did. I had no idea what they thought of me or my words as I tried to answer their questions. I was still in a state of near euphoric shock as a result of helping my son after a long trail of senseless pain and anguish. There was one thing of which I was totally convinced, no one in the room could comprehend how essential it was for me to rescue my son from his suffering.

Whenever a question was directed my way that Fieger did not want me to answer, he stopped me before I could open my mouth. "Everyone in the room knows Dr. Kevorkian helped my son die, regardless of individual interpretation of the fact or how each thinks about it personally," I whispered to him. With that, I was permitted to answer questions regarding the fact that the doctor helped my son die, but I was forbidden by Fieger's interjections to discuss specific details. When the arrangement of cameras and the bustle of activity subsided with the departure of the press, I was presented with another twist in the aftermath of my son's death. Fieger's office received a word from the sheriff's office that a call had been received from someone who claimed to be the father of the deceased. According to the caller, Nick and I were using assumed names. The sheriff wanted copies of both of our driver's licenses faxed over to him. This was absurd, but there was more to come.

This man who claimed to be the father also wanted to see the body. Thus, the sheriff refused to release the body to the mortuary. The law intended to open its arms to embrace the man who abandoned his children and forced them to live in poverty. It was an act which only proved to me that the law can be ugly and evil. Once again it was aiding and abetting a father without a conscience. I knew my acts as a loving mother were good and beneficial for my son. But, I never dreamed the man who had abandoned us would come crawling out of the woodwork like a spineless creature in the night. Due to his interference, I wasn't going to be able to see the body one last time before the late night flight I was scheduled to take. The sheriff was playing a political game and used my son's body to place me in checkmate. I wasn't going to stand for it; I decided to change my flight.

Carol Loving

The sky was overcast with quiet, gray clouds when I was driven back to the inn. It had been an exhausting day with a string of unbelievable events unfolding. I was tired, hungry but still keyed up from all the activity generated by the clash of good and evil forces. I turned on the television and saw the dissemination of propaganda at its peak. Reporters were having a field day with the news out of the sheriff's office that Nick and I were using aliases. The media was making it sound like we were Bonnie and Clyde on the run. There were photo clips of hoards of reporters waiting at the back entrance of the sheriff's department hoping to focus the camera on the man coming to see the body so they could stick a microphone in his face. It was insane. All to further intensify the hype they were generating.

I changed my airline reservation to Sunday evening and let Nick's press team know about the change. John Kirk planned to leave that night. Gayle wanted to remain behind and accompany me to the mortuary. They invited me to go out to dinner with them. It was then that I realized I hadn't eaten all day and was hungry. I could not help but wonder how Nick's death and the events of this momentous day had affected them.

When we met at the restaurant, we immediately began talking about the politics involved in the aftermath of Nick's death. Then, John tried to express his personal feelings as we sat down at our table, "I'm so glad I had the opportunity to get to know Nick and respect him before he left this world behind."

We ordered a bottle of wine. First we made a toast to Nick. Then, we raised our glasses to the compassion, concern,

reserve, and respectability of Dr. Kevorkian, who was courageous enough to help me help my son when no one else
would lend a hand. "He took the burden off my shoulders. He
saved me and my son from the horrible prospect of ending
his misery with a plastic bag. From being followed by the
long arm of the law and from having to cope with the awful
memories of Nick's last moments on earth. Instead, Dr.
Kevorkian gave my son a gentle death."

While I was with the media team, things were hopping
at the medical examiner's office. The father who never
fathered his son arrived on the scene surrounded by gossip
mongers who called themselves reporters. They followed him
with the camera lens. Stuck a microphone in his face. Spun off
questions. It was all so stupid to chase after a man who didn't
even know one twin from the other because he was never
there.

On Sunday, I was up at dawn. I made arrangements to
go to the funeral home early, but a phone call put an end to
that. The kindly owner of the mortuary called. The body was
not released by the sheriff's department as earlier promised.
He had to postpone my visit. He called again a little later and
told me one of the television stations was camped out across
the street waiting for me to show up. In order to spare me their
predatory behavior, he planned to leave open the garage doors
of his establishment at noon so I could drive right in and leave
the media behind.

I went to the funeral home in Royal Oaks with the photographer assigned to Nick's story. We arrived to see the last of
the television crew, who had given up their I-Spy game, taking

away their equipment from the vacant lot directly across the street from the funeral home. At exactly noon, the garage doors opened and I was inside without anyone the wiser.

The owner took me to the room where he had my son's body ready for me to view. For some reason, the mortician lingered in the room. I wanted to look at my son's body privately and touch him one last time with no one there except for the camera to record history. At last, he stopped talking and left the room. I stood close to the body that once belonged to my son and looked down into the face. So lifeless. So vacant. So still. Far more dead than when Nick slipped out of his body two days previously. All that my son had been through washed over me as I stood over the body of the one who brought so much love into my heart. He was the light of my life. I had been able to control my emotions before the outside world and cry only in private, but as I looked down at the lifeless form, tears forced their way to the surface and spilled over onto the dear face below me.

It was too early to go to the airport and Gayle wanted to stop and eat. I sat quietly as she drove along a never-ending stretch of road. We stopped at one place, but it was so crowded, it didn't make sense to wait. We stopped at another place and found it to be filled up as well. Eventually we found a restaurant without a line and sat down at a table, only to see on the menu that it was Mother's Day. With all I'd experienced from the very moment I arrived in Michigan, I'd forgotten that this Sunday was Mother's Day. I was a mother who helped her son die. I was a mother who helped lift her son from the bondage of suffering. Nevertheless, the son I loved would never be with me again in the simple, joyful way those around me having their celebratory meals with their children were.

I was hungry, but I found the food impossible to eat. All I really wanted to do was return to Phoenix and get back to the rest of my family so we could comfort each other. We left the restaurant and drove to the airport. There were scattered showers and a chill in the air. I looked out at the gray sky as the car sped along and wished the trip was over. I needed to be home.

At the airport, I got the wheelchair which I had to return out of the trunk of the car. I wanted to check it as a cargo item. As I wheeled the empty chair in front of me, my eye caught a glimpse of the young skycap who helped Nick and me on Friday when we first arrived.

As I drew closer his face became puzzled. I felt compelled to walk over to him and explain. He asked me where my son was. "He's the young man Dr. Kevorkian helped Friday morning," I said and thanked the skycap again for his kindness. He looked stricken for a moment, and I then said, "He's in a better place." He nodded. We shook hands and wished each other well. Then I returned to the empty wheelchair which I eventually exchanged for a baggage claim check. It was hours before boarding time and the wait strained my already fragile nerves. Gayle liked to talk while I longed for silence.

When Nick made his selection of CDs to bring on the trip, he included the Moody Blues. He told me he wanted me to have something to uplift my spirits on the flight back to

Carol Loving

Phoenix. He knew the Moody Blues would console my heart. I sat quietly, letting the music comfort me.

Finally, the loudspeaker announced our flight. Time to return home. Gayle and I said goodbye. I walked onto the plane and settled into my seat. I put the headphones back on and lost myself in the music again. Midway into the flight, I decided to get up and stretch. I walked down the aisle of the plane only to overhear a conversation about losing a loved one. I stood and listened as a young dark-haired woman spoke to those around her. Leaning over, I said something about the blessing that goes along with death. She looked up at me. "I know you. I know who you are," she said.

I knew who she was too, even though I never laid eyes on her before. I somehow knew I was looking at the young woman who had called Fieger's office to offer support. She said quietly, "The news of your son's death had a real impact on me. I cried all weekend. I don't know where you got the strength to help your son." We talked for awhile, and she stood up to hug me several times before I went back to my seat.

The plane landed in Phoenix, and I discovered my supportive family waiting for me at the airport. I was home. The mission was a success. My children, my brother and Del hugged me, all looking much better than they did the night Nick and I left. The torment of Nick's suffering had gone just as his soul had departed from the body that had become a chamber of hell. Everyone talked about how Nick's story was told via the media and said the media there did a good job reporting. I had no idea of the dimension or scope of the article in the *Arizona Republic* when we first allowed the press into our home. I had no idea of the tribute it would end

My Son, My Sorrow

up being to my son or the comfort it would prove to be to those who knew and loved him. And I had no idea how it would affect the people of Phoenix. It was a eulogy for my beloved Nick. It was heartwarming.

After we returned to my place, we stayed up late talking about the sequence of events as they unfolded in Michigan. I told them how beautiful the dawn was from Nick's and my view high above the city, about the kind young man who helped us out of the airport, the tranquil limousine ride, the suspenseful wait, our first view of the good doctor, the comfortable home donated for Nick's deliverance. Most of all, I communicated Nick's joy: the long beautiful sigh as Nick's soul departed, the divine experience that death was for him and should be for all people, and how happy Nick was to finally bring his suffering to an end. We all rejoiced to know that Nick was no longer in pain. So I would not have to be alone, Drew, my surviving twin, offered to spend the night. I laid in Nick's bed, because I needed to be close to the memories.

I had returned. I had to face the continuation of life in this world. ALS had forced its way into my life and had taken my beloved child. I had no idea why all this happened, but I knew there was a good reason why God would want my son. Nicholas John was special. God had entrusted him to me, and I had now reciprocated by entrusting my son to God. However, I had to move forward. As there was a new beginning for Nick, there had to be a new beginning for me. Tonight, I told myself, I could rest. Tomorrow, I would begin to figure out just what it was that God expected of me next.

18

Life After Death

I was home now. All I could do was feel my way through the numbness that sheltered me from the pain that was bound to return. Monday, after I took Drew home, I answered calls from producers of news programs, who wanted to talk to me. I knew instinctively that it was the right thing to do, and that afternoon I spent several hours answering questions from reporters. It was good for me to talk about Nick and how wonderful he was and the beauty of his death. People were interested in knowing about my son. People wanted to know who Nick was. What he was like. And, why he went to Dr. Kevorkian. I was not cognizant of what I was saying as strangers asked me questions. I was in a mist as time filtered through me.

Once I closed the door to reporters, and returned to the environment that only a short time before my son had shared with me, I found Nick everywhere. Everything I saw and touched had memories attached, good and bad. When I came upon the hospital's aluminum cane leaning against the wall in Nick's room, my immediate impulse was to get rid of it. It was a symbol of the cruel disease that seared our souls with endless pain. I grabbed the cane like it was the illness itself, ran outside the house and threw it into the garbage so I would never be choked by its image again. I took comfort in Norm who was back home mourning the loss of his master. We lay together on Nick's bed; I let the hours pass.

Tuesday was a repeat of Monday. Once again, my afternoon was consumed with reporters wanting to know about Nick and his death. It was a euphoric experience to speak of my son, but by late that afternoon, after two days of talking, I was drained. I was running on empty. When I was finally alone, I broke away from the house and went to the grocery store. I had not had a meal since Saturday. I sustained myself on water and coffee and felt like I was going to drop to the ground if I didn't eat. I was trembling from lack of food. I drove to a nearby market and once inside, went to the deli counter to get Swiss cheese. There was only one customer there, a large woman with tattoos on both her arms who had been handed her order. She talked a blue streak and didn't intend to stop regardless of my standing there, waiting my turn. The kindly, balding man behind the counter didn't know how to break away to get to me. Finally, I interjected with a firm, "Excuse me," and told the man behind the counter what I wanted.

The woman immediately lambasted me. With the justification of a distorted temper, she rammed her cart into my hip. She went on and on. She threatened to wait for me in the parking lot to beat the shit out of me because I interrupted her.

My Son, My Sorrow

Suddenly the scene seemed humorous. I had to laugh. I was back in Phoenix. This was reality. It was also insanity. On the way out I told the check-out person about the woman and her threat. He called over the assistant manager who apologized to me and walked me to my car. Once I was back in the car, the momentary diversion of the ill-tempered woman vanished. I was plunged back into my loneliness. I made it home and found the only comfort possible in my life within the four walls of my son's room, where Norm and I stayed, awake or asleep.

Wednesday was my birthday. I spent an hour in the morning appearing on a radio-television broadcast that included some calls from the listening-viewing public. Everyone said I gave a good interview. I was happy to tell people how peacefully Nick died, and that I was glad his suffering was at long last over. My son was in a better world. At the end of the day, I was on the radio again. Another talk show. The night went on and on. Many, many people called in with their own horror stories about doctors who had turned away and about dying family members who had suffered beyond belief. They supported Nick and his right to die with courage and dignity. People applauded me for helping my son. For having the courage to help him. I didn't need words of exaltation. "I am not a hero," I said. "Simply a mother who did her best to help her son in his hour of need."

The days crawled by. One full week had passed since Nick and I said goodbye. One week since his lilting sigh that was music to my heart accompanied the lifting of his soul. One week since I put my son's body in the back of the van and turned it over to the authorities.

That day the body was returned to me in the form of cremated remains delivered to my door by the postman. I opened the container to find the ashes inside a clear plastic bag. I opened the bag and the smell of a crematory permeated the pores of my face. Nick wanted his ashes spread to the winds atop his favorite place, Squaw Peak. It was too soon to let them go. I decided the appropriate time to cast the ashes would be the 12th of May, 1996. One year from the morning of his departure. I called my children to tell them, and they all agreed it was the right thing to do. I had a year to embrace the cremated remains of my son.

On Saturday, a Michigan State death certificate for Nicholas John Loving arrived in the mail. A piece of paper to tell me and my descendants that Nick was once alive. That Nick passed through death. A piece of paper that was an official state document. A document to reflect the truth and not error. And, certainly not falsehood, propaganda, or deliberate omissions of pertinent information. However, as I read the certificate, I realized the document was a malicious extension of the evil that shadows life and death on this planet. Nick's death was recorded as a homicide, a homicide due to poisoning by carbon monoxide. Nowhere on the record was there mention of the terminal condition which precipitated his death. Nowhere did it say Lou Gehrig's disease. The very disease which the medical examiner used to rule out suicide. With the exception of the video interview and documents which Dr. Kevorkian said I would receive and a few personal items still in possession of the authorities, there was nothing left to expect from Michigan. Feeling the emotional weight of my son's ashes and seeing the doctored death certificate were

My Son, My Sorrow

enough to strip away the final layer of protective cushion that had sheltered me over the week since I'd returned. I began to cry without restraint. Cry the way I cried that morning in October, 1993, when I hung up the phone after Nick called and told me the news wasn't good. Cried when I'd learned what Lou Gehrig's disease was going to do to my vibrant, handsome, exuberant young son. While he was with me, I had tried to restrain the flow of tears to times when I could be alone, out of respect for my son. When he was completely helpless and I had to serve him night and day, I didn't have the strength to cry, let alone the time.

Now was the time to cry my heart out completely, to absolutely lose myself in the agony buried inside me. Out of the depths of my sorrow, I cried, crippled in my heart like the disease that crippled my son. His life played over and over in my mind. Things he did. Things he said. The joy. Oh, the joy he had given me and the rest of the family, the comfort in the midst of our hardest times. Every memory forced more tears out of me. I cried. I sobbed. I groaned and contracted with pain that came from the emotions that surged within my soul.

How had I lived through all the pain and torment and suffering that went on within these four walls that echoed my son's struggle? What on earth was to become of me now that it was all over? I had enough money left not to worry about paying my bills for the immediate future, but I had no idea what I would do to earn my next dollar. I felt I couldn't deal with people and a world so far removed from the heartache and experience of my own being.

During the next few weeks, grief engulfed me, but as May gave way to June, the process of restoration began for my soul. I was compelled to sit down at my desk and pick up a pencil, my companion in times of sorrow. Before I could realize what was happening, I began to pour out Nick's story. It was the beginning of rebuilding myself. I organized the pain inside and began to purge the ocean of sorrow upon which I had set sail. Daily, I sat down at my computer and through a wash of tears, I began to heal my soul from the wounds incurred in Nick's and my war with Lou Gehrig's syndrome. I had to write. It was all I could do to save myself. And yet, it made the grief of each day even more intense. I relived everything in my mind, over and over and over again, in order to unravel the message of the resident spirit in charge of my life. But it became so intense I had to stop for a while. To counter my isolation and grieving, I began going to meetings of the International Sister City Program.

The Sister City Commission asked me to host a Chinese couple visiting from the ancient city of Chungdu in southwestern China. Upon their arrival, we became very close. We talked much of the children's and my interesting times in their country. They wanted to know about Nick and the nature of the condition that took his life from him. They, too, believed no one should have to suffer, and they considered the act of Dr. Kevorkian to be, as they said, "benevolent." It was an honor to have Chinese people in my home after years of study and the experience of living among them. I stayed busy taking them sightseeing and out to dinners, meetings, and popular attractions. Their stay lasted ten days and took me away from my writing, but also from the crying, and the mourning of my soul. I cherished their visit. When they left, I returned to the privacy of my life and the pain that still hobbled my heart.

August was a sweltering, rain-filled month. It felt like the tropics more than the desert. The eleventh was the twins' birthday. But, this August, Drew turned twenty-eight alone. I had left the planning of Nick's wake up to the children, believing that it would be good for their recoveries. When they kept putting it off, I realized that they too were having trouble and pain dealing with Nick's death. I urged them on and finally the day after Nick and Drew's birthday, the wake was held.

As if in preparation for our celebration of Nick's life, a fierce thunderstorm the night before created cool, clear weather and an ethereal blue sky. I felt moved to create a tribute to my son using pictures taken throughout his life. I painted a wall in the living room a highland green color to serve as a background for a collage of photographs. The wall of pictures and memories gradually took the shape of the great state of Texas where Nick was born. The wall gave everyone who came that day a place to stop and see Nick throughout his life, and a chance to think about him, to remember his uniqueness and talk about the significance of having him in each one's life. We had a barbecue. People ate from afternoon until late at night and stayed into the wee hours. It was a joyous event, the type of party Nick liked to throw for his family and friends. Even my brother Rick, to my delight, took control of himself for the event and kept his sobriety.

I was recovering. I set aside the day to worship the Lord and pay my respects for the life he had given me. On that day, August 21st, I woke up around dawn with a dream still vivid in my mind. Nick was far off in the distance, on the other side of the horizon, looking at me. Checking to see that I was okay. I was so happy to see him. I extended my hand, but the gesture was in vain. The distance between us was too great. He stood there in the distance and watched me. I could feel him with me. After it ended, I realized the dream was a gift. I savored it. I viewed it again and again in my mind as I enjoyed the light of another day. Around noon I sat down to watch the news. A young blond reporter announced that, "It just came in; Dr. Kevorkian has helped another person to die. A woman suffering from Lou Gehrig's syndrome."

News of Nick's passing was on the television. I couldn't believe what I was seeing. A flashback to the doctor's last assisted patient: my son. There was the van, right where we left it and the body for the authorities. Pain coursed through my body like a knife as the reporter said, "It has been three months since the doctor helped the young man from Phoenix, Nicholas Loving, who suffered from Lou Gehrig's disease." All of Nick's suffering was condensed into my being. Tears poured out of me in wave after wave. I couldn't contain myself. I was out of control. I went into the bathroom to splash cold water on my face. But I couldn't wash the pain away. Everything my son and I experienced, the suffering and his death passed through my mind. My heart was a tender wound that had been torn open and bled.

The entire day was labor for the soul. I tried to understand my sorrow and the direction which I was to follow. I was led to focus on the chain of events that took place over my lifetime, events that prepared me to give all in body, mind and

My Son, My Sorrow

soul to my son as he was led to the doorway of death. I began to understand that in writing the story of my son's suffering and death, I was living out God's plan. I was being given an opportunity to mourn my son, and to recover. I had to finish it if ever I was to let go of the anguish and suffering that still strangled my soul and held it captive.

Though it was an intense, difficult experience, I began to see that the process of grieving was a blessed event which removed the pain and sorrow of loss and separation. I walked through the endless grief before me each day. I waded through private memories of our struggle with the killer disease. I passed through the searing memories of how creeping paralysis drained the life from Nick's every muscle; how insidious chemical toxicity turned my vibrant young son into a crippled old man. And, eventually, into a living corpse. I reflected with great consternation on the way institutionalized medicine dictates the lives of the helpless and dying. I forced myself to write each day regardless of the tears that came every time I sat down to release the pain from my heart.

The process of releasing the pain through the written word proved to be fruitful. By August, I was halfway through the first draft. The multiple wounds, though still open and tender were beginning to heal. The writing drained me of my energy. Yet, I was stronger than I had been all year. When I wasn't writing or crying or immersed in thought, I spent my time going through things that belonged to Nick—in search of memories waiting for me so that I could put together the pieces of the past. I was making progress, but still I had a long way to go to clear my heart and head.

There were many bumps in the road to my salvation. Times when I felt the creeping paralysis that had destroyed Nick's body would nearly destroy my mind. The mourning process was no less a hazardous path for me struggling to keep afoot as I tried to rebuild my life.

The intense heat of August was finally coming to an end. I took a break from my writing and drove with Norman to Tucson where I had been invited to talk on euthanasia to a large audience of people drawn together by the Tucson Hemlock chapter.

I told them about the suffering Nick was subjected to, because as a society, we have created a medical system that refuses to aid the dying. I brought the audience to tears when I told them of the pain and torment my son was forced to endure, all because the public has lost sight of the sanctity of human life and entrusted the value thereof to the power of the government. When I returned to Phoenix, the communications department of Arizona State University contacted me. They wanted my consent to include the interview I gave in Tucson in their international journal on death and dying.

Autumn came and went.

The impact of Nick's desperate need to die motivated the Tucson Hemlock Society to draw up an aid-in-dying bill. That December, the chapter was able to persuade a local legislator to introduce the bill to the Senate. I went there. I stood before the State Senate Health Committee the following January. With strong emotions that almost overpowered me, I reminded the committee of recent Phoenix history about the Valley man, my son, who was forced to turn to a doctor two thousand miles from home, the only person in the medical community who would help him. I told my senators that I would be incarcerated for causing the death of my son were it not for Dr. Kevorkian who stepped in and removed that burden from me. "This bill will not empower the doctors or permit them to abuse the dying, but instead, it will empower the dying and allow them to control their personal destiny, as well as free them from existing medical abuse." I told the senators I welcomed any questions they had about my son and his death through the grace of Dr. Kevorkian. But they did not ask any. They sat, dumbfounded.

No one knew what to say. The chairwoman broke the silence and thanked me for my comments. Shortly thereafter, I watched as the bill was voted down, six to two. Two minority members on the committee voted for the bill. The ones in control of the power voted against it.

In February, I learned Dr. Kevorkian was going back to court over the deaths of two suffering people he had helped before Nick. The media wanted to know if the good doctor's acts were murder or mercy? I accepted the offer of one television producer to appear on his program to speak about the subject only to find my microphone cut off for the entire program while pompous authorities had their say in a one-sided discussion. They fancied themselves so important that they should be the ones with the power to designate the rules and regulations of the human dying process for everyone in the country. All spoke rhetoric and pap, and supported anti-compassion as a means of dealing with terminally ill people as well as the all-out prohibition of death.

I learned more about the structure of media power from this broadcast than the public learned about the tyranny

and subterfuge under which we presently live. Right after the
program, I ran into Helene Poigt, a journalist who wanted to
put together a documentary for the Polish community on
assisted suicide. She wanted to know if she could interview
me. We exchanged phone numbers and, in March, she and a
photographer came to Phoenix for the project. The weekend
Helene arrived was the same one in which Kevorkian's
lawyer, Geoffrey Fieger, was scheduled to speak to the
Tucson Hemlock Society. It also turned out to be the weekend Dr. Kevorkian was acquitted of the two 1992 "assisted
suicide" charges brought against him. I took the journalist
and photographer to the Hemlock Society. It turned out that
Fieger was unable to attend because he was defending the
doctor in court. His partner came instead and gave a talk to
the membership.

Helene and I spent much time together over the weekend. She interviewed my sons. For the first time, my youngest
son, Luke, had the opportunity to speak publicly about the suffering his brother endured, how much his brother meant to
him, and why it was important to help Nick die. Helene, who
felt it important for the piece to be objective, was just, precise
and fair in her selection of questions while I remained firm and
staunch in my belief that no institution has the right to dictate
the manner of death for my son, myself, or any dying individual. "Death is a sacred act involving the spirit, mind, and soul
along with the physical body. Death is the process of birth for
the evolving soul and no institution on earth has the right to
hinder the birth of the soul," I said.

A few weeks later I finished the second draft of Nick's
story. A draft that also purged the tears and pain from my

My Son, My Sorrow

bruised and lonely heart. In the four months it took to write the second draft, sorrow began to subside. I could actually go a day or two without losing myself in the fountain of tears that came through me. I was slowly healing. I wasn't finished with either the story or my mourning but I had reached an important turning point. I still had to write another draft, a final draft. The bones of my work had to gain muscle next time around. But I wasn't ready; I had to put my work down. I had to leave it alone for a time. In addition, I had to attend to the necessities of everyday life, like finding work, paying rent, earning money for groceries. When the time was right, I told myself, the final draft would come.

My brother was also moving through the grieving process in his own heart and way. The pain that accumulated inside him as he watched Nick lose his life to the deadly power of a killer condition receded as the months went by. My brother and I had lost our elder brother in 1977. Our mother in 1980. And, our father in 1987. None of the deaths prepared him for the tragic loss of his favorite nephew. Nevertheless, as I began to mend, so did he. He could still be brought to tears in moments of reflections, but the pain now moved through him and out. My dear brother Rick started to feel peace.

In the moments when grief still haunted him he tried to think about what Nick always told him: not to dwell on unchangeable things. And that gave him the incentive to heed the advice and look forward.

My youngest son, Luke, was also healing from the loss of his brother. Luke had also lost his hero. But his wife gave birth to a child in July, and the gift of a new life enriched and nourished him. Though a day didn't pass that he didn't think of his brother, Luke's own life took on a new direction through the experiences of caring and providing for his new-born son.

At first, losing Nick ate his twin brother up, and turned him into a ghost of himself. However, in the grieving process, Drew learned that Nick was always there in his memory. Drew was proud of Nick and would always remember how his twin faced death without fear. Drew believed life was eternal. He slowly became comfortable knowing Nick was in a far better place. The painful images of the crippling and final year of Nick's life dissipated as waves of mourning washed his soul clean. As Nick had predicted, Drew was strong.

Hannah's life was forever changed. My daughter and her children lost a brother and uncle in one. Her son would never forget Uncle Nick, but the memory would fade in the mind of her darling toddler daughter. Nevertheless, Hannah had fond memories to comfort her. With her domestic life in turmoil at the time, she hadn't seen as much of her brother as she would have liked and at times she felt guilty. But I told her it might have been a blessing in disguise. "Nick didn't want to be remembered as the helpless victim you saw just weeks before his death." And yet, that last meeting gave her comfort, for she had reassured her brother of her love and he had given his in return. She could rest her spirit knowing Nick had a special feeling in his heart for her and for the children she brought into the world.

As we moved forward, my sons honored their words to Nick that they would look after me once he was gone. As they unraveled their ways out of the pain that accosted them, they became more aware of the reality of my loneliness and

My Son, My Sorrow

the heartache still residing within me. My younger son moved his family closer, and this provided me the opportunity to be a part of my grandson's life. Each of my children worked through his mourning with resilience.

As the anniversary of Nick's departure approached, I was scheduled to talk to a group in Prescott on the eleventh. That Saturday, I gave a twenty minute talk about my son, the medical condition that took his life, and the medical profession that inflicted more suffering upon him. My speech was fervent, because the matters of which I spoke mattered so much. When I finished, there was silence and then enormous applause.

Mother's Day was again drawing near. The time had come for Nick's ashes to be dispersed on Squaw Peak as he had requested. I told one of the newspeople who had kept in touch with our family that we had agreed that one year from the date of Nick's departure, we would go there and in that private time, we would say our goodbyes to the person we had known and loved.

The plan was to arrive at the site at dawn, but the heat in Phoenix was already hitting the 100° mark in the mornings, making it impossible for me to go. I am unable to tolerate intense heat and, as the children know, I become very ill.

I wanted to postpone the event, but after a discussion with Nick's twin I realized how important it was for him and the others to have this day as planned. I told the family, "You must go without me. I was afforded the privilege of being at Nick's side for his deliverance. You will bid our final goodbye." Drew, Luke, Hannah, my brother Rick and Charley, Nick's old friend, joined together to bring closure to their mourning. They climbed to a point where the sprawling city could be seen for miles. They cried as they searched through their memories of Nick. Each contributed one and, in turn, everyone took handfuls of Nick's remains and flung them to the four winds. To their astonishment, with each dispersement, fragments of Nick's remains drifted back to cover the face of the one who tossed them.

Then came another disturbing intrusion. When everyone was ready to leave, they saw television broadcast vans driving up and down the park road. The vehicles stopped for a while where the road ended and hiking paths began. Searching, Waiting. It was obvious they were looking for us. Though I was not with them, my children were recognizable. Even though the sun grew hotter, the family decided to wait it out rather than hike down to face an invasion of privacy. I realized there is nothing off the record to the press. Despite the bad taste shown, I didn't know whether to laugh or cry when I caught the early news and saw reporters talking to hikers at Squaw Peak. The camera panned the area and the streams of heat waves rising up from the blistering hot road as they waited in vain for my children to descend the mountain. I gave one interview that afternoon and was especially pleased with the piece on the anniversary of Nick's death that aired that night. It was good journalism and a tribute to my beloved son.

I am glad the family had their private moment with Nick's ashes. I was afforded the honor of being with my son when he left this world, and their gathering at Squaw Peak was as close to a last private moment as they could have. Wanting to be alone, I spent a solitary Mother's Day reflecting on the past year and on how far I had come in the process of healing. Nick had valiantly left the world twelve months before. I

My Son, My Sorrow

remained to continue my obligation to my son and to our special bond.

A year had passed. Nick was in heaven. Yet, Nick was always with my children as he was with me, in heart and memory, and in the light that glows and kindles the soul. My children told me they were proud to call me Mother, because I gave my complete devotion to Nick during his tragic decline, and because I spoke out publicly about the suffering involved in dying from a debilitating, fatal illness. They stood behind me as I spoke about the medical abuse Nick was subjected to as he was dying. They encouraged me as a writer. They believed, as I did, that Nick's story needed to be told. Like Nick, my children would face death one day. They understood from Nick's experience that everyone has the right to control his last moments. The dying need to die. Now with the dispersal of Nick's ashes my children were able to move on, each knowing more about life and death than before. This knowledge I prayed would enrich both their future days on earth and their partings from it when their own times came.

What a blessing it was to have had Nick in my life. What a blessing it was to serve him on his death bed and deliver his soul to the kingdom of Heaven. I know now that the import of the experience only served to strengthen my own soul and move me forward in service of my fellow human beings. There is much that can be learned from the tragic circumstances involved in my son's medical condition and the behavior of the medical profession and authorities. Nick wanted his death to spark a debate on the right-to-die. I planned to speak out against the atrocities and tyranny of dying in our society until I no longer had breath.

Carol Loving

I am the voice of my son. I also speak on behalf of the suffering who don't have voices and have no control over the end of their lives. I must tell you that the same suffering that happened to my son can happen to you or your family. You or someone you love may be helpless, trapped in the prison of a pain-ridden body without a way to end the agony. Is your departure from earth an act to be dictated by the State? Regardless of what you want or think might happen at the end of your life, the State is in control as long as the circumstances of your death are dictated by the medical profession, the law, or anyone other than yourself.

It is my prayer and mission that compassionate provisions and concern for the dying become a paramount issue to those in power, and that society develops a greater understanding of life and its symbiotic partner, death.

As Nick went from the world of childhood visions to the perspective of a young man, he gave me his word that he would be here to take care of me as I began to decline into the infirmities of old age. He promised me he would provide for me. His words ring true. For my soul is enriched by having known and loved him. The spirit that sustained me through his loss has provided me with this legacy of words and deeds to be done. I will move forward into the future, rich with memories that will sometimes cause me to cry, and rich with joy for having given my son life, shared his vibrant youth, and brought him to his peace.